BOUNCERS AND BODYGUARDS

Former bouncer, mercenary, bodyguard and trainer of bodyguards, Robin Barratt is the author of the genre best-selling *Doing the Doors: Confessions of a Doorman* and *Maria's Story*. During 20 long years on the doors, Barratt worked all over the UK, from Manchester and London to Mansfield, Nottingham and Norwich. He also provided personal protection, mainly to the corporate community, in high-risk areas, including the Democratic Republic of Congo, Nigeria, Israel, Bosnia (during the conflict) and Russia, a country he specialises in. He hopes to retire soon to the west coast of France, where he can live peacefully and write fiction.

Website: www.robinbarratt.co.uk
Email: robinbarratt@yahoo.com

BOUNCERS AND BODYGUARDS
TALES FROM A TWILIGHT WORLD

ROBIN BARRATT

MAINSTREAM
PUBLISHING

EDINBURGH AND LONDON

This book is dedicated to all those men and women who put their
own health and lives on the line in order to
keep other people safe and secure

First published in Great Britain in 2008 by
MAINSTREAM PUBLISHING COMPANY (EDINBURGH) LTD
7 Albany Street
Edinburgh EH1 3UG

ISBN 9781845963026

This book is a work of non-fiction based on the life, experiences and
recollections of the contributors. In some cases, names of people, places,
dates, sequences or the detail of events have been changed to protect
the privacy of others. The author has stated to the publishers that,
except in such respects, not affecting the substantial accuracy
of the work, the contents of this book are true.

A catalogue record for this book is available
from the British Library

Typeset in Caslon and MetaPlus

Printed in Great Britain by
William Clowes Ltd, Beccles, Suffolk

CONTENTS

AUTHOR'S NOTE

This book is a combination of conversations, one-to-one interviews and specifically submitted written contributions. People working the doors and as bodyguards come from a whole variety of backgrounds – they are all so very different. They talk differently, write differently and explain things in a huge number of different ways, so, wherever possible, I have tried to retain and maintain each contributor's specific and unique character and style, even when the grammar is occasionally incorrect, the tenses muddled and the verbs confused. All these stories are based on actual events; however, some contributors have opted to remain anonymous.

The power of hiding ourselves from one another is mercifully given, for men are wild beasts, and would devour one another but for this protection

Henry Ward Beecher (1813–87)

INTRODUCTION

DIAMONDS AND CUNTS

Although now more or less retired from operations, I worked the doors for almost 20 years and off and on as a bodyguard for almost 15 years. At the time of putting this book together, I am 45 years old and, if I am brutally and truthfully honest, getting a little too old for it all. Working the doors and out in the field as a bodyguard is most certainly a young person's job. Although there are still many mature doormen and bodyguards out there, it has to be said that most are between the ages of 25 and 35.

It isn't that we 'oldies' can't do the job. I can honestly and modestly say that with the experience and reputation we have gained over the years in the field, we can probably do the job as well as most, if not better. Personally, however, it is the conditions and the environment in which I have occasionally found myself working that make me now tend to turn away from operations for a much quieter and far easier life. For example, in the car I now more often than not listen to Classic FM, as the serene music relaxes me when I drive and helps me control any early symptoms of road rage. Therefore, the repetitive thump, thump, thump of a noisy nightclub would most certainly send me insane and into a high-risk mental institution. And when I travel, I must admit that I do rather like the comforts of a decent hotel and tasty meals taken at leisure, so putting up with long hours and the frequently uncomfortable conditions of many high-risk close protection operations would almost certainly result in a grumpy, aching, moaning old bastard, whom I would not want to inflict on anyone! So, a relatively sedentary life in front of the computer screen is for me, I think, much preferable.

Rarely, for someone not from a predominantly military background, I went from being a timid, naive doorman at The Ritzy nightclub in provincial Norwich to an eventual trainer of bodyguards in high-risk countries worldwide. And over the years, while working on the doors and out in the field as a bodyguard, I have met a great many extremely interesting people, leading diverse and remarkable lives. I have been enthralled by hundreds of stories: funny, horrific, astounding, sad, tragic, inspiring, upsetting – the list is seemingly endless! Most of us working in the industry have had unique experiences, so I thought it would be a fantastic idea to chronicle some of our exceptional tales. And so this book was born.

During my time on the doors and out in the field as a bodyguard, I have met some wonderful and very genuine people – some real diamonds. Sadly, the opposite is also true: I have met some complete and utter cunts. I suppose it stands to reason that because of the nature of the industry – who we have to deal with, the environment in which we sometimes find ourselves and what we are occasionally asked to do – there are probably more extreme personalities working on the doors and as bodyguards than in most other professions. Most people are genuine, hard-working, honest, loyal, conscientious and utterly professional, while others are a complete waste of time – boastful, disloyal and dishonest wankers who you wouldn't even want to wipe your arse with, let alone trust with your life.

When I first started this project, I asked around to see who would be willing to give up four or five hours of their time over a three- to four-month period in order to write about their experiences. I asked all sorts of people, from good friends who I have worked with and have infinite and everlasting respect for to friends of friends who I didn't know personally but who were referred or recommended. I asked criminals serving life, well-known gangsters, cons and ex-cons. I spoke to the inexperienced novice door supervisor starting on the doors for the very first time and a bodyguard on his very first assignment. I asked members of Special Branch, bodyguard training companies and 'old school' roughneck doormen. Many said that they would be glad to contribute and a few said no – they either didn't have the time or were just not interested. Regardless of whether they agreed to participate or not, most people I spoke to were real diamonds – but some were utter cunts.

THE DIAMONDS . . .

It has been a real pleasure working with each and every one of the contributors in this book. You are all diamonds. Some of the people who gladly gave up their precious time and interrupted their busy lives to put together some great stories for me were already best-selling authors and immensely respected in the security industry. For others, this was their first piece of written work. For some of them, contributing to this book has sparked a desire to write more, and a couple of people have even asked me to help them write their autobiographies!

We have more than 20 enthralling chapters from some amazing people: Charlie Bronson writes about the early 1970s before he was put inside; Dave Courtney reveals how much he misses the violent times of the 1980s; Mickey Francis chronicles the rise and fall of Loc19, one of Manchester's most feared door firms; Alex Powell tells me about the time he and his close protection team protected the votes of the Iraqi people; and Inna Zabrodskaya recalls the time she fucked up a security and surveillance operation for the managing director of a multi-national corporation in Moscow.

A really big thank you goes to all of the contributors, with special mention to a few friends, including Charlie Bronson. Charlie has perhaps a little more free time than the rest of us, but within a few *days* of me asking he sat down and in his own distinctive style wrote a unique and funny little story about his experiences and thoughts on doormen and working the doors. Charlie was banged up well before I

11

sprouted pimples and has been in solitary for almost 30 years. I can't even imagine the thought of any human being locked in solitary for so long – it utterly defies comprehension. Murderers and child molesters don't serve sentences as long. I was told by someone visiting another prisoner in Wakefield prison that the child murderer Ian Huntley is free to walk around the visitors' area while families are visiting. Yet Charlie is escorted to and from his cell chained like an animal.

Charlie now spends his time making art and writing books and poetry. Is he a danger to society? I doubt it very much, although it is difficult to know how he would cope in this mad, crazy world after such a long time caged up. Charlie, you are a diamond, mate. Thank you for your unique contribution, and I sincerely look forward to having that pint with you one day soon.

Paul Knight, you are also a diamond. Paul spent a whole weekend writing three great stories from his time working on the doors in London – all distinctive and interesting and representative of what true door work is all about. Paul is an utter professional in his trade, and my hat goes off to you, buddy. (Sorry, Paul, but we can only use two stories this time – but the third will go into *Bouncers and Bodyguards 2*!)

You either love him or hate him, but Dave Courtney is also a real diamond. Thanks for entertaining me for a couple of hours at your place with your stories, your thoughts and your comments on the industry. Dave's ornaments and wall decorations have to be seen to be believed and woe betide any unwelcome visitor.

I have to admit, like Dave, I am very old school and believe that true door work is occasionally about teaching scumbag scrotes who misbehave and cause others distress and inconvenience a fucking hard lesson. In my opinion, we should go back to the good old days when coppers gave scumbags a fucking good kicking – we would then all live in a much better society. But as Dave says, there will never be the quality of fighters on the doors again as there were back in the 1970s and '80s. There will never be the same characters, the hard cunts whose reputation preceded them.

Steve Wraith, thanks for your stories from your life on the doors up in Newcastle. Steve is another complete professional – hard as fuck

12

but immensely polite, respectful and humble. Steve sat down for a good few hours – admittedly with a good few pints beside him – and wrote away. It is a pleasure to have you by my side, buddy, and it will be an honour to work alongside you one day.

Sadly, at the time of writing, Bob Etchells is still returning to his tiny prison cell every night and being tucked into bed by his freakishly large and somewhat intimidating cellmate. It was way back in my very early 20s, after dropping in and out of numerous dead-end jobs, grubby bedsits and quite a number of exceedingly tarty women's knickers, that I started working the doors at The Ritzy in Norwich under Bob's supervision. He was head doorman at the time, and I was a spotty and skinny wimp. I honestly thought being a door supervisor was a bit like being a hotel doorman – opening the door and welcoming people as they came and went – and truthfully didn't know what a real one did. (I knew what bouncers did, of course, but I didn't think that they were the same. It wasn't until it kicked off big time that I realised it was the same job!)

If I hadn't become a doorman, I wonder what would have become of me – and I wonder where I would be now if I hadn't stuck it out during those first few months (perhaps even years) of naivety and inexperience? Probably an old, fucked-up, boring-arsed factory worker married to an overweight, nagging ogre. (Come to think of it, maybe things haven't progressed much after all!) Bob had faith in me during those early months, and I fondly remember the very first time he sent me in to evict someone. I think Bob knew I was a bit of a wanker, and he told me to evict a man-mountain called 'Pint'. He was called Pint because he apparently loved to attack doormen with a pint glass – but I didn't know that then. Fulfilling Bob's orders, I just marched up to Pint and asked him to leave. As he put his glass down and rose above me, I looked up at him and gulped. I was in for a severe bashing, but surprisingly he said, 'OK mate,' and left. I later went on to prove myself to Bob and his team in hundreds of battles over the years, but back then I almost puked with fear when I had to eject this man-mountain.

Back in the 1980s and '90s, Mickey Francis ran Loc19, one of Manchester's most feared door firms. I first met Mickey in about

1997 when I was asked to run a club called Equivino in Wilmslow, Cheshire. Equivino had a regular Saturday-night promotion called Peruvia, and I was asked to move from Reading to try and sort things out, as the venue and the event attracted almost every gang in the North West. Needless to say, the task was way beyond my capabilities, so I called in Loc19. When I first met Mickey and his partner Steve Brian, I thought that if they couldn't sort things out, nobody could. They were fearsome. Of course, things were sorted, and I have kept in touch with Mickey ever since.

Thanks also go to Timm Smith at Ronin Security in South Africa. He didn't have the time to write a full feature for this book but said he would do something for *Bouncers and Bodyguards 2*. However, he did tell me a few hilarious stories about his (very rare) fuck-ups while protecting the rich and famous. On one occasion, he almost puked over Queen Elizabeth when he opened the door for her after having run next to her vehicle for three and a half kilometres in a suit with a steel-insert bulletproof vest in the midday South African sun. He also almost knocked out a blind guy while working with Nelson Mandela's bodyguard team. Mandela was opening a school and was giving a speech in a fruit grove. The blind man was due to meet Mandela and was being escorted by Timm towards the podium. Timm looked down and noticed a tree root sticking out from the ground, but he was too late to do anything, and the blind man fell arse over tit. Mandela commented to the red-faced bodyguard that even in his early boxing days he never managed to put someone down so quickly.

Ken Wharfe is an ex-Special Branch protection officer who wrote *Diana: Closely Guarded Secret*. Ken couldn't contribute to the book either, as he had just too many other commitments, but he did tell me about the time he looked after Prince Charles. One day, the prince was wandering around the grounds and gardens of Highgrove House, as he frequently liked to do. Ken was keeping a discreet distance from Charles, giving him some solitude and peace. Suddenly, he heard the prince shout, 'Ken, Ken, quick.' Ken sprinted over to Charles, who was standing staring down at the ground. It looked as though he had either seen a ghost or there was someone hiding in the bushes, pointing a very large gun up at him.

14

'Yes, sir, what is it?' Ken panted, almost drawing his weapon.

'What's that?' Charles said angrily, pointing down to the ground.

Ken looked down, and after a few confused seconds said, 'It's a banana skin, sir.'

'And what is a bloody banana skin doing down there?' Charles replied.

Ken didn't really know what to say and eventually replied, 'I will have it removed for you, sir.'

According to Ken, Prince Charles isn't of this planet – he lives in a world of his own, totally oblivious to what is 'normal', and cannot relate in any way whatsoever with normal people.

Ken told me another funny story about when Charles was presented with a beautiful new Rolls-Royce. The luxury car manufacturer had spent hundreds of thousands of pounds making an exceptional bespoke vehicle for the prince and was presenting it to him at a special private ceremony. Top managers, key workers and other special guests were invited to attend. The managing director of Rolls-Royce proudly showed Charles the plush, luxurious interior, and the gloss and sheen of the paintwork, but as they walked to the front of the stunning vehicle Charles pointed to it and said, 'What is that?'

'It is a Monte Carlo grill, sir,' the managing director proudly replied.

Charles looked confused and then disgusted. 'No, don't want it,' he said and walked off, leaving the rest of the party standing in amazement.

Last of all, a real big thank you to all the other great contributors. Thank you for your hard work and time, and thank you for your kindness and hospitality – you are all fucking diamonds.

AND THE CUNTS . . .

Working the doors and bodyguarding is a business built on trust, loyalty, dependence and honesty. We trust that the people we work with will be there for us in good times and bad. We are loyal to our team. We depend upon them, as they depend upon us, and we are truthful. Without these things, there is no security industry.

I don't mind somebody telling me that they will do something for me but then realising that they perhaps just don't have the ability or the time and changing their mind. I have been in that position before: circumstances change; unexpected things happen. To those people who had the decency to let me know well before the book's submission deadline that they couldn't contribute for whatever reason you are also diamonds for not letting me down. Thank you.

But to those who repeatedly said yes to me and then let me down at the last fucking minute, you are, without doubt, utter cunts and should not even be on the planet, let alone in the security and protection industry. I was seriously considering naming and shaming you for all eternity, but then I would be a cunt, too, and I just hate calling myself a cunt. However, you all know who you are. You should not be in any position of trust, and you certainly should not be working on the doors or as part of a close protection team. You deserve everything that befalls you – and I hope it is a fucking huge piano from a seventh-storey window.

Apart from a few hiccups, especially at the last minute, putting this book together has generally been great fun, and I have met some great people. But it has taught me one thing: if you promise to do something for someone, then do it or be honest and say you can't – don't just leave things, hoping that they will go away, because, believe me, they won't!

Stay safe.

Robin Barratt
robinbarratt@yahoo.com
August 2007

1

BACK IN THE EARLY '70S
BY CHARLIE BRONSON

Way back in the summer of 1974, I was a 22-year-old 'pavement artist' (i.e. armed blagger). When I got nicked and put away, the Three Degrees had a number-one hit with 'When Will I See You Again'. I was never to see the streets again for 14 years. I deserved all I got. I was a nasty, vicious bastard – that is how it was with me. You *never* hear me crying about punishment.

I only survived in the 'free' world for a couple of months. My whole adult life has been in maximum security – I am still in a hole, but I am alive and kicking. So, from 1974 to 2007 I have been caged up, apart from a couple of months of freedom. Thirty-three years of porridge! And out of those years, 30 have been spent in solitary. And I am still in solitary. Why? Because I am Charlie Bronson . . .

Although I'm a 55-year-old man and now anti-crime, anti-violence and anti-drugs, my past has buried me deep inside the 'Belly of the Beast'. So bear with me . . . I am a bit lost and confused as to how doormen and minders conduct themselves today. This is my story from years back.

All you really needed in my day was a sharp eye and a good right hook to diffuse any situation. And my hook was second to none! Although my profession was blagger, I often done some collecting and security work, and on a Saturday night you would often find me on a door just passing the night away.

One memory that often makes me smile in my hours of boredom is of a crazy lunatic who just wouldn't stop causing problems. I was on a club door when he came in. I said to the other bouncers , 'Watch him.' I just have this inner sense about trouble. You either have it, or you don't. It is a vibe you pick up – I can smell it, feel it . . . and I am 99 per cent always spot on. This lunatic was oozing madness. His eyes were spaced out, and he had that walk. His whole posture was saying, 'Come and fuck with me if you dare.' It didn't take him long to kick off.

We had no earpieces or CCTV in them days. All we had was speed. We were fast – get in hard, ask questions later. He had put his hand up some bird's skirt, and a fight broke out with the bird's fella! I got in fast – I stuck my two fingers up his nostrils (my speciality!) and led him out into the car park. Simple as that. Or so I thought. (You really can't plan for a lunatic.)

As I let him go and wiped my fingers on his jacket and told him to fuck off, he dived at me and tried to bite my face off. The rest you don't want to know, but he was never the same again. He's sure got through a million colostomy bags, and he's never put his hands up another bird's skirt since.

Another time, I was on the door of my mate's club when a giant of a man came in. I mean awesome. (Incidentally, the tallest man I ever chinned was at Broadmoor. He was six feet ten and a half inches.) This guy was about six feet nine inches. A fucking giant or freak. He became very abusive to the bar staff. I am five feet ten inches, and I strolled up to him and said, 'OK, mate – LEAVE!'

He looked down to me and said, 'Fuck off.' Well, I tell a lie. It was just, 'Fuck . . .' He never had time to say 'off' before I hit him. It was like a tree going over. I was told the following week that he had come back twice to see me. The third time, he found me and said, 'Sorry, mate. I was out of order.'

And that is how crazy it can sometimes be on the doors. Guns can be pulled, knives, all sorts. I once had a transvestite slice his wrist in the toilet. I wrapped a towel around his wrist and tied a tie around his bicep till the ambulance arrived. I've seen it all: birds getting shagged in the gents, poofs at it, threesomes in the cubicles, blow jobs under the table. You could write a library of books on what doormen experience. Every club, pub, nightclub is different. It's exciting but not as good as a blag. Counting up the loot is the world's best buzz, and spending it even better.

I was with a doorman when he had his eye ripped out. It is a lot to lose an eye on a job. Others have been shot dead, stabbed, burnt, all sorts. It's a fucking mental job with little thanks. But it's a way of life. Doormen are a special breed. They're all a bit strange to want to do that job, but they're a good bunch. Wars are won with such men! They sure don't get the respect they deserve, and everyone has a story to tell.

Another job I had was looking after a serious 'Bizz Man' when he used to deliver a briefcase full of dosh. I mean *big* bucks. I had to make sure he got them from A to Z in one piece with no problems. On one run, I knew we were definitely being followed. I slammed on the brakes and ran out with an axe. I never got a chance to use it, and I have never seen a car go so fast in reverse. Apart from that one incident, the rest of the journeys we did were trouble free!

A man has to do what *needs* to be done, no matter what the odds are or the consequences. You do it fast and furious; otherwise, you're a total cunt. I despise people who talk the talk, walk the walk, then bottle out. You learn who's who in your own journey of life. There are some doormen, minders, who have yet to be tested. Until a man's tested, you don't know him. It's the same in war – some *can't* do it. It is the ultimate test of life.

My journey in life has forever tested me. It still does, even today. I've survived it all: multiple stab wounds (all in my back), guns to my head (Old Bill and villains), serious brutality. Read my books – it's all in there. Although I am now a changed man and deserve any act of violence, it's best you don't test me. It's so much nicer to be nice.

But if you really want to test me, let's go into the darkness alone and 'discuss' it!

Doormen, I salute you!

Charlie

P.S. If I had my time over again, I'd be a porn star. What a fucking job!

BIOGRAPHY OF CHARLIE BRONSON

Charlie Bronson was born in Aberystwyth on 6 December 1952. His real name is Michael Peterson. Bronson states on his website that contrary to reports frequently made in the media, his name was changed by his fight promoter in 1987 and was not a choice he made in relation to the screen actor Charles Bronson.

Initially jailed in 1974 for robbery, Bronson has been in prison more or less his entire life since the age of nineteen, and he has spent only three months out of custody. Due to repeated attacks on prison staff and inmates, including a number of hostage situations and rooftop protests, Bronson has spent most of his prison life in solitary confinement. In 1999, a special prison unit was set up for Bronson and two other violent prisoners to reduce the risk they posed to staff and other prisoners. In 2000, he received a discretionary life sentence for a hostage-taking incident. In 2001, Bronson married Saira Rehman, but the marriage didn't last.

Bronson also supports a charity called Zöe's Place Baby Hospice in Liverpool (www.zoes-place.org.uk). They do amazing work with severely disabled babies, so if you have some spare cash, send it to them – it will make Charlie very happy.

For the past ten years, Charlie's art has occupied him and is now the main part of his life. His artwork is unique and is sent to all corners of the world. Bronson has also published ten books and has received numerous prizes for his poetry. His books include *Solitary Fitness*; *Heroes and Villains: The Good, the Mad, the Bad and the Ugly*; *Insanity: My Mad Life*; *The Krays and Me*; *Legends*; *Silent Scream*; *Bronson*; *The Charles Bronson Book of Poems: Birdman Opens His Mind Book 1*; and *The Charles Bronson Cartoon Autobiography: Hostage of My Past*.

You can contact Charlie at www.freebronson.co.uk

2

MICKEY FRANCIS – THE RISE AND FALL AND RISE AGAIN OF LOC19
BY MICKEY FRANCIS

I am 46 years old and was born in Moss Side, Manchester. I was brought up by mixed-race parents in a really rough area. My father was Jamaican and my mother was a Scouser. They met after the war but are now separated. My dad used to beat us badly – he had a saying: 'Spare the rod to save the child.' He was a big chap, a wrestler, and we used to be scared shitless of him. Basically, he used to beat the fuck out of us. As soon as he came into the room, we would walk out. He was a bastard to his children and a bastard to my mum – he used to beat her up, never treated her right and was always fucking around behind her back. But they say that what goes around comes around, and he has got his just deserts – he has Alzheimer's now. He stays with me a few days a week – I am looking after him. His partner died a short while ago, and he is now on his own, spitting bubbles, having his arse wiped. But I have to put everything that he has done to me and the family behind me; the past is the past. I can change the future, but I can't change the past. It is about today, and he is still my father after all.

I was on the streets from the age of about 12 or 13. I grew up on Acomb Street, about five minutes from the Manchester City football ground, which was why I became a City football fan. My very first means of collecting money was minding people's cars. People used to park up on the street for the match, and we would ask if they wanted their car minded for 50p. If they said no, we would puncture the fucking tyres. We had our territory. Kids called the Ryans had another street and the Daltons another. We all kept to our own streets – no one stepped on anyone else's territory. It was the way that I first made money on the street, really. I would make £15 or £20 a match – going back 25 or 30 years, that was a lot of money. When most kids were delivering papers, I was minding cars – and damaging cars if their owners didn't pay the fee! In the end, everybody paid the fee.

Then I started to get involved in a bit of football violence. It was a great buzz, and I loved it. My first real fight was at Wigan football club. It was in the Doc Martens area, and I got knocked fucking out! This lad had banged me straight out. The police picked me up and asked me what I was doing in that area. Then they banged me in the stomach and told me to fuck off back to Manchester. That was my first-ever experience of football violence – getting knocked out and then battered by a copper! I was hoping to get my own back when City next played Wigan, but that never happened, as Wigan were always in a lower division than us.

I started off as a little soldier and worked my way up. I showed that I had a lot of bottle. I would go in first and could fight hard, and I became a leader at a very early age – about 15. I did it until I was about 28 years old. I liked the buzz of it all.

From about the age of 18, I arranged everything. Every Saturday for about 15 years, we would meet up at The Parkside pub. There used to be about a hundred of us all searching for violence. When I look back, I think, 'What an idiot. What was the reason behind it all?' But it was just one of those things: some people chose to be bikers or rockers; I chose to be a football hooligan. I know it wasn't the right choice, but at that time I liked doing it.

We came on top at Millwall and West Ham and Middlesbrough, and afterwards all of us would get on the coach, bleeding and buzzing and telling our stories – adding a little bit onto them, as you do. It was great. I liked the fear and the buzz of it all. I never thought that people could get killed – they did, of course – it was just a bit of excitement. I got into football violence in a big way, and eventually I was the head man at City. Whenever there was trouble, I would be at the front of it.

The Manchester police eventually caught up with me. They set up an operation called Omega, infiltrated us and watched us for 12 months while they collected as much video evidence as they could. Looking back, I had an idea something was going on, but at the time I couldn't tell who the coppers were. For almost 12 months, I got away with murder. I could do almost anything, and I didn't get charged once, even though I was arrested 28 times that year for football-related violence. They were letting me get away with it because they were building a case on me.

Eventually, when I was 29 years old, and after dawn raids at my house, I was arrested. I was put on remand for six weeks and then let out on bail for about a year until the trial took place. I was sentenced to prison and banned from attending any football match in the UK or Europe for ten years.

I was a scaffolder by trade. However, before I got arrested, and because I had a reputation for football violence, I was asked to work the doors at a club called Fagan's by a friend of mine called Mike Faux, who ran an event security company. I was training at a gym when Mike came over and asked if I fancied doing a bit of door work. At that time, I didn't think it was really for me, but I had just bought a house in Prestwich with my girlfriend, and I needed the extra money. It paid £14 a night, and so a few days later I started working for him. I then went to work at Rotter's nightclub on Oxford Street, Manchester. I think it was called Rotter's because it was full of rotten people! It was where all the stag nights came for a night out, arriving in coaches from St Helens and Liverpool and from the outskirts of Manchester, and every single night there would be running battles outside the club between Manchester lads and those from outside town. It was mayhem, and we used to really fight for our money. The funny thing was that we all had to wear white blazers and dicky bows, which ended up covered in blood every night.

At that time, I did a bit of boxing and fancied myself as a bit of a boxer – although I admit I was never very good at it. One night, I was on the door at Rotter's when I banged a kid and knocked him out clean. However, he swallowed his tongue, and I really thought I had killed him. I almost shit myself and rushed downstairs into the club, got changed and suddenly became a waiter, walking around the tables, trying to keep out of the way. Because I was the only black guy on the door at that time, one of his mates who was still inside immediately recognised me and rushed outside and told the rest of his pals, who then all tried to storm the door. It started to get a bit out of hand, but the kid came to and was all right in the end – it was a scary experience thinking that I had killed him, though. After that, I started to get a name for myself as a bit of a knockout merchant. I was then made second in command of the door.

One night at Rotter's, I was working with a doorman called Jed. There was a pissed-up hen night at the club, and the girl who was getting married that weekend fancied a bit of sex with Jed. She and Jed went off to the staff changing-rooms, downstairs at the back of the club, and most of the rest of the door crew and I followed and started watching through a crack in the door. There were so many of us all trying to have a peek that the door gave way, and we all tumbled on top of each other into the room.

I worked on the door at Rotter's for about two years – it was where I met my first wife Margaret. I have two children with Margaret, but I made a right fucking mess of that relationship, shagging around. I admit it was my fault; I just couldn't keep my dick in my pants. I got arrested for the football violence while I was with her. That scared her, and, needless to say, the marriage didn't last very long – it was over about two years after we got married.

At that point, I started to get asked to supply doormen to various clubs. I had been asked before but hadn't really known anyone suitable. However, my contact list grew as I spent more time in the business and got to know other doormen. I also asked around at the gyms if anyone fancied doing a bit of door work and hand-picked guys who I knew or had heard were quite capable, and I started to get my own firm together. That's how things started. Over a period of time, I started to get a few doors in and around Manchester, and it was then that I met Steve Brian, who was into the same sort of thing as me. He also had a few doors, so we decided to link up together and set up a joint company called Loc19.

The name Loc19 came from the Manchester canal. There was a bar on the canal called The Canal Bar and behind it was lock number 19. Steve and I sat in the bar one night, and I asked him what we could call the company? We were thinking of names when he saw the sign on the lock and said let's call it Loc19. The rest is history.

We built the company on having bottle and balls, and the thing that made us strong was that we didn't come from one particular area, unlike say the Gooch, who came from Moss Side. We were a central firm that didn't have allegiance to any one area. We also dealt with situations as hard as we could, which rapidly built our reputation. But when we first started, we didn't get any good venues, as the good venues didn't need anyone like us. Also, most of them were controlled by firms outside town, so we only got the shit clubs. But over time we got a reputation for doing a good job and of keeping trouble out of clubs, and more and more venues therefore took us on. What we had back then was loyalty and friendship, which you don't get now. Back then, we worked together, trained together, fought together. We all had a good bond. And we got involved in all sorts of things as well – lots of 'behind the scenes' stuff. People came to us wanting doormen to do this and that, and we kept things nice and tight and controlled things.

We got put to the test a couple of times by a couple of different firms. One night, we got tested by the Gooch. We were running a venue called The Limits in Manchester, and the Gooch were coming to the door in big teams and putting my doormen under pressure. I had had enough of it all, so I told the doormen to let them all in. Once they were in the venue, I made a few phone calls and got as many guys together as I could. There were about 50 of us in all. We shut all the entrances and exits and went into the venue tooled up, and we really hurt some people. But it caused a massive stink, as it was another firm. Their head guys came down, and we respectfully put them in the picture: they could do whatever they wanted, but we were standing firm – we were up for it and had made our stand. The Gooch knew we were not going to the police and that we would fight fire with fire. Because of that, our reputation developed even further.

We had guys from Salford who could sort the Salford side of things out and guys from Cheetham Hill who could sort the Cheetham Hill side of things out. As a result, there was a time in Manchester when most venues ended up using Loc19. We could control most clubs, especially raves and special events, which no one else could. We had allegiance to Loc19 from all quarters and areas of the city, even into Liverpool and Merseyside.

Although Steve and I ran Loc19 and we had over 200 guys working for us, I always worked the doors myself. I wanted to be on the front line. I liked the job. There would be trouble at some of Manchester's late-night venues after 2.30 a.m. once all the main clubs had closed. People would want to come into certain of our venues, but we had to turn them away, which would cause us big problems. There were times when I worked the door every night wearing a bulletproof vest, tooled up with coshes and CS gas. And there were times when I would even wear a vest going to the corner shop for a pint of milk.

In actual fact, violence was rarely used, but it was the fear of *who* we were and what we *could* do that made us what we were. However, saying that, when violence was used, it was used in such a manner that you would never want it to be used on you again. Once you had had a taste of Loc19, you were a broken person, and that was well known.

One night, we had a major confrontation on the door with another firm. One of our doormen, wearing a Loc19 jacket and badge, pulled out a gun and shot one of their firm twice, once in the chest and once in the leg. All hell broke loose, and Loc19 soon crumbled. Once the police got wind that Loc19 were using guns, they wanted to destroy us, and we lost venue after venue as pubs and clubs were told not to use us – we were animals and obviously any licensee or venue owner definitely didn't want doormen working their venue who went around shooting people! Licensees, managers, club owners – everyone became afraid of Loc19, but as a gang our reputation soared. We were fearless;

we were people that didn't fuck about, and as a firm we were left to our own devices. However, Loc19 was slowly pushed to the outskirts of Manchester, because neither the police nor the licensees wanted us running doors in the city centre.

The doorman who had shot someone really fucked our business, and club upon club let us go and found other companies to run their doors. Things really came to an end for Loc19 – as it was back then – at Applejacks nightclub. Applejacks brought in an outside firm called Platinum Security to run their door. One night, one of our lads tried to get into the club and got punched in the mouth by one of their doormen. He told me about it, so my brother Chris, Steve Brian, about 20 lads and I went down to sort things out. We were tooled up just in case, but I said to everyone not to resort to any violence unless I gave the nod. But when we arrived, the doormen wanted a confrontation – they wanted to make a statement. So, I gave the nod, and we annihilated them. It was a massacre that night, and we did some really serious injury, but we all walked away from it. As I turned to leave, I smashed the front door of the club with my fist.

The police didn't get involved straight away, but everything was on camera, including me giving the nod, and the manager had given the CCTV footage to the cops. Two weeks later, a police armed-response unit conducted a dawn raid, and I was arrested and charged with, amongst other things, attempted murder for stabbing a doorman in the chest. On camera, you couldn't see who or what I smashed. At the trial, a bulletproof vest turned up with three stab marks in it, but, unfortunately for the prosecution, I was only seen banging the door, so the charge of attempted murder was eventually dropped.

We were on remand for nine months, straight off the streets. We went to trial, and I was found guilty. Chris, Steve and I all got four and a half years. I was sent to Strangeways, which is another story . . .

Without me or Steve running things, Loc19 more or less fell apart. Once the company leadership had gone, it went to pieces – people helped themselves to our business, and venues found other door firms. We were left with just a couple of units and a handful of doormen.

When I came out of prison, we had to form again, and over time we got things going. Now Loc19 is not as big as it was back in the late

27

1980s and early '90s. Because of the new Security Industry Authority (SIA) rules and regulations, we have taken a step back from the doors, and the business has diversified and now has other interests. It is a different industry to what it was back then. All the guys we used to work with who had street cred can't get a badge – they can't work the doors anymore.

When we were re-establishing ourselves, we looked at other places in the North West where we could run the doors, because we no longer ran as many venues in central Manchester. Chester was one city where Loc19 had a couple of doors but hadn't yet developed a big presence.

TALES FROM CHESTER BY STEVE, AREA MANAGER FOR LOC19

I was working as a doorman in Chester on one of Mickey's doors when, unbeknown to me, Mickey got called by another doorman – who already ran a couple of doors in Chester – to discuss some sort of sharing of the door at my venue, as apparently he had overheard that the owners were looking to get rid of Loc19 and pass the job over to him. Mickey agreed to a meeting at a service station on the motorway and, because I was in charge of the door, asked me to attend.

The other doorman and I arranged to go to the meeting together. Apparently, he was a bit of a name in Chester, but once I told him about Loc19's reputation he crumbled and was on his hands and knees, begging me not to leave him alone with Mickey. He genuinely thought that if Mickey pulled up in a van, he was going to get shot and dumped somewhere.

We met Mickey and one of his colleagues at the service station, where we discussed this doorman's discourtesy to Mickey and Loc19. Because of what he had said and done, it was agreed that he could no longer operate in Chester from that day onwards, and he agreed to hand all his doors over to Mickey and Loc19 as a punishment.

I had been working the doors in the local area for many years and had a strong martial-arts background. I was quite well known, and Mickey asked if I would like to look after business for him in Chester – I agreed. The buzz quickly went round that Loc19 were fully in town. There were mixed emotions: a lot of people were happy that certain local characters would no longer rule the roost, whereas others were not so pleased. However, many of the local gangsters initially kept their heads down and remained out of sight.

Loc19 were like a ghost; people were aware of the name and feared them, but no one had actually seen them, so I thought I'd ask Mickey if he could come down with a few lads and show his face. One night, we were doing a bit of a collection for one of our guys who had cancer. We were collecting at the door and had various fundraising things arranged for that evening, and I asked Mickey if he could come down. I was hoping that he would turn up with a few lads from Manchester as a bit of a show for our boys in Chester. Halfway through the evening as I was inside patrolling the club, one of the doormen rushed up to me and said I had better come to the front door pretty quick. Mickey had come down with about 50 doormen in the biggest black coach I have ever seen. That was the start of Chester police's interest in Loc19. Mickey's presence that night kept the lads safe – they knew they were part of a decent firm.

Later that evening, we all decided to go to another club. I called the head doorman at a place about a mile up the road and told him we were coming – and that there would be a lot of us. I suppose 'no' wasn't really an option, but he said no problem; we were all welcome as his guests. We didn't think that there would be any trouble. We were all there as guests and were all behaving. A few of the lads, because they were new in town, had girls flocking around them. Mickey and I were in a raised area of the club keeping an eye on them all when all of a sudden a local lad from one of the estates smashed a champagne bottle over one of our lads' heads. It immediately turned in on itself; it was like a feeding frenzy against the locals.

The fight was eventually quelled, and the troublemakers were either ejected or sent off to hospital. The head doorman had seen exactly what had happened and was very apologetic, but about ten minutes after everything had died down he came rushing over to me again and told me that the chief constable was outside and wanted to talk to me urgently. I went to the front door and was introduced to a uniformed officer with all the pips and decorations everywhere. He knew my name and told me we had a problem: he knew who we had in there, he wasn't comfortable with what was happening in the venue and all of our lads had to leave immediately. I replied by saying to him that there weren't enough of them to evict us all, and he replied by saying, 'Believe me, there are enough of us.'

The copper told me that the general manager of the venue, who wasn't working that night, had been told about what had just happened at his venue and wasn't at all happy. He had also been told that the police were going to close his club. I couldn't believe it and went over to Mickey and told him what was going on.

So we knew who was who that evening, we were all wearing black. We were like a drilled army. We all stuck together, and within just a few minutes everyone filed quietly out of the venue. As we left the club, there was a big camera pointing at us, filming us as though we were on stage. As we walked back to the coach, which was about a mile up the road, you couldn't see any pavement – it was a mass of black. There were helicopters in the air and police everywhere, and van doors were opened as we marched past, revealing snarling, barking dogs. Later, we had heard that they had even closed all the roads in and out of Chester.

The chief constable and his entourage walked with me, and he told me to stay well away from Mickey and his firm, but I politely reminded him that they were not causing one jot of trouble. No one was being abusive to the police or causing problems. They were just filing out quietly and calmly.

Once we got onto the bus, we decided to go to another venue that we all knew in Ellesmere Port. I called the manager and asked if we could all come in. He said by all means and agreed to meet us at the gate. We drove off under police escort, like we were royalty! But the manager was then contacted by the police, who were obviously listening in to our calls, telling him we were on the way to his venue and he was to close up and turn all the lights out. He refused, telling the police that we were his security company and that he could have whomever he wanted in his venue, and he kept the club open for us. Most of the police convoy left us once we had turned off the motorway, apart from a few vehicles, which were placed strategically around the venue.

30

What really infuriated me were the headlines in the local papers the next day and for about two weeks thereafter. 'Marauding gang of Manchester doormen wreck Chester after bursting through the doors of Rosie's nightclub' was one example. We were accused of attacking the doorstaff, turning tables and chairs over, and only being in town with the intention of causing mayhem. It was reported that the local police sorted us all out and removed us from the town under police escort. It was a complete fabrication, and it lost us a couple of doors. We were even accused of supplying drugs and being drug lords. When I told Mickey about the headlines, he just laughed and said, 'Welcome to the real world.'

Chester is a tourist town and a place for entertainment; for example, we have the very famous Chester races, which are attended by people from all over the country. We have visitors from Manchester, Liverpool and London. Admittedly, they don't always get on with one another, but when most serious players see the Loc19 badge that *all* our doormen and security staff wear they behave and show us respect. And that is how we have gained a lot of doors and venues, as the managers see this too. Loc19 is not afraid of taking anybody on.

There are a couple of big estates just outside Chester. Some of the lads who live there have held siege to our venue on a couple of occasions, surrounding us and throwing bricks through the windows. The police didn't really want to know, so after the second time we had to sort things out ourselves and make sure that it didn't happen again. We visited one particular estate, where we knew the main players were based, and spent an evening walking into pubs, asking around. We made sure people knew who we were, that we were in the area and exactly what we wanted – in other words, we made sure that the word got about. Later that night, I got a call from one of the head lads asking for a meeting. We arranged to meet in one of our bars in Chester on a Tuesday afternoon at 2 p.m. There were about six heads of the area plus a few of their soldiers. I arrived first and was just about to buy everyone a round of drinks before we got talking when the whole place was flooded with police. They had blocked the road at either end and took everyone outside and lined them up against the wall, apart from me and my driver. The police had heard that we had been looking around the estate, and they told the locals that we were very dangerous people. Anyway, we assured the police that we were just having a meeting and that nothing was going down. Things eventually died down (although one person got carted away for non-payment of a fine), and the police left. We had our meeting and told the heads of the estate that Loc19 wanted them to work with us; we wanted them behind us, not against us. By the end of the meeting, they were all beaming – they could go back to their communities proud.

When they went to pick up their lad who had got nicked, the police wanted to know what had been said and what was going down. They told the coppers that in those few hours Loc19 had done more for their community than the police had done in years. All the cops had done was to chase kids around and nick them for this and that, whereas Loc19 gave them respect.

Of course, we understand that because the police have their hands tied they can't do what we can do. We can go and sort out these problems in our own way, but we have never been bullies. As a company, we have never taken a fight to anybody first; we have always responded. If the police could only work with us and other firms like us, there would be a lot less trouble.

Not long after, we took on a club on the outskirts of Chester in Ellesmere Port, a tough residential community with some tough people living there. No one wanted to run the bar. It was a really rough place, a bit like something from the Wild West. One particular family had a reputation as being one of the worst in the area, and within that family there were twins who for some reason thought that they were the Krays.

One night, these twins caused a bit of mischief at our venue. They were pissed up and having an argument with what seemed like another member of their family. A couple of my lads and I tried to settle things down, but the twins took the piss a bit. I really didn't want the story getting back to Mickey, as the fight was eventually quelled and things were sorted out, but the manager was adamant that Mickey was told.

Mickey was in the area at that time, so he suggested we give the twins a visit. To be honest, I didn't think it was a good idea – there was only me, Mickey and Mickey's driver! Anyway, we went to the twins' house and rang the doorbell. As soon as one of them answered the door, Mickey said, 'All right, mate?' and punched him straight in the face. Mickey then said, 'Listen, you took the piss with the doormen at our venue. Because you disrespected Steve, you have to pay him £1,000 by next Friday for his discomforts, and if I have to come back to your fucking house, I won't be *talking* to you.' The guy looked nothing like the hard man he was supposed to be. On the Monday, he paid me, and we never heard from him again.

I have to say that Loc19 is one of the best firms I have ever worked for. The employees have huge respect for the company, something rarely seen in other door firms. The doormen covet their badges more than anything. For instance, one of our doormen had a £700 coat stolen that his wife had bought him one Christmas, and he was nearly crying because his badge was on it. Lads want to work for us because of the firm's reputation. For most of them, working for Loc19 is a big honour.

BIOGRAPHY OF MICKEY FRANCIS

Mickey Francis, AKA 'The Guvnor', is the All Nations Heavyweight Wrestling Champion of the World and one of the UK's premier wrestlers. His book *Guvnors: Story of a Soccer Hooligan Gang by the Man Who Led It* was published ten years ago and is still a best-seller in its genre. Mickey continues to run Loc19 and supports various children's charities. He can be contacted via his website www.the-guvnor.co.uk

3

DAVE COURTNEY TALKING ...
BY DAVE COURTNEY

You will never be able to replace the quality of fighting doormen that you had back then with what you have on the doors now, purely because it was an era when fighting was popular, you know. 'Are you looking at my pint?' and it would all go off. And the emphasis on the door and number-one rule from the owner was 'WIN!' If you lost a fight on the door, the manager would basically sack you and employ a better fighter. It actually made doormen famous throughout the land for being good fighters, e.g. Lenny McLean and Roy Shaw. Every town up and down the UK had their minor celebrities. And it made tasty bastards – it just made fucking tasty bastards. Back then, we would have 3,000 people in a nightclub, at The Hippodrome say. You would have two doormen outside, one doorman inside and one doorman upstairs. That was 750 people each. No fucking walkie-talkies or CCTV or that shit. When it kicked off, we just fucking shouted, 'HELP ME!'

Fighting is like any other contact sport – including sex – in that you cannot get good at it unless you do it. You cannot stop playing football for six months and come back being as good as you were. Back then, the doormen were fighting four or five times a night, five nights a week for fucking years. And if you decided to kick off, you were in fucking trouble, because doormen were fucking good fighters. But now your doorman has his name and photograph and all his fucking details on a badge. If he hits a punter back once – if he hits him back! – he is brought to the police station by the owner, and he will never work again. So please can some cunt tell me how you are supposed to get good at something that you aren't allowed to do. Right? If you hit someone now, you are sacked and never allowed to work as a doorman again. How the fuck is someone supposed to get good at something that they aren't allowed to do? This is fucking diabolical. You will never replace the Lenny McLeans. And the way it's covered now is to have loads of doormen. You can't just send one doorman in to sort things out; now you have to send four fucking doormen in to get a fella out! And now you have 28 fucking doormen in the same place that I used to work in on my fucking own – 28 fucking doormen, all with walkie-talkies and CCTV.

Society outside the nightclub might be more violent, but inside it is no more violent. There is no way in the world there are more fights in the nightclubs now than in my time. There fucking aren't. With all those cameras! Twenty years ago, we fought every week – we had to. How the fucking hell do dickheads standing ten-handed on the door think they are a proper door team. If any one of them is banged once, they are dead. They're just dickheads on the buzz, suited up, but if they hit anyone, they will never do the job again. How can they justify their fucking bravado? You cannot be what we were back then – doormen became famous worldwide. You will never have doormen taking on a pub full of Arsenal supporters like you did back then. Some of these people were – rightly so – legends. Whereas before there was one doorman onto twenty, now it's twenty doormen onto one.

And bodybuilding wasn't as popular back then as it is now. There were big ol' lads, but they weren't really bodybuilders. Listen, if you are fucking frightened of spiders and then you go away for two years, wear leotards, stick things in your bum, look at yourself all the time in the mirror and come back, you are still fucking scared of spiders! You just don't *look* like you are. It's not like you've gone away for two years and learned karate, unarmed combat, ju-jitsu – these bodybuilders have actually worn leotards, looked in the mirror, popped a few pills and . . . I am not saying that this is all bodybuilders, but fucking most.

Take Lenny McLean, for instance: he was a fucking tasty cunt at 16 stone, and that is well known. When he decided to do all that bodybuilding and went up to 20 stone, he was a *fucking* tasty cunt, because he was already a tasty cunt at 16 stone! If you are not already a good fighter and go away and become 20 stone of meat, it won't actually make you any better when you tell some cunt to leave and he tells you to fuck off. (And you are not allowed to hit anyone now, anyway.)

You can see naughtiness in a man; you can smell if someone is capable of it. Say you are gay and you go into a nightclub, you can spot another gay. If you are a heroin addict, you can pick out someone else who uses straight away. And if you are a naughty man, you can pick that out, too. You can pick up the mannerisms.

They say the eyes are a window to the soul. I know if someone is fucking handy from their eyes. I know if they can hurt me or if I can beat them from their eyes – nine times out of ten. Some of the naughtiest men I know look as though they couldn't harm a fly, but they have it in their eyes, and some of the scariest looking fucking creatures you have ever seen in your life are like fucking kids. When you go to work on the building site, you wear overalls or a mask if you are a welder. As a doorman, you are *supposed* to look scary.

Believe it or not, what is actually happening now is that doormen are just policemen! You are not a proper doorman if you are not allowed to hit anyone back. As a doorman now you are someone who is going to arrest someone, take them down to the police station, stand in court and point your finger at them, and all that. And if you don't point your finger and put them in prison like the governor wants, you are sacked. And because they have never experienced the old ways of the doormen, the new doormen of today actually believe that this is the way it should be, that this is really it, even though they are not allowed to hit anyone, not once – *ever*. They have never experienced the old ways.

In the old days, doormen saved each other's lives three times last week. When there was a big fight and everyone used ashtrays and glasses and fuck knows what, and you thought you had cashed your chips in, you came out of that saving each other's necks – fuck me, you were fucking buzzing. How can that be the same now? You cannot find that in any other walk of life, bar maybe in the forces. The forces are so good at building on the strength of companionship. (Although I am not too keen on their aftercare when you leave. You grow as a unit and then one day you are out with fucking nothing.) You will never find that anywhere else. You used to be able to find that working the doors.

Having a good partner on the doors was essential, because if you didn't, you would get your fucking head kicked in. He saved your life. It is a lot fucking easier to be a doorman now when the governor has got 28 of you and you search everyone 20 fucking times even before the punters get in the club, and the club is all camerad up. And if after all that the fucking bollocks does go off, you are not allowed to do anything anyway.

The doorman today is only a doorman in name. Real doormen are no more. They are all like special policemen now. It is not like you can sort things out there and then in your own club any more. If you catch someone with drugs, you can't clip them round the ear and throw them out. If it goes off now, you hold them and call the fucking police. It doesn't make fucking sense.

The business was not just about what you knew but who you knew. There was no industry in the world like it. But not today. Back in the old days, if you ran a firm, your firm was run military style.

Nowadays, teachers are not allowed to tell you off. If your mum gives you a smack, you can take her to court. What sort of a world are we living in? Back in my time, if you did something wrong at school, you got the cane, your mum told you off and your dad gave you a beating. Now, if you do something wrong at school, you get detention, and if you tell them to fuck off and don't get detention, then what? We should tell the fucking do-gooders to *shut the fuck up*! Same in the clubs: if you tell someone to leave and they tell you to fuck off knowing that it is all camerad up, what the fuck do you do? Doormen are fucked, yet they still try to drag a little fame and glory out of the job when it is just a title. Again, a doorman is now just a police officer.

The government is turning the whole country into a country of informants. This is the God's honest truth. When this country came out of the war era, the word on the street was 'loose lips sink ships'. And the whole fucking nation grew up with that instilled in them – that was the number-one rule. The policemen at the time knew their job was very hard, as everyone said, 'I ain't saying nothing.' And that came about purely because of the war years, but in the last 40 years it's all changed. The government has, on purpose, made everyone informants. I paid policemen – I *know* what I am talking about. Please believe me, I know I am right. They made a conscious decision to make informing right. If you said to me 20 fucking years ago that there would be a programme on TV just for fucking grasses, I would have bet my life, or my kids' lives, that you were lying. But cleverly, on prime-time television on every single station there are now trailers advertising entertainment programmes for grassing people up. There is a grass line if you are claiming the dole, a grass line if you have a gun. They have made it so matter-of-fact. There is a thing that if you know someone who has drunk too much and the cops catch them, you get £500 for grassing them up. There are people who go into a pub, buy their mates a few drinks and then grass them up. There is even a grass line for other doormen to grass on their mates, the people they work with. People grassing up their friends, their mothers, their dads is fucking Hitler Youth stuff. The government has turned it all around. There are no more Sherlock Holmes policemen; coppers now just rely on fucking grasses.

They can take photos of you from the fucking moon, and new cars have to have a tracker installed so that they know where you are. Mark my words, one day every single car in the country will be bugged – a fucking police bug so they know where you are. There is no freedom of speech. The journalists have freedom of speech, but the editor doesn't. The journalist writes a good story, but the editor says that it's not allowed.

I get booked to do talks around the country, but the police usually come and say if you have Dave Courtney talking, cancel it or lose your licence. Then I get a call with some excuse – the landlord's nan's died or something – but they don't realise how many calls I get. They think they have a good excuse to get out of it, but I hear it every week. All the time Dave Courtney is alive, living in the UK and not in prison, I am rubbing their faces in it, and the police hate it.

Because of the situation nowadays, the smart nightclub owner does this: he greases the authorities by having a certain amount of doormen working legitimately and trying not to beat anybody up on the premises; meanwhile, he employs another four people at the bar, not in doormen attire. If someone does need a fucking good kicking or the doormen are finding it hard to eject him, then they pass the job off. If anyone says anything, the unofficial doormen just leave. When the police and ambulance turn up, it wasn't the doormen.

Back in my day, the industry was a job centre for 'doormen for hire'. It wasn't just about the job doormen did for five hours a night. If you wanted anything doing, a doorman would do it – hired muscle, rent a thug. If you wanted your neighbours smacked in the mouth or your girlfriend's ex to be told to fuck off, everyone knew someone who could do it, and doormen were the people to go to. To go and get muscle and things just grew for me that way. My personality is that I am easily approachable, and the door industry was a massive job centre for me. People contacted me from all over the world. Dave, can you get this? Dave, can you do that? I would get calls from people with £10-million debts. It was a job centre for *naughty* men. They were doormen for five or six hours a night, but for twenty-four hours a day, seven days a week, they were muscle for hire. If they beat people up in the clubs six nights a week, then they would do it to your neighbour for a grand. Now, this is all completely crushed. I am afraid the poor old English person is brainwashed.

I have actually read an article in the newspaper that Dave Courtney might be an informant, alongside my photograph! When I saw it, I said, 'What?' When I went to court, I was found not guilty and the coppers guilty. But they didn't put that in the paper! The power the government has over British subjects is fucking frightening.

I really miss the old days. I actually bang one off thinking about them. When my cock won't get rock hard or something, I don't think of a bird, I think about the old days.

BIOGRAPHY OF DAVE COURTNEY

According to his website, ex-London gangster Dave Courtney has been shot and stabbed, had his nose bitten off and has had to kill to stay alive. He has had long-standing friendships with many notorious hard men including 'Pretty Boy' Roy Shaw, the late Lenny McLean and the Krays. Amongst many other things, Dave has managed nightclubs and run security and debt-collecting companies – and he has been called 'King of the Underworld' and the 'most feared man in Britain'. In 1995, Dave arranged security for the funeral of Ronnie Kray.

Dave lives at Camelot Castle, south-east London, and has had number-one best-sellers with *The Ride's Back On*, *F**k the Ride*, *Stop the Ride I Want to Get Off*, *Raving Lunacy*, *Heroes and Villains* and *Dodgy Dave's Little Black Book*. Dave has also appeared in a few films, including *The Krays*, *Clubbing to Death*, *Six Bend Trap* and *Hell to Pay*.

Dave now does a lot of charity work for the Prince's Trust and is a patron of the children's ADHD charity Misunderstood.

Dave can be contacted via his website www.davecourtney.com

4

TOO BIG TO BE A GLASS COLLECTOR

BY SCOTT TAYLOR

'**Y**ou're a bit big to be a fucking glass collector, aren't you?'
Those were the words that led me into my 15 year love–hate affair with the door. They came from a man called Ramsey, a huge highlander who worked as the bouncer in the bar I had just got a job in. I was a 17-year-old, acne-riddled boy working in a shit hole of a bar collecting glasses at weekends, the first job that I'd managed to get since moving to Aberdeen from a small town called Thurso in the far north of Scotland.

'What in the fuck are you doing collecting glasses, Scott?' Ramsey said, flashing me his trademark huge grin whilst knocking back his usual pre-shift treble vodka and coke. 'You should be on the fucking door with me!'

I couldn't figure out what to say to him. How could I explain that I was as timid as a field mouse and that the very thought of standing at a pub doorway telling people that they couldn't get in scared the shit out of me? How could I explain that I had no self-confidence thanks to a neglected upbringing by an alcoholic mother and that I was terrified of confrontation thanks to repeated beatings throughout my school years by older kids? I'd been working as a glass collector for a month, and it was hard enough to deal with people accusing you of stealing their drinks, even though their glasses were empty when you picked them up, or the assholes who wouldn't move out of your way when you were trying to manoeuvre through a packed crowd with armfuls of pint and shot glasses.

Before I could tell Ramsey that there was no way I could be a bouncer, he had stormed off toward the bar, where he'd spotted the manageress. After a few minutes of arguing with her, he walked back towards me with a big grin on his face, threw me a bow tie and said, 'You're on the door with me tonight, lad. We're going to have fun!'

So that was it – I was a doorman. The only good I could see in all of this was the big jump in wages, but then I didn't think that it compensated for the fear that was pumping its way through me the first night working on the door. My voice was squeaky, making me sound like Mickey Mouse whenever a customer asked me a question. I must have run to the toilet for a terror-induced shit about five times in that first hour, and I was sweating more than Michael Jackson having a browse through Mothercare.

Ramsey, however, loved the whole situation; finally, he had a fellow highlander with him on the door – he had a deep distrust of the city 'lowlanders'. We also discovered that our parents used to live a few doors apart in the same street, so most of our chat was all about the home country that we'd left to find work in the big city. Having Ramsey there made it easier for me to relax, and over time he helped me (unwittingly, it appeared) to develop my self-confidence and put my fears aside. No longer was I frozen stiff when speaking to people I didn't know; no longer was I terrified of confrontation. Hell, being on the door was probably the very best therapy I could have had, and it was thanks to that big, usually drunk highlander who threw me a bow tie.

After a while, I discovered that I loved my job. I loved meeting new people and working in new venues. I loved watching the ebb and flow of a crowd as the night grew long, watching and scanning for any possible 'hot spots'. And as much as I abhorred violence of any kind, I loved the 'I survived that shit!' feeling you would get as you wound down from the adrenalin surge you'd just had after you'd been in the middle of a massive 'Battle Royale'. That's if you managed to make it out unscathed, of course.

In my 15 years working the doors, I've seen too many good men and women getting seriously hurt because of the stupidity of the half-pint heroes – people who can't go on a night out with friends and drink sensibly. I've seen friends go to hospital after having their face sliced open by broken bottles, being left with partial vision after being smashed in the face with a stool or chair, or having their skulls fractured by a well-placed kick when they're down on the ground. These are people whose lives have been irrevocably changed thanks to the actions of some pissed-up bastard who thinks that it's his God-given right to get drunk and fight, and that a night out isn't a good one unless they come home covered in someone else's blood or wake up in a cell covered in their own piss, vomit and shit after 'sleeping it off' for the night. To these vermin this is the sign of a good night out, a night out that they can boast about to their workmates the next day over the water cooler. To me it's the sign of a deep-rooted problem with their upbringing and their psychological make-up.

I have personally suffered numerous concussions, broken fingers, broken ribs, 14 or more broken noses, several scars thanks to glasses, ashtrays or bottles being raked across me, attempted stabbings, one successful stabbing and teeth smashed out thanks to several boots to the head. But if I bloody someone's nose in self-defence, suddenly I'm an out-of-control monster and a thug who thrives on bloodshed and bullying – or at least that's how I'll be portrayed in the newspapers, which will invariably carry the story in big letters on their front page the next day.

My views on the state of today's drinking culture and my complete disdain for the weekend whisky warriors aside (and before I go completely off topic), I mentioned the elation you feel after surviving a battle in your venue. The feeling you get as you sit down with your team after your shift knowing that you've all had your shit on the line and you've survived is one of the best bonding experiences you can have. That's a reason why I love the job and all the crap that goes with it. You have to trust that the guy beside you in the black tie can hold his shit together when the proverbial hits the fan. When he does, it builds a trust between you and your teammate that is, in my humble opinion, rarely found in any other line of work. These are men and women you are counting on to save your ass when you're up the creek without a paddle, the very same people who through their actions demonstrate that they are to be trusted and in doing so become some of your closest friends.

I have made friends through this job that I would go to the grave for, people whom I would trust with my life – if it came to the crunch, friends I would do anything for. I've travelled the length and breadth of the country to help these people out. I've kicked down doors with my big, black Magnum boots to stop people threatening and intimidating those close to me, and I've lent a shoulder to those friends whose lives have crumbled and fallen around them. And never have I doubted that they would do exactly the same for me or that they would go out of their way to support and protect me. That's what doing the doors means to me: building friendships so intense that people become family. And throughout my years of bouncing, I've built up a massive family.

However, on the flipside, the job also brings you into contact with people who will become your mortal enemy, the weekend whisky warriors who take you throwing their drunken ass out of a club as a personal insult and will hold that grudge against you for a very long time. In the past, I've had to change my mobile phone number more times than I can remember to avoid the prank calls and death threats from those I've thrown out of bars, sometimes for something as simple as them being too drunk to stand. These people, who take being asked to leave as a slight on their holier-than-thou character, will go out of their way to hound and harass you. Most of the time, a quiet word in their 'shell like' normally stops the harassment quick sharp, but at other times it goes well past the point of annoying phone calls.

I remember one time I came home to the flat I shared with a former girlfriend to find my front door loose on its hinges when I put my key in the lock and opened it. My girlfriend, who'd been home alone, came running to me and dove into my arms, sobbing uncontrollably into my chest. After a while of reassuring her, she managed to tell me that she had been lying in bed at about 1 a.m. when she had heard someone pounding at the door, shouting my name. She kept the lights off and looked out into the hallway toward the front door. Back then, most flats in the area had strengthened, frosted-glass doors, and she could see that there were at least three people outside, pounding on the door. Luckily, she had more sense than to go and answer it; instead, she sat down in the hall and watched in terror as the three figures continued shouting my name and booting at the door.

For about 15 minutes, they continued to pound on the glass, trying desperately to break their way in – all the while my ex sat on the floor, hugging her knees and sobbing quietly, terrified that they might make it into the flat and too scared to move toward the phone in case the three figures, which she guessed to be all male, noticed the movement through the frosted glass and intensified their attack on the door.

Finally, they gave up after realising that they weren't going to get through or that there really was nobody home. It was about 15 minutes after they left until my ex finally felt that it was safe to move. She got to her feet, double checked the locks on the door were still secure and then ran to the bedroom, where she fell to the floor beside the bed and sobbed uncontrollably until I came home little over an hour later.

Initially, I was furious that someone would attack my home, although I had no idea who had done this or why. I banged on my neighbour's door until they answered and demanded to know why they hadn't seen fit to call the police when they could hear the commotion outside. All I got was apology after apology as the young lady I was speaking to stood crying at her door asking if my partner was OK. Sadly, this was an area of the city where incidents like that happened all the time, and the residents who weren't drug dealers, prostitutes or junkies were too scared to report any crime in case the criminals found out it was them and targeted them next.

I was furious. Almost blind with rage, I stormed out into the street, my ex-partner pleading for me not to leave her in the flat alone. I stood in the road furious, yelling out for whoever it was that attacked my home to come and get me, but apart from curtains being twitched all along the road by concerned neighbours, nobody responded to my call. There was nothing else I could do that night except go back into the flat and reassure my partner. Over the next few days, I put out feelers all round the city trying to find out who the lads were, and it wasn't until the following weekend that the information I wanted came my way.

One of my good friends who worked at another venue had found out that the three lads had come looking for me to give me a beating. It seemed that I had thrown one of them out of the club I worked in because he was drunk, and in doing so I had embarrassed him in front of the lady he was with. In an attempt to save face, he had orchestrated the attack on my home when he knew that I would be at work so that the two friends he'd roped in to help him out would think that he was some kind of hard bastard when they beat up on my door.

The lad had taken the simple act of me throwing him out of a bar as such an insult to his manhood that he attacked my home and terrified the woman I lived with. My good friend supplied me with the young man's address, and he and I enjoyed a good talk over tea and biscuits. Well, that's maybe a slight simplification of what happened, but I'll leave you to do the colouring in.

This was one of the few times that nearly killed my love for the door and almost wiped out any fondness I had for my profession and nearly poisoned me against ever stepping foot on the door again. I can deal with a lot in my life and have a very long fuse when it comes to people attacking me either verbally or physically on the door, but when it arrives at your home it's a different matter entirely. Luckily, with the support of those around me, I put my anger behind me and got back to doing what I love.

However, like any love, it's constantly tested. Time can pick holes in it and start to blur the parts that encouraged your affection. Time erodes things that in the past seemed new and vibrant, and outside influences spread a cancer in the thing you love that force it to die in front of your eyes. I've tried looking through rose-tinted glasses as the job evolves around me, with promises from those in power that things are changing for the better and that what will emerge out the other side will be a more controlled, regulated, professional and better industry than we have presently. However, all the signs so far look like the industry is heading for an iceberg and we should man the lifeboats as soon as possible.

Since the implementation of the SIA in the UK, good stewards who've done the door for years have been told that under the new regime they will no longer be able to work, as they picked up an assault charge, for example, a couple of years previously. Hell, one lad I know had his application for a licence turned down and put to appeal because he was detained for a weekend by the police because of a breach of the peace after having an argument with his former girlfriend in their home. I've watched as lads who've done the door for years hang up their boots and call it a day rather than throwing nearly £400 at the SIA to get a little badge that says they're fit to do the same job they've done for the last 20 years.

These are the very same men and women who put me through my apprenticeship when I started on the doors. If you can show me in black and white how certificates earned over a few days sitting in a classroom make you more proficient on the door compared to a rookie working with a team of experienced, professional doormen who over time can show him exactly how to spot trouble and deal with it proficiently and swiftly, then I'll wear my SIA badge on my chest with the pride and justification it deserves. Until then, I'll continue to piss and moan to anyone who will listen about how the SIA are killing the doorman community and making it near impossible for us to do our jobs.

I've sat back and watched as young students are brought on board by security agencies, put through their courses and then paid a damn near minimum wage for putting their safety on the line week in, week out while the agency rubs its hands at the increased profit margins. These are the very same agencies that filter out the more experienced lads because the profit margin is too low and then fill the gaps with young boys and girls who are thrust clean into the firing line. I've sat back and watched the SIA put the control of the UK's pubs and clubs back into the hands of the weekend whisky warriors, and it hurts me to see the industry I love dying on its arse.

Modern stewards are now concerned about getting involved in separating troublemakers in case one of the parties reports their badge number and makes a false claim against them. Hearing the words, 'What's your fucking badge number?' from some pissed-up asshole you've just thrown out for groping one of the barmaids is guaranteed to make you think twice. And now that these half-pint heroes know they've got control over you, there's no respect for the stewards in a venue any more. Effectively, the SIA have tied our hands in political correctness. All we can do now is sit back and watch the show while the monkeys take control of the circus.

I still work on the doors and still suffer weekly abuse from those whisky warriors who plague the city. I sit here twiddling my thumbs waiting for the SIA to send me a badge in Scotland, saying that I'm a fit and capable human being to stand on a cold, wet doorway of an evening!

My love affair with the job is still there – for the time being. However, as time goes by and the job becomes more and more tied up by the politically correct brigade and the wonderful SIA, I may have to cut ties with the old lady of my life and move on to pastures new and find another job to love. When the industry does die, would the last member of the SIA please put the lights out after them?

BIOGRAPHY OF SCOTT TAYLOR

As well as working the doors, Scott works for a large entertainment company based in Aberdeen as the security manager for their venues. In 2004, as a side project while he taught himself web and graphic design, he built a door-steward-related website called www.door-network.com, which has over 1,000 registered members and is getting more and more popular by the week. Scott uses his spare time training to compete in strongman events, writing stories about his time on the doors and spending far more time than is feasibly healthy on the Internet.

At the time of writing, Scotland had followed England and just implemented new rules regarding security-industry licensing. Scott is still waiting for his licence to arrive, four months after attending yet another SIA accredited course.

He can be contacted at scott@door-network.com

5

CHARLIE BRONSON, DOING THE DOORS AND ME

BY STU CHESHIRE

I've been working the door for some time now, and it was actually the infamous and notorious Charlie Bronson who initially helped me with my SIA licence. It was a few years ago and I was on holiday with my girlfriend in the Gambia, sunning ourselves by the side of the pool. Nearby were a couple whom we had said hello to a couple of times when we occasionally passed each other in the foyer or in the bar. As we all sat quietly baking in the hot African sun, I couldn't help but overhear them chatting to each other, and from their conversation I quickly understood that they were both prison officers. I also noticed that the man was reading Charlie Bronson's biography – Charlie's first best-seller. Being an inquisitive soul, I politely butted in and asked if he was actually guarding Bronson himself. He said that he didn't work in that prison but that he knew a couple of wardens who did work with Charlie, and he also told me how good the book was. I cheekily asked if I could borrow it after he had finished, and he said, of course.

Because it was such a great read and he wanted it back before he returned home, it was probably the quickest I have ever read a book – much to my girlfriend's annoyance. She kept moaning that I was concentrating too much on the book and not enough on her! I was enthralled with Bronson's story and his mad, crazy life. It was a great book and an unputdownable read, and as soon as I got back to England I decided to write to Charlie and tell him how much I had enjoyed it.

A couple of days after returning home and settling back into my mundane life, I put pen to paper and wrote Charlie a long letter telling him what I thought about the book and how much I had enjoyed reading it. I never really expected the letter to reach him and thought that it would not get delivered or else be added to the large pile that Charlie must receive each and every day. To be honest, I thought he must have hundreds of people writing to him, and I didn't expect a reply. Surprisingly, he wrote back to me within just a week of me posting the letter – I was really pleased when a strange-looking envelope appeared through my letter box!

I replied back to Charlie almost straight away. After reading his book, I felt we actually had quite a bit in common – we both loved boxing, keeping fit and unarmed combat – and over the following 12 to 18 months we became friends, writing backwards and forwards about the stuff that we both liked.

In one of my letters, I told him that I was working the doors. He was very supportive and wrote back to me with quite a bit of advice – and advice from Bronson is definitely something to take seriously! Although he had spent much of his time behind bars, he did know a lot about life, dealing with violent situations and handling violent people. A life behind bars must also be an extremely violent life.

I was in the middle of buying a house with my girlfriend, and for a long time we had both saved really hard in order to get just about enough money together for a deposit. Times were tough, and the laws had just changed with regards to SIA licences. Like a great many other people in the same position as me, I had to get a licence in order to carry on working. It was bollocks, as I already had a licence from the local council in which I was operating, but now I had to go on another stupid course for another piece of paper to allow me to do the job I had been doing for years. However, because I was in debt up to my eyeballs with my new house, I just didn't have the money to attend the training course, let alone pay the money needed for the licence – every single penny I had was in the property. I needed the work desperately, but couldn't get it because I didn't have a licence, and without the work I couldn't afford the licence. The uncaring SIA had made it unfairly difficult for me and many people like me. I was trapped.

I moaned about all of this to Charlie in one of my letters, telling him how unfair the whole system was. Completely out of the blue, Charlie, via a friend of his on the outside, sent me one of his works of art to auction off. He said that I could use the money to pay for the door supervisors training course and the SIA licence, and anything left over should be sent to a children's charity in Liverpool he had been supporting for a number of years called Zöe's Place Baby Hospice. I was completely gobsmacked that someone who I hadn't even met should decide to help me in this way. I thought it was wonderful that someone had that much trust in a friendship that had only been developed via pen and paper in an occasional letter and card. It was great.

Altogether I raised just over £900, and I was able to send a nice fat cheque to Zöe's Place as well as getting my SIA licence. Charlie told me in a later letter that a few of the people he had helped had not been so honest – either pocketing all of the money themselves or not being so truthful about the total amount they had raised. He had never heard from those people again. But we were friends and had been writing to each other off and on for quite a while – I wasn't going to spoil the relationship by being dishonest with him, and to this day I am still his friend. I still write to him and even get up to Wakefield to see him now and then.

Because of his status in prison, it is very hard to get a permit to visit Charlie Bronson. First, you have to apply and Charlie also has to submit a formal application. CID visit you and ask you lots of awkward questions about why you want to visit him, and they thoroughly check your background. Even after all of that, there is still no guarantee that when you turn up you will be allowed in. I have heard that quite a number of people are turned away and refused access with no reason being given.

Charlie Bronson is Charlie Bronson, and personally I think he is now inside only because of his name, not because he deserves to be in prison any more – most prisoners have been set free after serving less time for committing crimes a lot worse. Even murderers get less time than Charlie has had, and 30 years' solitary is completely contrary to any human-rights policy almost anywhere in the world – even third-world countries don't treat prisoners so badly. Anyone who is now in contact with Charlie says that he is a decent guy who once led a violent life – but that was 33 years and another lifetime ago. I have always found him helpful and kind, and if it wasn't for Charlie I would not have worked as a bouncer for as long as I have. I am proud to work the doors – it is a great job.

As the years go by, I am constantly amazed by the scumbags you meet while working on the doors. I am sure there is not a doorman (or doorwoman) in the land (or in the world) that hasn't got a good story to tell from their time in the job. Funny or frightening, violent or sad, comical or miserable, we've had them all. It's an occupational hazard: nutters wanting to cut your throat, stab you and shoot you all because you have refused them entry into your venue on the grounds that they're a scumbag! And evidently your judgement has served you well – that is the reason why they are going mad outside, making threats and not just walking away. They are pond life and scumbags.

Don't get me wrong – it's not all bad. There was one night my fellow doormen and I turned a group of foul-mouthed girls away who had clearly drunk far too much. One of the group came back to the door. She was about five feet five inches and probably well over sixteen stone. She was a fucking monster and a right 'space hopper' – God was she ugly. She had a face like she had battled parked cars and very little personality to match. She was staggering all over the place telling all the door staff exactly what she thought of us. Suddenly, she fell over and landed flat on her back right in front of us. All 16 stone of her was on display, her fat legs splayed in the air and her skirt horribly hitched around her middle – not a pretty sight, I can tell you.

And it was made fucking worse by the fact that she wasn't wearing any knickers. Why is it that the fat, ugly girls are generally the ones who cause most trouble and are the worst to deal with? Seeing her fat legs in the air and a grotesque tuft of back fluff between that mound of ugly white flesh, I couldn't stop laughing. It is comedy moments like this that make the job worth doing.

There was another incident when a guy was asked to leave the venue by the manager and he refused – as they all seem to do. I was asked to deal with this, and the bloke went for me. I restrained him, and he was quickly removed. Outside, he was still playing up, coming back for more – as they all also seem to do! I was trying to be reasonable and polite, which he obviously thought was a weakness. Big mistake! To be fair, he brought out the worst in me at that particular point, and the guy ended up actually shitting himself. The smell was fucking awful. It wasn't a proud moment, but sometimes things like this just need to be done.

The worst incident that I have ever been involved in was out the back of the club. The venue was rough: fights almost every night; a guaranteed glassing at least once a week. A group of lads were thrown out of the fire exit at the back of the club, and a big fight started to unfold. Unluckily for us, the club toilets were being refurbished at that time, and the builders had left the scrap piled up in a skip around the back, which quickly became weapons in the hands of the group of not too happy scumbags. Bars and pipes were flying everywhere, and blood started to flow. I ended up in hospital with severe internal bleeding after being bashed hard in the side with a piece of pipe. But times like that are all part of the job, part of being a bouncer. We won the fight that night – perhaps we might have been accused of being a little 'heavy handed' – perhaps – and looking at the blood-stained white bonnet of a parked car nearby it certainly looked that way. But for me it is just personal safety – we were fighting for our lives. People who criticise and condemn bouncers very easily forget that it is our job to keep a venue safe, to keep the scum out and to create a civilised place for decent people to enjoy a good night out. And if that means battling hard . . . well, so be it.

In this occasionally tough job, those were the sorts of places I first cut my teeth in. Tough, hard, demanding places, where I had no choice but to learn quickly and react fast. These are places I think all beginners should start at; if they can't face the worst, then they should not be given the best. 'Jacket fillers' who have been on the doors for a while but have never experienced the worst should not be doing this job, as the worst *will* happen at some point to everyone. If you have not had the experience or don't know how to react and deal with it, then you are putting yourself, your team and your customers in great danger. But nowadays most doormen don't want to battle – they want an easy life, posing, chatting up the girls and looking cool. There are many doormen working the doors now that have never been involved in a violent incident. I find that amazing.

I am not sure if I would still be on the doors had it not been for Charlie Bronson sort of sponsoring me. At that time, I was definitely unable to afford the course fees and the licence, and maybe, as time passed, I would have never been able to get them.

They say that you miss the doors for the first few months away. You really miss the people, the music, the fun, the other doormen, but after a while away from that life, away from the doors, it becomes harder and harder to go back again. At one time, a weekend at home with the missus was a luxury and a rarity, but after a few weekends at home it becomes the norm and leaving is virtually impossible.

These days I work an altogether different venue: The Boars Head taphouse in Kidderminster – a large, friendly pub that puts on live bands and prides itself in attracting decent customers. Pop in sometime and say hello.

BIOGRAPHY OF STU CHESHIRE

Stu was born into a decent middle-class family in a nice area of Worcestershire but had a strict upbringing and was often caned by his father. As a teenager, he was always in trouble: hanging around with bad lads and causing bother in the rougher parts of town. His father then introduced Stuart to boxing, which occupied his mind and his time. He gained self-respect, a high level of fitness and skill, and, above all, self-control. In his late teens, he made friends with a well-known doorman at a local club who saw potential in him and introduced him to working the doors. Charlie Bronson helped Stuart get his SIA licence when the laws changed. Although Stuart now has a great day job, he still works the doors two nights a week and loves it.

6

SHOWDOWN AT HAMPTON COURT AND KILROY-SILK GIVES US THE BIRD

BY PAUL KNIGHT

In the summer of '95, I was given a ray of hope after three long years of very dark times. I had started the year off by going to see a specialist in the field (i.e. a shrink) who talked me through why I had developed a 'hit first' and then 'many more' times philosophy. I wasn't suicidal, but I did put myself in extreme situations that suggested suicidal tendencies, in particular several confrontations that I handled in a less than diplomatic way. I saw my shrink for a little over four months, and we established very quickly that it was not because I had issues with my mother, which seems to be a psychiatrist's answer to 90 per cent of all their patients' problems. Instead, I had suffered a huge betrayal years previously that had put me in a very angry place, and I was venting my anger towards everyone but the person who had caused it. I had nurtured a destructive outlook and knew that I had to channel that destructiveness into something constructive. And the answer was baking.

The idea was to vent anger through kneading dough, mixing ingredients, using controlled measurements and having a finished product that would then provide happiness and substance for others to enjoy rather than causing pain and suffering. It had its desired effect, and I became a dab hand in the kitchen, much to the delight of my colleagues who had to eat the sweet spoils of my anger.

This, however, created two new problems: the first was that I was becoming the cause of mild diabetes amongst the team; and the second was that I wasn't feeling like a naughty bad boy any more, which was rather bizarre, considering the lifestyle I was living and the kind of working environment I was in. Therefore, instead of becoming the heavy-handed puncher, I became the scam artist of Scorpion Security Services, the company I was working for, pulling strokes on every door I worked and finding out every way there was to make a pound from a penny. In fact, I believe I am one of the main reasons why life on London doors has changed so much, with the introduction of venue rules and door policies. Sorry, guys and girls, for spoiling the big earnings, but I feel in a roundabout sort of way that I have created opportunities for you to find *new* ways to scam nightclubs and pub doors to help supplement your meagre hourly rate and make the job worthwhile.

Anyway, back to the point of this little story. I pulled the mother of all door scams at the Shepherds Bush Empire. It is, as they say, a story for another day, but it was so big and so bad that I became too hot a commodity to stay working in central London. My boss, John Smith, had to show his clients that he acted swiftly and severely when any of his employees broke the rules. In reality, if he did feel that way, I would have been fired on the spot and reported to the police rather than given a pat on the back and a sweet position as head doorman at a new brasserie-cum-nightclub in Hampton Court called Pals.

Pals was just one of many in a chain owned by Danny Rose and his business partner Geoff. Danny used to own The Limelight club in Shaftesbury Avenue back in the late 1980s, early '90s. I used to work

The Limelight in those days; it was just around the corner from The Hippodrome, where my friend and occasional work colleague Lenny McLean used to run the door. In those days, London's West End was a great place to work the doors – before licences were introduced. So many angles; so many perks – it was good times for all!

Anyway, the timing, as usual, was perfect for me – one door closed and another opened, and I started my 18-month stint working at Pals in both Hampton Court and Croydon. I have to say that Pals in Hampton Court is one of my all-time top doors that I have ever had the privilege and pleasure of working, but as with any new establishment, it wasn't always plain sailing, and in its opening week I was involved in a near-death confrontation. Had I still been thinking the way I had been at the beginning of the year, I would definitely not be around today to tell this tale.

Danny opened the doors to Pals on a Thursday night. Although he already had a string of them across the country, it was this one that was his pride and joy. He had finally acquired a prime location opposite Hampton Court Palace and had plans to develop a wealthy and occasionally pretentious clientele. The cream-and-blue decor was standard, but each venue had tailored fixtures and fittings to complement the local area – this particular two-storey building had a cosy restaurant on a raised section that was separated from the bar and a sunken chill-out area filled with comfy sofas and moody lighting. The upstairs function room was for private hire during the week, but on Friday and Saturday nights it acted as a separate area for punters to dance the night away.

The door rules were simple: between Sunday and Wednesday it was virtually anything goes, which meant over 18s and trainers were allowed; Thursdays were over 21s and smart dress; and the weekends were strictly over 25s and *very* smart dress. Danny was adamant that these rules were never broken, because he knew what the area lacked: a venue where the older, richer clientele could go and relax and spend their easily (I always presumed) earned wealth.

The venue had a capacity for 550 people, but Danny always made a point of never going over the 500 mark. He figured that there was no need to squash people in – the customers were given decent elbow room so that they would enjoy themselves more and therefore come back for more. For Danny, it wasn't just about the money – it was about reputation. When he owned The Limelight, it was the place to be seen; paparazzi, celebrities and high-profile customers would often be spotted coming and going from its large glass doors. Of course, the place went downhill the minute he sold it, and if it had not been for the door team that stayed on, it would have easily gone the way of other clubs that underestimated the value of a good door team. The proof of that pudding is that when they did change the security company, the place eventually hit rock bottom, and it was sold on again to an Australian company that came in and shut the doors to The Limelight altogether. They eventually rebranded the place to match their franchises worldwide, and the doors reopened – only this time the venue marketed itself to a different sector of revellers, and business never reached the same levels it did when shrewd executive Danny Rose owned the place. Danny knew how to add the extra magic to make the punters come back time and time again – he was a born nightclub promoter.

Before Danny's reign, Pals had been a pub with an 'anything goes' policy each and every day of the week: underage drinkers, no dress codes and all the fights that could be started. Its regulars were travellers and nasty characters from East Moseley – the noisy, violent, working-class district of the peaceful and wealthy Hampton Court area. The landlord who ran the pub back then was spending more money replacing windows and furniture than what was being rung through the tills, so it wasn't too long before an alleged insurance job was organised – a fire that actually killed the landlord and the two idiots he hired to start the blaze. Needless to say, Danny did not want the same kind of crowds coming back to his new venue and gave his word to turn a blind eye to anything that went on at the front door that enforced that rule.

Thanks to the inexperienced doormen that the door supervisors' licence scheme was allowing through its vetting system, I had not yet arranged a fully hand-picked team. Hampton Court was a far cry from the West End and did not have the additional financial rewards that working 'in the smoke' offered. Scorpion Security supplied me with a few people until I had the chance to build a team I was happy with, but they were mostly a complete bunch of utter wankers – the licensing scheme had eliminated a tasty workforce and left mainly rank amateurs who could not stand up against a gust of wind let alone a team of scumbags from hell. Thankfully, I had managed to get an old acquaintance to agree to work with me. His name was Kevin, and he was a seasoned professional who had moved to Surrey after making a few quid in the construction game.

I first met Kevin back in 1992 when I was freelancing. I had just enjoyed the atmospheric event of the World Wrestling Federation's SummerSlam at Wembley Stadium, before heading down to Break for the Border, just off Tottenham Court Road, to work the night as a fill-in. It was a special night for me, not because I met Kevin, but because some of the wrestling stars came down to blow off some steam – they were staying in a nearby hotel. One of the stars who came in was the immortal Hulk Hogan – he was a boyhood hero of mine after I first saw him on late-night wrestling back in 1984. However, by the way he was acting in the club, I was glad I no longer thought of him as a role model, otherwise I would have been severely crushed – but, again, that is a story for another time.

Kevin worked with me on the front door at Pals, vetting the punters and keeping the trouble out. Inside the club, I was lucky enough to have been supplied with Paul 'Professor Hightower' Smith, a six feet six inch mass of a man from Streatham. His Frank Bruno looks and stature made him stand out in a crowd, and the Professor had a right cross to equal the boxing champ he resembled so much. Paul got the nickname Professor Hightower because when he was not on duty he wore spectacles that seemed to hide his aggressive nature – you could understand how Clark Kent got away with it. They also made him look like a schoolteacher, hence the moniker. This was the full extent of the back-up I could rely on. The other two guys in attendance were a waste of space, and the sixth member of the team had yet to show up – it was not a good start.

The doors were set to open at 7.30 p.m. for the club's grand opening. The general manager was Michael Camp, and he was giving his staff a last-minute pep talk. At one time, Michael, or 'Campy' as he was called, had run The Limelight for Danny. Campy was a thinly built man with a little Friar Tuck patch starting to show through his thin blond locks. He was a good manager – he was realistic and understood the fact that the door staff occasionally had to do what they had to do in order to get the job done and would back them up 98 per cent of the time.

It was 7.25 p.m. when the last member of the door team finally graced the squad with her presence – her boyfriend, who was also in the security game, as well as being a part-time DJ, had insisted on dropping her off. In true West Indian style, he ran late for everything, but as far as I was concerned – especially in the muscle game – the only thing you should run late for is your own funeral. I told her that if her boyfriend couldn't get her to the venue at least 15 minutes before the start of her shift, she should perhaps work at a different venue. From the following night onwards, Allison drove herself to and from work.

With all the door team together, I gave a brief talk on the history of the area and what the management wanted to happen with the club. I pointed out that trouble was expected for at least the first month or so, so everyone had to be on their toes and give full back-up. Although everyone nodded in agreement, I still had very little faith in some of the new faces and made a mental note to make phone calls the following day in order to get a few more reliable people to make up the crew.

The locals were alerted to the opening of Pals by a highly organised invite system. Danny had done his homework on the surrounding community, and he targeted people who lived in certain streets based on house prices, as well as business owners who had a specific turnover. He then sent personal invites to all those who matched the criteria and let their bragging at being selected act as word of mouth. By 9 p.m. the place had reached capacity, and the atmosphere was a happy one, helped by the fact that Danny had laid on free drinks for the first two hours. He had special gold cards printed and was issuing them out to a select few. The card allowed for priority entry to Pals if a queue had formed outside or if the door was running on a one-out, one-in system, and it also gave the holder entry to the upstairs VIP club. The gold card soon became a highly sought-after acquisition.

The night was running smoothly until some old faces turned up to reclaim their drinking haunt. There were eight of them in the group – all roughnecks who were up for a row at the drop of a hat. Kevin stopped them at the door and in his politest voice explained that tonight was invitation only and they would not be able to gain entry. In addition – as he pointed to the youngest-looking members of the group – it was strictly over 21s, so some ID would be required.

They did not like the polite knock-back and started to argue their case. I then stepped in, redirecting their attention towards me and giving Kevin some manoeuvring space. Three of them were definitely underage and two had trainers on, but the remaining three were OK, and I was willing to let them in. I put the ball in their court and asked them what they wanted to do. The group huddled together and thrashed out their views. They decided that the three youngsters could go off and spend their evening in Kingston town centre, leaving the older ones free to enter. As the three youths begrudgingly walked off towards the town, one of the remaining three asked if the two who had trainers on could go home, change and come back to join them. Kevin told them that would not be a problem, so off they went.

Divide and conquer was the name of the game. Neither Kevin nor I had any real trust in the door team to handle this fight-hungry crew, so dividing them into more manageable numbers seemed a much better plan.

The three guys walked into the club with smug looks on their faces, thinking that they were the dons of East Moseley or something. As soon as they entered, I radioed the Professor and got him to target them. He was to leave it for about five minutes and then ask them to leave. The bar was four deep with people cashing in on the free booze, and these guys didn't stand a chance of even getting a free beer before they were going to be turfed out. The Professor cut his way through the crowd and told the roughnecks in no uncertain terms that it was time to leave. They kicked up a fuss. It was bad enough being shown the door, but the fact that it was by a black man made it even more insulting in their eyes. They chanced their arm by laying into the

Professor, but Kevin and I came in swiftly behind them, and it was on – a few digs and choke holds as we quickly dragged our prey outside to continue the pasting.

The frontage of Pals was made up of French doors that gave the place a Continental feel. The commotion outside caught the attention of the wealthy customers inside, who watched through the glass as the same three doormen who had acted so politely earlier punched the crap out of three scumbags.

When the other two scumbags eventually returned after changing their footwear, they were disappointed to hear that their friends had already left – although they didn't know how or why – and turned around and started their journey back into town to find the youngsters. The rest of the night was a peaceful affair, and the evening had not been too tarnished by the earlier display of violence.

Overall it was a good grand opening – guests had a great time, friendships had been made, regular customers established, the network system was in place and hopefully word would quickly spread that the old crowd that used to terrorise the place before were not going to be tolerated in the venue any longer. If all was done and dusted on the first night, what was the second night going to be like?

It was a staggered start for the security team at weekends: two started at 7 p.m., two at 8 p.m. and the final two at 9 p.m. The Professor was one of the 9 p.m. starters, due to his regular job finishing late. I made sure that Kevin and I were the 7 p.m. starters – so we both knew that someone trustworthy was there to watch the other's back, which was just as well because payback from the night before was going to start early.

It was Friday night, and it had just gone 7 p.m. Kevin and I were standing on the door shooting the breeze, greeting the early arrivals and saying farewell to the afternoon crowd as they made their way home from work with probably one or two too many glasses of bubbly flowing around their systems.

The evening had a scent of danger in the air; we all somehow sensed that something was going to happen and that we should be alert and on our toes. It is a strange feeling and hard to explain, but we just felt that something was in the air. It is a feeling experienced door staff know and understand, a feeling that we develop after years in the business. It is a kind of sixth sense, and we are right almost every time. It may have been a wealthy area, but trouble still lurks in the dark corners of almost every aspect of society.

Pals was situated opposite a small roundabout that had fairly light traffic activity during the evening. The local police shop had closed for the night – the need for a 24/7 station was unheard of in Hampton Court, so any call-outs had to be dealt with by the understaffed force at the Kingston nick. All this stood the army of travellers who were blocking up the road outside Pals in good stead. Old beat-up vans and transits screeched to a halt, cutting off all access to the roundabout, and the passengers who emerged from the vehicles were the biggest collection of Desperate Dans I had ever seen. All of them looked like professional pie eaters and all of them were tooled up.

The leader of the pack stepped out of a white Rover. He was a huge figure of a man who bore the markings of a true scrapper – what the size of his hands and his gnarled cauliflower ears did not tell you, his collection of tattoos and sovereign rings did. He was the king of this clan, and he obviously had some business to take care of with me and my team. The thick Irish accent seemed to add to his threatening demeanour as he called out to us standing side by side outside the newly opened club.

'Are you the two fuckers who be't me lad?' Images of the night before ran through my head. Sure we gave out some punishment, but it was to grown men, so why such a heavy response? The angry father pointed to the passengers who were seated timidly in his car. They were the three youngsters who had been knocked back by their own entourage and went off to town to find their evening's entertainment. I stepped forward away from the door and closer to the menacing man-mountain who was looking for retribution.

'No, no one here laid a hand on those three. They were turned away last night and took their business into town.' It took all of my self-control not to show that I was just a little worried by the present situation. There was a look of disgust on the frustrated father's face at the cheek of the cockney who stood in front of him 'lying' about what had happened.

'Well, big man, me lad sez you and yer banana boy did this for na' reason. Are ya saying he's a liar?' His voice rose an octave, indicating that he was not willing to listen to reason – adrenalin was fuelling his temper. To be honest, I sensed a beating was about to take place and therefore had nothing to lose but to use the most useful tool a professional doorman has – his voice. Over many years of facing violence, I had learned that size meant nothing and your voice could be your strongest weapon. It can control a situation, it can calm a person down or it can incite a revolution. You can throw an opponent off guard by speaking softly, especially when followed by a strong physical attack. Your voice can charm and persuade, it is the source of all solutions and it was all I had to put a stop to the confrontation that was now before me.

'You are a huge man with a loyal following. It's obvious you are a man of position. You have their respect, and judging by the turnout you ain't scared of having it with anyone, but you ain't no Bartley Gorman [a champion bare-knuckle boxer in the UK and Ireland between 1972 and 1992 and more commonly known as the 'King of the Gypsies'], and I would fancy my chances in a straightener against ya. Now, no one from this club hurt your boy. We did mix it up with some of their pals, but that was all. Now, if you want to step up, then do so. If your back-up steam in, then know one thing: I will put you down before they even get close enough to stop me.' I wasn't a small man in those days, and the truth is I'm still a large-built fella – my seventeen stone, muscular build sat quite nicely on my six feet two inch frame back then, and I was a professionally trained fighter who had lost a fair chunk of my conscience and was brought up to endure pain. If it went off, I would not be going down without taking out that fat sack of shit in front of me. However I *had* changed my school of thought. If the same situation had gone down a year earlier, I would not have said anything and just steamed into all of them. Like I said: extreme situations that sometimes suggested suicidal tendencies. But I had changed, and for the first time in my life the thought of actually dying on the pavement I was standing on seemed a real and possible outcome.

Upon hearing my challenge, Kevin stepped forward. His left hand was in his pocket, and the knowledge that his dusters were resting against his knuckles added a little reassurance that he could be busting some faces of his own before the night was over. The look on the leader's face turned from disgust to confusion. Was he hearing right? This cockney bouncer was facing down a 20-strong army that could pack up home and disappear from the face of the planet if the need arose. He must have wondered whether I was brave, stupid or just hoping to bluff my way out of all of this. The tension shifted up a gear as the protective father beckoned his son out of the car. The young lad, who was sporting a painful black eye and swollen jaw, stood sheepishly next to his angered dad. The behemoth looked down at his offspring and asked him one last time, 'Is this ta man who done this to ya?'

The boy looked ashamed, embarrassed and a little scared. He shook his head. His ability to speak had left him, because he knew what his father's reaction would be for causing this situation to happen. Without warning, the man slapped the boy across his good cheek and motioned for him to get back into the car. He then returned his attention to me. 'Yer right. I ain't no Bartley Gorman, but I would have given ya a decent stand-up. I'm a big a'nuff man to admit I was wrong. I will speak to the boy and get ta the bottom of it all.' He then held out his hand in a gesture of respect. 'No hard feelings?'

'Not at all. You are a good father who wanted revenge for his son's injuries. I respect that, and I respect you for taking the time to make sure you had the right bastards. It could have been a nasty mistake.' The two of us stood and chatted for another minute or so – the rest of the clan were already driving off. I told my very large opponent that it went without saying that his boys were not welcome but that anytime he wanted to come down, perhaps taking the missus out for meal, he could come in as my guest. Thanks were given, and the big man got back into his white Rover and drove off.

As I said earlier, I am a big fella – I am also big enough to admit that I was shit scared when facing that gang down. It was evident that at any given moment my angry opponent could have figured that the time for talking was over and that it was time for retribution. As handy as Kevin and I were, the odds were severely against us, and we would have gone down hard – there was no two ways about it. But in the muscle game, perception is everything in moments like those and bravado carries you through. I had got lucky, and as a result both Kevin and I were still standing.

I turned to Kevin with a sigh of relief, and as we walked back to the door we saw that everyone in Pals had their faces stuck to the French doors like Garfield's on a bird's car window. They had witnessed the whole thing, and the police had been called, although they were obviously in no rush to face 20 or so gypsies. The fact that no blood was spilled meant they would not be breaking any speed limits to take statements, either.

We entered the bar to a thunderous round of applause and cheers; men came up to shake our hands, and some of the women rushed over and kissed our cheeks. A new sheriff and his number-one deputy were in town. Wyatt Earp and Doc Holliday basked in the glory for a little while longer, grabbed a mug of tea and returned to the front door of the OK Corral.

Respect had been earned that night, and whispers of the tale of the two doormen who had been outnumbered ten to one but had stood their ground soon began to spread throughout the land. By the time Allison and the other 8 p.m. starter turned up, the story had already escalated to it being a fifteen-to-one ratio and the opposition all had guns. I actually dreaded to think what it would be by closing time. Everyone who ventured in that night was told the tale: some believed it; others didn't care. Capabilities had been put to the test, and no further proof of what me and my team were about was needed.

Even Allison went up in my estimations that night. When some punter didn't want to stand in line with the other waiting masses and tried to gain entry to the upstairs club – he wanted in and no girl was going to stop him – Allison head-butted him clean on the bridge of his nose before (wo)manhandling him down the stairs and out of the side fire exit. And in her brief absence, no one took advantage and jumped the queue to get into the club. She too got cheers on her return. Personally, I was just glad when the night was over and I could make my way back to Walthamstow.

The next night, neither Kevin nor I wanted a repeat of the night before, so we came a little more tooled up. Hampton Court and its surrounding residential area were easy pickings for 'Chinese Whispers'. The escapades of the previous night's entertainment had been doing the rounds all day among local shopkeepers and their customers, and every time the story was told the odds and details were increasingly exaggerated. This kind of response could actually push a volatile situation into overdrive.

By showing restraint and tact, the main man of the local band of travellers showed why he was the leader. He was an angry father who wanted blood for his son's assault, but he still waited to confirm that the events told to him were true. In front of his clan, who turned out in full force to back him in taking retribution on those responsible, he walked away after being faced down by a cocksure bouncer. Now, to some people that might have seemed weak, but he knew that right was right and attacking an innocent man was not going to do him and his clan any favours. He showed real class that night by getting to the truth and leaving the situation with the best possible outcome. But when the gossipmongers got going, he might have felt that he should put the record straight and destroy me and my colleague, and even Pals, just to save face and restore fear in the locals. Thankfully, that was not to be.

Later, we found out that the night before the showdown the three youngsters had got a little mouthy with the doormen of Options, a club in Kingston upon Thames. Options' door team had given them a slap for their troubles. The three bruised youngsters had then met up with their friends who had earlier got a slapping from me and my team and decided that we were the ones who should be blamed. Upon returning home, they said that my people, including a black guy, had set upon them. Understandably, the chief got angry and wanted his pound of flesh. After his son finally admitted who the real culprits were, the tooled-up team of travellers drove into Kingston and set the record straight by annihilating the door crew of Options. This show of force gave the fear back to the travellers, and the need to save face with me was resolved.

I often think back to that night and hold that fella in the highest regard because of his display of leadership on the doorstep of Pals. He showed a level of class that I have only witnessed a handful of times in my life, and it was partly because of that display that I started to change my ways and approach to working the doors.

I did eventually get the opportunity to meet the head traveller and his wife and to have them as my guests in the restaurant, with all the trimmings on the house, and I never had any trouble from that particular group again. A lesson learned from a man who could have easily taken my life rather than giving me a new lease on it. If by some chance you are reading this . . . I thank you.

By 1994, I was a bit of a recognised character within the circles of Scorpion Security. Not only had I got a reputation for being quick tempered, psychotic and, in some people's eyes, suicidal, I had also become known as being a 'poster boy' for door supervisors.

In 1994, the regional door supervisors' licence was introduced for all those working in the borough of Westminster. Everyone in the trade back then will remember that it was the kiss of death for the industry. All the big, respected and well-known names in the game were faced with being ousted because of the fact that anyone with a criminal record – especially for ABH, GBH, aggravated assault, affray and the like – was a no-no under the new guidelines. No licence; no working the doors – it was that simple. But it was these people that set the standard, kept the trouble controlled and added status to the clubs in question.

To get around the problem and still have their 'deterrents' on the door, venue managers would make up new titles for the high-profile guys who couldn't get a licence – front of house liaison officer, security consultant, meet and greet specialist, and so on. In fact, any title that would give them a reason to be there without calling them doormen, bouncers, door supervisors or face punchers, which would be breaking the rules. Even my friend and co-worker Lenny McLean fell under this banner, even more so because at that time he had only recently been released from prison after being jailed for an incident that took place at The Hippodrome, Leicester Square, with a naked punter.

This was the government's way of regulating the world of nightclub security and forcing out all those who were a real deterrent – those that could handle 20 drunken punters ready to take on the world. The government wanted to make way for the smaller, easy on the eye, 'I'm only doing this part time because I'm a student' type of security guard. Again, it was a kiss of death for the industry.

Now, I was a breed of doorman all on my own, and I had very strict East End values on life. I was a known face in my neighbourhood, and, to be honest, I was a villain. I was still living dangerously, taking far too many risks and ready to stare down Armageddon if the situation called for it. As I've already said, I was a big fella, and I can also humbly say that I was a fairly good-looking guy (old age is setting in now) with a personality and most importantly a functioning brain that allowed me to hold an intelligent conversation with patrons and clients alike. Yes, I was the doorman who could walk, talk and chew gum at the same time. What can I say? I had it all. Oh and did I mention I was also modest?

Hopefully by now you are getting the idea that I was a cheeky chap who was a tad arrogant and very confident. I had an old-school mentality and new-school looks, hence why I was classed as a poster boy. And just what is it you do with a poster boy when the world is saying that all doormen are thugs? You parade them to the public to dismiss such claims and present to the world a new and supposedly improved model to demonstrate that the industry is complying with the new guidelines. What a load of bollocks!

With this in mind, it came as no surprise that whenever a TV documentary, talk show or reality programme was being made about bouncers and Scorpion was asked to provide the people, I would be involved somewhere along the line. So, when Scorpion got the call to supply three of their staff for a stint on the *Kilroy* show – the programme was doing a piece on the changing face of dangerous professions – yours truly was called along with my brother Vaughan, who had my back at The Mean Fiddler the previous year, and the talented Mr Ben Perry, a very good friend of mine.

Ben is as big in personality as he is in stature. He stood at six feet eight inches and weighed in at three hundred and ten pounds. When he was once asked by an irate punter, 'Just who the hell do you think you are?' big Ben simply replied, 'God . . . because I have the power to separate your head from your shoulders with one smiting blow.' Yes, Ben Perry's haymaker was an equaliser.

I'll never forget the first time I worked with Ben. We were positioned in a fast-food outlet in Leicester Square, stopping non-customers from using the upstairs toilets. I know that must seem both petty and a waste of our time, but despite the jokes and insults it was one of the roughest gigs going. When Scorpion Security first got involved, the toilets were being abused by drug dealers, prostitutes, transients and kiddie fiddlers. At that time, it was a family restaurant that was *not* a safe place for families to be. And the 'rent-a-cops' who were in there before us didn't tackle the problem properly. Why would they? They were getting £4.85 an hour. We, on the other hand, were getting three times that and were up for a rumble, so after months of fighting, death threats, stabbings and major displays of dominance, Scorpion made an example of the transgressors and marked their territory with the scent of blood.

Of course, once you have it how you want it, it needs to be maintained, hence the heavy artillery being deployed to keep those who were not paying customers out of the comfy, upstairs bathroom area. Anyone who has ever walked through Leicester Square on an evening can testify that there is a huge amount of trouble with drunk and drugged revellers, and Triads and thugs (who can't enjoy a night out without either mugging someone or getting into a tear-up). They too needed to be stopped at the door, and that is why we were there.

I remember that I had to stand on the first step just to come to eye level with Ben. At that time, I was the new guy with Scorpion, whilst Ben was an established and respected body, but we clicked straight off the bat. Although an intimidating sight, with his skinhead and devil beard, he was more 'Gentle Ben' than anything else, and as any punters who used to visit the goth and punk nightclub Slimelights during the late 1990s would be able to tell you, he was also a good laugh.

It was hard for me to take my old partner in crime seriously after witnessing him curl his huge, bulky frame under a small oval floor rug to show the world that he was really a turtle whilst E-ing out of his face. He would stretch his neck from his shell (the small oval floor rug), while making a turtle face, and try to eat imaginary lettuce. It was all very surreal, but not as bad as when he and a small group of friends tried to re-enact *The Wizard of Oz* whilst tripping on LSD. Watching a grown man tuck a chequered tea towel down his pants while sporting a twine mop on his head, acting like he is stuck in a tornado and screaming 'Where's Toto?' is an image not easily forgotten!

When he wasn't living life to the fullest in his time off, Ben was a non-stop working machine. Because of his size, he was a very popular advertisement for nightclubs and would find himself working five days and seven nights a week. (With that work schedule you might be able to understand the extreme methods my friend went to blow off some steam on those rare occasions he wasn't earning a living.) Because he worked so much, he would always have a host of stories to tell you whenever you bumped into him. My favourite was the time he was working on his own at a pub in Carnaby Street, London. I think the pub's name was The Blue Trumpet, but don't hold me to that – like I said before, old age is setting in! It was a Saturday afternoon and a big game was taking place on the home ground of a London team against some other big team not from London – I don't want to start getting into the whole football rivalry thing, so that will have to do. The landlord of the pub told Ben that in no circumstances were any football hooligans or groups of people sporting team colours allowed in. There is nothing more satisfying than having a job that sets you such compromising challenges: keep out football hooligans and people wearing team colours on a Saturday afternoon in the West End of London when a cup game is on hosted by a local team. I can only assume Ben must have felt special knowing that the landlord was aware of what was coming but still insisted on having just *one* doorman on duty – nice to know that you're appreciated.

Between the hours of 3 p.m. and 5 p.m., there was obviously just the usual traffic in and out of the pub. The landlord was all smiles and kept teasing Ben because he had been worried about the day's events. Ben, however, was on the verge of decking the muppet landlord – it wasn't game time that worried him; it was what was coming.

Just after 5 p.m., a group of nine pissed off supporters whose team had lost were making their way towards the big double-door entrance of The Blue Trumpet with only Ben there to stop them. 'Sorry, gents. The doors are closed to sports clothing – dress code, I'm afraid.'

They answered with the typical response that every doorman hears at least a hundred times per shift: 'You're having a laugh, ain't ya?'

'No, geezer, I'm not. Those are the house rules. You can't come in.'

Using a dress-code policy as a reason to keep undesirables out of a place is common practice; using a dress-code policy when you are at a pub in Carnaby Street is not so easy to pull off due to the area's varied clientele – goths, punks, trendsetters and students all hang around this famous street in the heart of the West End. The group of supporters would have had a valid point of discussion on their side had they wanted to debate on the matter, but instead another member of the group opened up the talks with a truly well-established line: 'Fuck off, we're coming in . . . Who's gonna stop us? You?' And with bravado on their side, the group edged forward towards the doors.

Ben held out his arm, more to judge his punching distance than to act as a halt sign. 'There's no need for trouble, fella,' he said. 'It's not my policy. I'm on your side in all of this, but the rules are the rules.'

As the group responded, none of them seemed to notice that whilst talking to them Ben had closed one of the doors, bolting it shut, and had proceeded to pull his weighted gloves out of his jacket pockets and put them on. He had already got them at arm's length, surmised who was most up for it in the group and positioned himself in the remaining open doorway with a good, solid stance. They had allowed him this leeway without even realising it. Ben had set himself up in a position that he felt more comfortable in handling, no matter which way it now went.

He then changed his tune: 'Right then, you fucking muppets. There's only one way you can get in this place, and that's through this doorway. I'm six feet eight and weigh twenty-two stone, and I'm standing in between you and the bolted door. Your best bet is to rush me in single file and get through one by one. But I tell ya now: that's exactly how I'm gonna fucking knock you out – one by one. Who's first?'

By the look in their eyes, it was a chance some of them were willing to take, but common sense slowly kicked in, and those in the group not really wanting to put Ben's theory to the test started to take steps backwards. This left three out of the nine standing strong, although all were unaware that the rest of their group were not behind them as they thought. Like the scene from *Shrek* in which Shrek asks the commanding officer, 'Really, you and what army?' only for the commanding officer to turn and realise his loyal army has run off, these three turned to see that they were alone and ran off towards Oxford Street station. Crisis averted.

When Ben told me this story, he was not afraid to point out that he had been scared. Had all nine stuck together, he would not have stood a chance and would have wound up on the wrong end of a nasty kicking. However, when you put someone in a fight-or-flight situation, eight times out of ten they will take the flight option. Taking part in an actual physical confrontation is not something people want to do, despite how it initially seems. Fighting is still mainly left to the experienced, the drunk and the crazy – which is a very small percentage of people in the grand scheme of things.

That was Ben: a chancer, a rogue and one of the funniest people I have had the pleasure of knowing. A true gent and a diamond geezer.

Now back to the story . . .

The *Kilroy* show was live, starting at 10 a.m. and running for about 25 minutes. There was no room for second takes or do-overs – you had to be on your game, quick on your feet and ready to roll as soon as the camera crew gave the signal that filming had begun. This meant that all the guests had to be in the studio by 8.30 a.m., which for us meant being picked up from our homes at around 6 a.m. This was after we had all worked the night before. I had got in after my shift at 5 a.m., showered, changed clothes, grabbed a cuppa and was about to tuck in to some delicious warm buttered toast when the chauffeur rang my doorbell. The studio had sent executive cars to those involved to ensure that key guests would turn up, although I could not understand why they sent us a car each, as we had to drive past where Vaughan and Ben lived on the way to the studio.

I arrived at the studio at about 7.50 a.m. – Vaughan was not that far behind me, judging by his text message, so I waited outside for him. When he turned up, we chatted for a few minutes about the adventures of the night before and what was about to take place that morning. We had been told that we were there to talk about the changing face of nightclub security because of the introduction of the new door supervisors' licence. It all seemed innocent stuff, and we ventured into the meet-and-greet area, where we were signed in and shown the breakfast room. We were told to help ourselves to the tea, coffee, juice and breakfast buffet. Now, that is the last thing you should say to a sleep-deprived and starving person my size who knows how to put away a meal or two. Vaughan was no slouch when putting away a meal either. It must have been in our genes, and it was definitely a task for the caterer to be on his toes and keep our plates stocked.

The moment we entered the room we could feel that something was out of place: the people present were of mixed ages and ranged from students to grannies – all went a deathly quiet as we walked in. Whispers flew across the tables, and it was obvious that people were staring. We were the biggest people in the room and most definitely the very centre of attention. However, I was too tired and hungry to care, so I headed for the tea, pastries, and bacon and eggs from the buffet.

It took a while for the caterers to cotton on to the size of portions we were expecting, but they got there in the end! With our plates eventually piled to a size that constituted a *proper* breakfast, we shuffled along to the beverage section, where the next argument started. The cups were those pathetic little things that come with matching saucers and a handle that you can't even fit your little pinkie into. I politely explained to the young girl pouring that we were going to need three cups each just to equal the size of a decent mug of tea – I drink tea by the pint. For whatever reason, she was slow to oblige. I do not know why, as it was not her tea or crockery, but she felt the need to refuse, which meant I in turn got a little louder. The rest of the room had already been giving us dirty looks and talking about us, but now I was giving them a real reason to do so.

The head catering guy walked over to defend his young worker and looked as though he might have given us a verbal run for our money when Big Ben entered the room – his chauffeur had been a little late in picking him up. If we thought the room went quiet before, then this was the purest form of silence imaginable. Ben strolled over and peered over my shoulder, saw the tasty morsels on offer and my plate piled high, and simply said to the head guy, 'I'll have what he's having.' He got Ben a plate and proceeded to fill it up with all and sundry, whilst rushing the young girl on to pour out nine cups of tea.

We sat down at the nearest table and began slurping and munching our breakfast, all the while talking and, if I'm really honest, swearing a little bit too much in audible voices. We were three big bouncers, acting in a very stereotypical way, and we were doing ourselves no favours in the eyes of those present – but then why should we act any differently, I thought? We were going to be the real stars of today's show, weren't we? Our 15 minutes of fame brought with it a celebrity attitude, which we quite rightly made the most of.

Time flies when you're having fun, and before we knew it the participants were being called to take their places on the set – a semicircle of seats with four levels set out like a section of a Roman coliseum. Everyone was told where to sit apart from six people – us and three others. We looked around confused, wondering if we were not going to be on the show any more because we had made so much noise earlier. But if that was the case, why stop the other three as well? One of the studio hands then called the other three over, spoke softly to them and ushered them into the seating area. We were the last three left.

A few minutes later, the same studio hand came back and beckoned us over. 'Hi, guys,' he said. 'I'm going to take you through in a few seconds, and I'll tell you where you have to sit. Because you are such big-built gentlemen, we cannot have you all seated together. OK, now you all know what today's topic is, don't you? So remember: listen to Robert [Kilroy-Silk] and follow his lead. Let's go, come along.'

We followed him to the semicircle where everyone else was sitting and were shown our seats as the rest of the audience stared at us. Ben was seated in the front row next to Kilroy-Silk. This particular tier only seated three people, and accompanying Ben and Kilroy-Silk was a pretty little thing. She was only nineteen years old if she was a day, and she was wearing full make-up, her hair was done and she had on a push-up bra – the whole nine yards. Vaughan was directed to the right-hand side of the tier, third level up, and he was sandwiched between one elderly lady and a slim-built bloke in his early twenties. Finally, I was positioned on the top row. On my left-hand side were two hoodie-wearing tykes; although they were in their late twenties, they were still dealing with acne and, judging by the look of them, a severe lack of women in their life as well.

It was less than five minutes to go before we were on the air when Kilroy-Silk jumped up from his hiding place and told us not to stare straight at the cameras and that if we had something to say, we should raise our hands. He also said that we could only speak if we were chosen and to remember that we would be live so there was to be no swearing. We all had to be on our best behaviour and all that jazz.

The crew started the countdown, signalled by sign language: five . . . four . . . three . . . two . . . one . . . and we were on the air and live. 'Good morning. I'm Robert Kilroy-Silk, and on today's programme we will be discussing the heavy-handed tactics of those who abuse their power in the workplace. We have traffic wardens, wheel clampers and our "hit first, ask questions later" nightclub bouncers.'

Fuck it – we've been set up. The wankers! What now? The three of us looked at each other. We all knew that if we made a fuss, we'd only prove his point, live on TV. We realised we would have to wait it out; after all, how bad could it be?

Hands started going up in the air. For every offender, there were eight victims. The traffic warden and wheel clampers were all glossed over fairly quickly, and then it was time to focus on nightclub bouncers and on us. Tale after tale of 'over-the-top brutality' and people being hit for no reason started to do the rounds. I kept raising my hand so that I could have my say and defend my colleagues and profession, but Kilroy-Silk kept going to the victims. Vaughan joined in, putting his arm in the air, but still Kilroy-Silk refused to come to us. He seemed to be baiting us, hoping that we would snap and do something so that his ratings would soar.

Suddenly, out of nowhere, a bird flew in from an open window and started circling overhead. At first I thought it was a vulture, because we were well and truly dead, but thankfully it was too small, and I breathed a huge sigh of relief. However, it *was* big enough to stop the proceedings for a few minutes while the crew debated if it was going to be a problem; after all, this was live TV. They decided to take a chance and continue.

Kilroy-Silk laughed it off on camera, and the conversation then turned to the pretty little thing sitting on the front seat. 'Now, Sharon,' he said, 'tell us what happened to you?' Kilroy-Silk sat down beside her so that he could share his microphone with her.

'Well, I was in a club one night with a bunch of my girlfriends.' Her voice sounded like butter wouldn't melt in her mouth, and I knew what was coming. 'Halfway through the night, these two big bouncers came over and just started to beat this boy up who was talking to me for no reason [they beat the boy up for no reason, not that the boy was talking to her for no reason!], and when I asked them to stop . . .' The tears started to appear and trickle down her angelic face at that point. Kilroy-Silk comforted her and asked if she was strong enough to carry on. She wiped the tears from her cheek, nodded her head a little and continued. 'One of them punched me in the face and threw me down the stairs.' Kilroy-Silk jumped out of his seat as though he had just heard Mother Teresa say motherfucker and turned to Ben. 'Is that common practice amongst you bouncers?' he asked. 'Do you beat people up with your colleagues for no reason?' Kilroy-Silk then did a sweeping gesture with his arm, and the cameras panned and zoomed in on Vaughan and me, with our poor victims either side of us. 'And punch girls in the face before throwing them down the stairs?'

The microphone was thrust into Ben's face. 'There have been times when ejecting people that they have tumbled down a few stairs, but innocent people who get in the way . . .'

Kilroy-Silk had his opening, and he must have cum in his pants, judging by the smirk that lit up his face. 'So you have pushed innocent people down stairs? So you think there is nothing wrong with punching girls and throwing them down the stairs? This is something you admit to doing?'

Ben's face turned more angelic than the pretty girl's. He had an answer that was going to turn things back on Kilroy-Silk. You could see it in his eyes – our boy Ben was ready to give the mother of all answers . . . when the bird appeared again and landed at Kilroy-Silk's feet. He turned to the camera and said, 'And that's all we have time for today, but tune in tomorrow because we will be talking to pregnant women who have been sexually abused by their doctors. And we're out. That's a wrap. Great show everybody!'

Poor Ben was speechless. He sat there in complete disbelief. Because he hadn't been given a chance to defend himself, the programme had ended with its viewing audience thinking that he hit women and pushed them down the stairs. It was an ambush, plain and simple. If that damn bird had not eaten up four minutes of the programme's time, Ben would have been able to give his reply and leave Kilroy-Silk with no airtime left to retort. Kilroy-Silk had well and truly given us the bird on live TV.

We made our way down to stand with our fallen comrade when Kilroy-Silk came over, handed us signed photos of himself (I still have mine; a keepsake, I keep telling myself) and said, 'Great show, lads. Thanks for coming down.' He then walked off to get the layers of foundation and make-up removed from his wrinkled, ageing face – more 'sandpaper' than 'silk' if you ask me.

I couldn't help but start to laugh, which in turn started off Vaughan. Ben frowned disdainfully as we flippantly re-enacted his last moments on the show: 'So, Ben. You hit old ladies and young girls and throw innocent people down the stairs. Is that true? I'm sorry, we're out of time. We'll just take that as a yes.' Whack, whack, oops!

As the day went on, Ben saw the funny side of it. He had to, because he was back on the doors that night after a nation had seen him on live TV failing to deny that he hit women for no reason and pushed innocent people down stairs. If his customers didn't get him, other doormen surely would. Bouncers are definitely the type of guys who would kick a fella when he's down.

I have some absolute cracking memories of Ben, and it was a crying shame we fell out of touch. The last I saw of him was when he worked for Autoglass in Black Horse Road, Walthamstow. If any readers know him, please get him to contact me through my website – thanks.

BIOGRAPHY OF PAUL KNIGHT

Born within the sound of the Bow bells in the East End of London, Paul's real surname at birth is only known by a handful of people, and that's the way he likes it. Paul's grandfather was a known face out of Hoxton and was the reason why Paul had a notorious East End gangster as his godfather. In 1974, after his father left them, his mum settled down with Robert Knight, which is where Paul's adopted name originates from.

Boxing ran in the family's blood, and fighting became a way of life for Paul throughout his late teens and 20s. Door work was second nature and an easy entry into the world of debt collecting, hired muscle and criminal activities, a world that had him standing side by side with some of the most respected and written about people in the British criminal empire. In the following 12 years, he saw the passing of 23 of his closest friends and family.

Paul purposely stayed low profile and was therefore able to move out of that world and into the one that he now shares with his wife and young family without successful prosecution, stigma or reprisal. To air his skeletons and refocus the destructive energy that he used to carry around with him, Paul has turned his attention to literature. Paul's first novel, *Coding of a Concrete Animal*, is set in the true-crime fiction genre and has been compared to *Judas Pig* by Horace Silver because of its realistic take on a gangland family growing up in the 1970s and '80s. Paul's next book is *Concrete Animal: Hear Me R.O.A.R.*, the sequel to *Coding of a Concrete Animal*.

Website: www.paulknightonline.co.uk
Email: coca@paulknightonline.co.uk

7

DOING THE DOOR
BY STEVE WRAITH

Like most young lads on Tyneside in the 1980s, I was spending my
money as quickly as I was earning it. A lot of my time was spent
in my locals, The Ship and The Swan. In fact, at weekends the lads
and I almost lived in The Ship. It was not uncommon for me to start
drinking on Friday and have a lock-in till Saturday morning, go home
to get some kip or go to the match if Newcastle were playing at St
James's and be back in the pub again for another session that evening.
Great days – from what I can remember – and good *craic*, which is
always important!

When I was younger, I had a habit that was a pointer to my future
career: I couldn't mind my own business when it came to a fight or
an argument. I had to be in amongst it. I liked to stop any bother if I
could, one way or another. But don't get me wrong: I have never been
a fighter. I can handle myself, but I'm no Mike Tyson. I didn't go out
to pick fights, although if someone took a liberty with me I certainly
hit first and asked questions later on occasion.

My face became quite well known around town thanks to my television appearances as a fanzine editor covering local football for *Players Inc.* magazine, and I found it easier to jump the large queues outside the bars in Newcastle due to my new-found fame. I struck up quite a few friendships with the lads on the doors and would often miss a round because I found myself putting the world to rights outside with the 'men in black'.

By the time I had reached twenty, I was over six feet tall and a handy fifteen stone. As well as football, I had started to attend local boxer Glenn McCrory's gym, where I started to learn the noble art of boxing. I had also invested in a set of weights and a weights bench. When I was at college, I had bounced at a few roof-top parties in exchange for a few quid and as much beer as I could drink, and, to be honest, even though I had generally sorted out any bother, I still hadn't imagined that this would be my future career.

It all started one Christmas at a bar called Masters opposite St Nicholas Church in Newcastle city centre. Gary, or 'Lurch' as he was known to a lot of the punters, asked if I fancied earning a few quid over the festive period. One of the lads had broken his wrist, and Gary wanted me to fill in. I was game enough and couldn't think of a better way of earning a bit of cash than standing in a bar listening to all of the up-to-date tunes and looking at all of those beautiful ladies. My first shift was a Thursday night, which, as anyone in Newcastle will tell you, is as busy as a weekend in most other cities. I was dressed in a white shirt, black pants, Doc Martens and a black bomber jacket. I felt and looked the business. I wasn't at all nervous as Gary introduced me to the lads who would be watching my back – and vice versa. First and foremost there was Gary, then Irish Buzz, Wrighty Dave and John Lillico, who remains one of my closest friends to this day. What a night! There were two key positions – front door and back door – with buzzers and flashing lights to let you know when and where a fight had broken out. There were six fights in just over four hours – and that was a quiet night according to the lads. I've got to admit, though, that I loved every minute of it.

The festive season is crazy. Once a year, drinkers swoop on city centres up and down the country and drink too much, eat too much, score with the opposite sex, empty the contents of their bowels and stomachs on any available footpath or shop doorway, and generally do things that they wouldn't normally do. Up until that Christmas, I had been doing exactly the same thing, and it was only then that I realised that there was more to life than spending my hard-earned cash on booze and puking it up.

Christmas never changes: it seems to take ages to come around, then it's all over in a flash and you wonder what all the panic was about. January on the door is one of the quietest months of the year, as people are often in debt and have to stop in to sort out their finances. When the door staffs' hours had to be cut, I was first out because I'd been the last in, and I lost my Thursday to Sunday shifts. I was gutted. I missed the adrenalin rush that I'd got when those lights and buzzers came to life, and I missed the lads with whom I had become part of a team. I left the doors for a while, and it was not until I was asked by an old friend by the name of George Poulter, who ran The Filament and Firkin and Scruffy Murphy's, if I would be interested in sharing the head doorman's job with a lad called Paul Tinnion that I decided to give it another go.

By then, Newcastle City Council had decided that all door supervisors should be licensed. This meant four days' training, covering all aspects of the job, including fire regulations, health and safety, drug awareness, licensing laws and, of course, first aid. The final day saw each potential doorman sit a multiple-choice test on what he had learned. I passed with flying colours and was given a weekend shift as joint head doorman in George's bars at the Haymarket end of Newcastle.

So, Paul Tinnion and I started to work together. Paul's the kind of doorman you would want in the trenches with you – always on the ball and not someone to mess with – and over the weeks and months we handled every situation that came our way. The bars weren't as hectic as Masters had been at Christmas, but nevertheless we had our fair share of bother. The football matches always brought trouble, and more often than not rival fans would clash with Newcastle fans before and after each game. As a fanzine editor, I came in for a lot of stick, but I had broad shoulders and was never unduly bothered by the verbal threats from some of the narrow-minded yobs that called themselves supporters.

Doormen in general have a bad reputation. They are looked at by the public as paid thugs who chat up women and give any man who looks at him the wrong way a good hiding – hence the name bouncer. The council, in association with the police, wanted to change that image and rid the bars and clubs of the criminally minded doormen – hence the licensing. What publicans wanted was a customer-friendly doorman, someone who talked to the customers and only ejected them with *reasonable* force if they misbehaved.

I learned very quickly that doing the door was as much about 'front' as it was physical size: never back down when you have made a decision, because it shows weakness; always maintain eye contact with a customer whom you have a problem with; be aware of who that person is with; and, most importantly, make sure someone is watching your back!

I was making frequent trips to London to see the chaps, and when I was down there had been doing regular shifts at Diamonds, Dave Courtney's club in Hackney, and at the Ministry of Sound. Working those venues gave me a taste for club life, and for a while I considered moving to London full time, but I was told in no uncertain terms by Courtney that I should 'stay up north, mate, and make your mark'. I decided to take his advice.

I had been to see the various faces who ran the doors in the North East and made it known that I was looking for club work. I was told that they would be in touch as soon as a vacancy turned up. A couple of months had passed when I was called by Mike, the manager of Legends nightclub in Newcastle. He said that he had been given my number and that he wanted to offer me a job. I jumped at the chance, and four hours later I was signing on the dotted line with Geoff Capes's security firm. (Yes, Geoff Capes the famous athlete and former copper.) However, what Mike had neglected to tell me was that the previous doormen had just been sacked, that the police were keeping a close eye on the club and that they had compiled a list of criminals and doormen whom they wanted barred from the venue.

It was well known that the sacked doormen had been running the club like the Wild West – customers were getting beaten to a pulp, the CCTV tapes kept going missing and the club had quickly gained a reputation as a bit of a drugs den. So, one night the police decided to raid the club with over 150 officers. To their embarrassment, they caught no dealers and only a handful of people for possession. I had taken on a job and a half!

Doormen in every town or city are a funny breed. There is a lot of competition in the industry and a lot of pride at stake, and the one thing that doormen hate is outsiders, people from another part of the country in charge of the doors in their area. Capes UK was based in London and relied on 'outsiders' to work problem bars and nightclubs for them. The first couple of days at my new unit passed by without incident, but this was the calm before the storm. Despite receiving a substantial settlement, the ex-doormen weren't happy, and they were going to make us work hard for our money. Paul came on board, which give me a lift because up until that point I was the only Geordie. Paul and I were now looked on by the local door fraternity as being 'scabs' and were subsequently barred from most bars in the city centre – with the threat of a good kicking if we ever tried to visit any of these places.

I'll admit that each night was a nerve-racking experience; I changed my route to and from work, and I was careful not to let anyone know my address or telephone number. I even gave a false name to people whom I talked to in the club. Paranoid maybe, but you cannot be too careful in this game. Although some of the threats lacked any real substance, I had to take each one seriously, because one day someone might just call my bluff.

As time went by, the threats died down, and we had more or less weathered the storm. I had had a few run-ins with a few faces during that period, but as the months passed the lads from other bars started to respect the fact that Paul, the other lads and I had stood our ground and not bottled it.

I suggested to our gaffer that he lift the ban on doormen now that the trouble had cooled and that we let them in as long as they surrendered their licences to us for the duration of their evening. He agreed, which made our job that little bit easier, and one by one our own bans started to lift in the town. I was soon able to go for a pint in Newcastle again without looking over my shoulder. Special mention *must* go to those who stood their ground and watched my back at Legends: Paul Tinnion, Johnny Miller, Vaughn Basset, Maria Gillon, Mark Higgins, Simon McGhee, Biff, Adam, Naz, Andy, Gareth and Amanda Scott.

People often ask me what I get out of doing the doors. Well, it's simple: it is a means to an end. If you do six nights a week in a bar or club – say thirty-five hours a week at £12 an hour – you are pulling in more than some bar managers. It pays my bills, keeps a roof over my head and gives me money to spend on the finer things in life. Also, I have had some laughs and met some characters whom I wouldn't have otherwise met.

Some doormen use the job as a dating agency, and I would say I have worked with probably two of the worst offenders in living history. One of the lads has over three hundred telephone numbers of women he has bagged on the door filed in two cash bags and even has Polaroid photos of himself and his conquests to prove to the other lads that he is no liar. The other, whom I shall call 'The Hawk', specialises in collecting souvenirs at the end of the night from the cubicles in the women's toilets! It takes all sorts.

From a customer's point of view, I would say I'm quite tolerant of the pissed general public, and I always have time for the punter who is ejected early on from a club on a freezing cold night in the North East and proceeds to protest with the door staff for the next few hours, inevitably resorting to, 'My Dad/Mum will have this place closed down!' What people do not realise is that we hear this sort of thing *every single night*. If anything, it keeps us amused and passes the time, but, like referees in football, we never change our mind! (So, if you find yourself in that situation, do yourself a favour and go home; otherwise, you'll either end up in a cell or with a lousy cold – or both.)

Humour plays a large part on the door, and nine times out of ten you end up taking the rise out of each other. I love a good joke and am lucky that I can laugh at myself.

Legends – as I have already said – was once renowned for its customers using drugs, and I spent most of my time working on the front door, where I would have to carry out spot searches. I must admit, I hated it, as having experimented with drugs myself when I was younger I felt a bit hypocritical stopping people doing the same. It wouldn't have been too bad if all we had to do was knock these folk back, but, no, the police wanted us to detain people. So, reluctantly, I had to be seen to be doing the job.

One night, I decided to wear my brand-new suit. As I bent down to check the customer's legs for anything he might have concealed, I heard a loud rip; my new pants had given way and a cool draft was evident at the rear end. That was the only time in my life that I can honestly say that I had my back well and truly to the wall. Still, it certainly gave everyone a good laugh that night.

Working the door can be a bit messy at times, and it's not uncommon to see at least one broken bone or some blood spilled at least once a week. And you also witness some very strange human behaviour: exhibitionists who like a good shag in a dark corner of the club or druggies having a bizarre conversation with the wall. However, one of the most distressing sights I have ever witnessed was the lad we suspected of snorting coke in the toilets one night. I kicked the door in and could not believe what I was looking at. A male in his early 20s was kneeling in front of the toilet with his pants around his ankles, masturbating over his own shit, which he had placed around the toilet seat. Sick or what? When he realised he had been rumbled, he stood up, turned to me and put his hand out towards me to apologise. He had shit all over his hand! Needless to say, we all backed off until he'd cleaned himself up and then kicked him out into the street.

The job also has its glamorous side when celebrities visit the club. I've looked after hundreds of stars, from footballers to actors and pop groups, but I have to say the most enjoyable night I had was at Legends with snooker's Dennis Taylor when it was his 50th birthday celebration. All the top stars from the sport were present: Stephen Hendry, Ronnie O'Sullivan, Darren Morgan, Mark Stevens and, of course, Dennis. We had a great night and one that I will remember for a very long time.

When I look back at the years I have spent on the doors of the pubs and clubs of Newcastle, I think of Legends with immense pride and satisfaction. I stood my ground with the lads, and we sailed through a political storm with flying colours. Working a club is different to working a pub. For starters, there is the fact that you start and finish later. The clientele you are dealing with in a boozer are just there to get pissed, whereas those in a club are smashed and looking for a bit of a boogie or a warm bed for the night. Legends was definitely the place to be, but it had come in for a bit of a hammering from the press and the local council after the big drugs raid failed to net the police much more than a couple of people for possession. The sight of 150-odd police officers raiding a club only to arrest a few 'chavs' with a wrap each was highly embarrassing for our boys in blue.

In Newcastle, Monday night is generally student night in most of the clubs around the city. When the locals are slogging away at work five days a week to pay for their highly priced drinks at the weekend, bars and clubs depend on student 'tax dodgers' to pay the wages and bring in an extra source of income. We had all sorts in on those nights: hippies with green hair and flares; skinheads with pierced lips and noses; fat, ugly girls with tight denim jeans and boob tubes; and, of course, university rugby players whose fathers, as we were told time and time again, owned the very streets that we walked on. I lost count of the number of times that I was told by these pricks that they would be earning more than me in a couple of years' time, and that their dads could have me sacked and the club shut down if I didn't let them stagger back down the stairs into the venue. What a bunch of complete wasters.

George was one such punter. Not a week would go by without him being dragged out of the club for one thing or another. He really was a pain in the arse. He would be thrown out at about 10 p.m. and would still be there at 2 a.m. arguing the toss and threatening my livelihood. Needless to say, I'm doing OK, and he is still studying – six years later!

Another student that springs to mind is 'Posh Ron'. He was called Ronald and spoke like Harry Enfield's character Tim Nice But Dim. Every Monday, Ron felt that he had to perform for his fellow students by stripping off in our club. And when I say strip, I mean strip – the fuller monty, if you get my meaning. The lads eventually decided to teach him a lesson. One night in January – and I hasten to add that it was a *very* cold night in January – Posh Ron set off on his usual routine. As his final Dunlop trainer was flung off and he let it all hang out, the lads and I set our plan into motion and began gathering up his clothes. Once we had all of his gear, we grabbed Ron just as he was about to do the cancan and escorted him off the premises. It had started to snow, and Ron quickly realised the error of his ways, but this time we weren't going to hand him his clothes back. The sight of 'Posh' with his hands cupped over his nether-regions kept the queue entertained and had us all in hysterics until the police arrived to protect his dignity. We reluctantly handed his clothes over to the police who gave our friend a lift to the local nick to warm up – instead of cooling off!

Nigel was another character who graced our student nights. He was well respected and in general a nice geezer whose daddy had plenty of money, but you tend to find that a lot of these kids who were born with a silver spoon in their mouths and have a lot in their wallet haven't got very much between their ears. We had a restaurant upstairs at Legends that would double as a VIP room once in a while. We only entertained celebrities on a weekend, so a Monday would be business as usual for the restaurant. I would always start off on the front door and then go downstairs for an hour or so to warm up, before going back on the front door to finish. When inside, I used to stand on the stairs leading to the restaurant. For some reason, Nigel would come looking for me to ask if he could hobnob it with the stars. I would say, 'I shouldn't really, but if you make it worth my while, I will turn a blind eye.' Every Monday night, without fail, my palm was greased with a fiver from our Nigel, even though there were never any celebrities up there. He never did catch on. See what I mean? Not much between the ears.

However, life wasn't always fun and games at Legends. Every year the Hoppings fair would visit Newcastle's Town Moor for a week in June, and apart from bringing bad weather it would also bring a whole lot of trouble in the form of gypsies. Travellers, for me, are the worst type of gypsy you can come across. (Sunderland football fans come a close second.) Travellers are always looking for bother with anyone who so much as looks at them, and this particular night was no different.

It was a Thursday, and a couple of the lads were late arriving at the club, so there were only three of us on duty. Earlier on in the evening, we had let in a group of lads who were on a stag do from Edinburgh – now have you ever seen a sober Scotsman? No? Neither have I. Later on, the gypsies started to arrive in dribs and drabs – we were quiet so had no objection to letting them in. It took all of five minutes before the alarm was ringing. 'Fight in bar one,' was the call over the bar staff's radio. Sure enough, the Scots and the gypsies had introduced themselves to each other, and Paul and I had a riot on our hands.

As standard practice, Johnny, the other lad working with us that night, had to stay on the door. Inside, there was a ruck of about twenty blokes punching and kicking seven bags of shit out of each other, so Paul and I got in amongst them as best we could. I pulled the gypos back – sovereign rings and all – while Paul weighed into the kilt-wearing warriors. Our back-up arrived in the shape of Simon and Vaughn, and we eventually managed to get them all outside. It was like the Wild West, and blood and snot was flying as we 'rag dolled' the lads up the stairs and out onto the street. I like to go to work, earn my money and go home without any bother if I can help it, but this was one of the very few occasions when I actually had to hit someone – a record I'm quite proud off. One of the gypsies was from the school of dirty fighting and decided he fancied a bite of my arm. I just managed to pull it free before he drew blood and caught him with a cracking uppercut followed with a straight left. Sweet! My old boxing coaches Bernard and Tommy at Felling Victoria would have been proud of me.

A lot of doormen weren't at all happy when cameras were introduced into Newcastle city centre and then into the bars. Skiving and any misdemeanours were quickly seized upon by the management, who previously hadn't known what their door staff were up to. However, I was certainly happy that the cameras were in place and working in Legends on one of my rare nights off.

I was standing at the side of the main dance floor with a few of my mates: Ritchie, who worked at the club; Graham, a taxi driver from Gateshead; and Curly Keith and an Iraqi called Alan, two punters whom I knew from the club. A fight broke out on the dance floor, but it was all over in a flash, leaving a lad nursing a broken nose. I went up to him amongst all the ravers and tried to wave over Irish Mark, one of the doormen working that night, but I couldn't get his attention. By that time, the lad's mates had crowded around me asking what I'd done to him. I told them what had happened, but because they were pissed they thought I had done it. They wanted to get involved, but by that time Irish Mark had come over and was listening to the lad's mate's side of the story. The lads were convinced I was guilty and wouldn't let it lie, so I told them I was going to leave before the situation got out of control. I left through the fire exit and made my way home.

The following night, I arrived at work as normal and was called into the manager's office. I was told in no uncertain terms that I was no longer required for work. I was suspended. In a nutshell, the lad's mates were convinced that I was the guilty party and had called the police. As a result, the manager gave the police my name, and I was a wanted man! I told the manager that if he checked the CCTV for that night, the camera would clear my name. He said he would but that the police had it and would return with it the following week, so until then I was suspended. I could not believe it. In the end, the camera didn't lie, and I was proved innocent, but it still cost me the best part of £200, as the manager refused to pay me while I was suspended.

It's amazing how many 'friends' you have when you work on the doors. Most bars in Newcastle have a queue at some time during the evening, and this is when your so-called mates suddenly appear. If you are on the front door of a bar or club for a few weeks on the trot, people get to know you and say hello or shake your hand. Some even give you the time of day and comment on the weather or a football result. This is the punters' way of getting in with you. They see you as a way of jumping the queue – it is as simple as that. Now, I don't mind letting one or two people in for free who I have got to know over time, but I have had some people who really take the piss and attempt to get ten people in past the long queue. If you are one of those people, I'm telling you now: don't do it again. And for all of you working in clothes shops whom I have let in over these past few years, rest assured, I will be coming into your shop for a few freebies very soon – I have happily scrubbed your back on a few occasions, so now you can scrub mine!

I worked at Planet Earth (Dolce Vita when the Kray twins visited Newcastle) every Wednesday for a while. The promoter had a hard job filling the place. Most of my Wednesdays were spent with Mickey Armstrong and another lad called Anth. Malcolm, the manager, was always up for a laugh, so the atmosphere at that venue was usually fairly relaxed. One day, Anth made the fatal mistake of wetting Malcolm with a bottle of water – the battle lines were drawn. Malcolm and Mickey enlisted me in their revenge attacks – yes, attacks were going to be made on Anth.

First up was the standard 'wetting Anth with a bigger bottle of water when he least expects it' – simple enough. Result: Anth in wet clothes. The following week saw a little more planning. Mickey enticed Anth into a game of pitch and toss against the club wall. I went first with a poor attempt; Mickey went second. He retrieved his coin, which was a bit closer than mine. Next up was Anth, who was really up for the challenge. He'd done it – his coin was closer to the wall than mine or Mickey's. Splash – he hadn't banked on Malcolm throwing a bucket of icy water out of the window. Result: Anth in wet clothes.

By the following week, Anth was paranoid and was doing a new version of the green cross code, looking left, right and straight up! Our next plan had to be good . . . and it was. We asked one of the lasses from reception to pose as a collapsed punter outside the fire exit at the back of the club. We arranged for Anth to be on the front door with a new starter so that when the call for assistance came to the front door Anth would have to go and deal with it. It worked like clockwork! Anth went around the back of the club to rescue our damsel in distress, and by the time he realised he'd been duped . . . splash – another bullseye for Mickey and Malcolm. Result: Anth in wet clothes (and most of us in wet pants).

I was crying with laughter. Proof (if you need it) that doormen aren't the animals they are made out to be – we like a good laugh as much as anyone!

The Union Rooms was at one time a gentlemen's club in the heart of Newcastle city centre, but when it finally closed it stood empty for the best part of 25 years. The pub chain J.D. Wetherspoon saw an opportunity and grasped it with both hands, and Eric Pilman, Mark Higgins, Gordon Gray and I were asked to work the door. It was a new type of bar: no music, no televisions or big screens, just cheap booze and good conversation. Just like the good old days!

The place was commonly used – and still is – as a starting-off point for a night on the town and was generally heaving on a Friday and Saturday night. Also, being next to the train station, it attracted a lot of football fans on a match day. A lot of the lads I used to go to the match with in my younger days were still running with the hooligan firms at that time – the latest batch being known as the Gremlins. I didn't have a problem – and still don't – with any of the lads, but the manager of the pub did. The bar had a restaurant upstairs, and on one occasion the manager received a few complaints from customers about football fans singing. As a result, he asked us to throw out those responsible. So we did. However, the problem was that some of the lads involved knew me and knew that I was also a fan, which made me the target for their abuse. It didn't take long for the rest of them to join in. Soon, other fans were singing, and the situation was really starting to get out of control. Four doormen and four hundred fans equals? The police arrived soon after the manager had called them for assistance. The fans vowed revenge; they'd be back.

The following week, we were told to stop any fans wearing colours, which caused more animosity, and yours truly got the brunt of the stick again. However, any hooligan worth his salt doesn't wear colours, so it wasn't long before the singing started, and the manager was at a loss as to how his plan had failed. We went inside to tackle the situation, and it was obvious that the lads had come in for a bit of bother – and boy did they get it. We asked them to move outside. 'Are you gonna make us, like?' one of them said. Then the whole bar went up. One of the other lads threw a punch at Eric, just missing him, and the four of us waded in. It was like something out of *The A-Team*, without us having to build anything! Bodies were flying all over the place, glasses were smashing, bottles were flying here and there, and each football hooligan that got in our way found himself lying next to one of his pals in the gutter outside the bar. The video of the event should be used at door-training seminars, as we were all quite pleased with ourselves that day – and so was the manager. Needless to say, we didn't have any more singing on a match day, but was it really worth upsetting all of those fans for the sake of a poxy couple of people in the restaurant? I don't think so.

We had other rucks with visiting firms. The whole town would be on maximum alert for the North East derby between Newcastle and Sunderland or, to a lesser extent, Middlesbrough. The police would visit us to have a look around for any notorious faces, and once or twice they would update us on their whereabouts, but, as I have said before, I knew most of the lads, so didn't have much bother with them, as there was a mutual respect all round.

One of the worst match days I ever had to work was again at The Union Rooms next to the central train station. Mick, the other lad who was supposed to be working that day, didn't turn up, which left me in the lurch, and Newcastle had just lost at home to Sunderland, so the atmosphere was pure evil. In those days, the away fans were given a police escort to the station, but that didn't bother those intent on causing trouble. The police had for some reason underestimated their numbers, and I had a major incident on my hands. The bar was full of Geordies urging the Makems to have a go, and I was one man against the masses. A bottle was thrown towards the bar, and the window went. It was like the starting gun to a marathon – the whole place erupted. The Makems charged the door and the Toon fans charged the oncoming red and whites. Game on. It made *Braveheart* look tame.

I let those who wanted to leave go and pulled a woman off the ground who had been knocked over in the crowds – she was a little shaken but nothing was broken. Out of breath but all in one piece, I managed to bolt the doors. The sound of smashing glass was deafening. The aftermath? Well, it was like a bomb had hit the place. The manager was just pleased that no one was hurt. Mick chose the right day to be off!

Sea nightclub is situated on Newcastle's flourishing quayside and is a very sophisticated establishment, where ordinary Joe Public can mingle with the stars of the moment from sport, stage and screen – you name them and they will have been to Sea. I got the job working there through Alan Scott and Graham Hancock and was given six nights a week, Sunday being my night of rest! I was also working at Chase on a Friday and a Saturday with Richard, Andy, Hezzy and Julie. There was never any real trouble at either of these places, which made them a lot harder to work. Why? Because you can easily slip into a routine and, if you're not careful, lose concentration, which can be fatal in this line of work. That is why I must admit I preferred the hustle and bustle and time-bomb atmosphere of the Bigg Market than the serenity of the quayside.

The people on the quayside were pretentious and most were pretending to be something they weren't. A lot of them worked in clothes shops and as a result had all the latest gear, which made them look as if they were in the money. They would buy a bottle of champagne between six or so of them and make it last all night, whilst looking down their noses at those lesser mortals who could only afford a bottled lager! Wankers. However, I made some good mates at Sea – Wayne Keepin, Wayne Pinkerton, Ian Young – and we had a lot of laughs.

Some people have no consideration when it comes to parking their cars, and that was the case when we arrived at Sea one evening to find that some plonker had parked his vehicle in front of the doors of the club. We tried every possible way to contact the owner, but to no avail, so there was only one thing for it. Four of us surrounded the Vauxhall Vectra and, in our own Geoff Capes style, lifted it out of the way of the doors. You could tell we weren't used to that sort of thing, and the car was left with a few bumps and scratches that it hadn't had an hour or so before. We denied all knowledge when the owner returned and drove away with the car's bumper trailing along the ground.

One night during our first Christmas at Sea saw a heavy fall of good snowball snow. It was a quiet evening, so we started throwing the odd snowball at a few of the friendlier customers leaving the venue. A couple of brave ones threw some back at us. As the night progressed, customers started to get braver and began to team up. By closing time, we had a full-scale war on our hands, with about eight doormen against twenty punters. With the odds heavily against us, I nipped inside and got the glass collectors to fill up the big bin that they collected the bottles in with ice and water. The punters were just under the swing bridge, so I got the glass collectors to sneak around the back of the club and up onto the bridge with the bin. We then stood back and laughed as the enemy got a bloody good soaking!

Christmas is supposed to be the season of kindness and goodwill. Humbug! Sometimes we do have a good laugh, but the 'once a year drinkers' cause mayhem for a solid fortnight, and, boy, have I had them all: work colleagues who have discovered that they are shagging the same bird – except one of them is married to her; brothers who have fallen out over the same woman; a reveller who grabbed a woman's arse only to receive a right hook from her boyfriend who regularly sparred with Mike Tyson in his spare time. Ding dong merrily on high! I've lost count of how many girls I have seen spewing through their fingers, only to be necking on their latest victim ten minutes later. So remember lads: the next time some lass is dangling mistletoe over your Santa hat, check for carrots.

On a more serious note, the quayside sadly attracted a lot of jumpers, and that's not because it was cold. I mean suicide jumpers. It wasn't uncommon to have more than one a shift. The Tyne Bridge was a favourite, as it was the most well known. For many of these people, it was a desperate cry for help; for others, it was how they wanted to end it all. The worst I witnessed was outside Chase when a man jumped and hit the pavement – not a pretty sight. Another man attempted to jump on three separate occasions on the same day. After the third attempt, the police had him sectioned.

Drunken exploits could also lead to disaster down by the water. Students would often dare their mates to hang from the fence above the water. Most of them completed the stunt without harm, but the odd one wouldn't be as lucky and fall in. One night, Alan Scott and I were on the front door when we were alerted by a passer-by that someone was in the water. Alan ran to the fence and looked over. It was dark, and he had to guess where the person was. He threw the ring over, and the young lad managed to grab it and hold on. I called an ambulance and the police, who arrived a few minutes later. Alan had saved the lad's life, yet there was nothing in the papers, no recommendation from the police, not even a thank you from the lad. Don't get me wrong: I don't do the job for a pat on the back, but if Alan had been arrested for something, it would have made front-page news because he was a doorman!

With Sea being a relatively new club, we were visited by a lot of big names. The stars and celebrities arrived thick and fast. Graham Hancock knew that I had looked after a few people whilst I was living in London, so he designated me, along with a couple of other lads, to look after any VIPs who visited the club. Looking after the stars is the easy bit – keeping the public at bay is what really tests your patience.

With Robbie Williams, we weren't really sure whether he would be turning up at all, so the whole club was opened just in case. Then he arrived out of the blue with about 30 people in tow. We were told to go and ask ordinary punters who had settled in the VIP lounge to leave their seats and make room for Robbie and his entourage. Needless to say, there were a lot of people with their noses put out of joint that night. 'Why should we move for him?' 'Has he paid to get in?' 'Will *he* be here next week?' I agreed with them, but I was just doing what I was told.

Once the area was cleared, Robbie appeared, and the drinks started to flow. Bottle after bottle of the finest champagne was downed, and more and more people flocked upstairs to get a look at their idol. He was a lot smaller than I imagined and was madly jumping about all over the place – if he had been anyone else, he would have definitely been chucked out onto the streets. A lot of girls were trying to get past me to get to Robbie, some even offering their 'services' if I would just let them through. Not a chance. Even people who should have known better said that they would report me to the owner if I didn't let them

101

pass. I couldn't understand why someone would want to embarrass themselves like that.

Just as we had things under control, Robbie jumped up and started to sing his number-one hit 'Angels'. Well, the place went mental as his fans sang back to him. I wasn't impressed and was just glad that I wasn't in his personal security team, because they really had their work cut out. The next day's paper reported that Robbie had bought everyone in the club a drink – although I didn't get one – and there was talk of an alleged £3,000 bar bill left outstanding. That's rock and roll for you.

Pop band Steps caused the same kind of mayhem. They didn't have as many followers as Mr Williams, but their security asked us to make sure that no one took any photos of them. Talk about mission impossible. The usual faces tried to gatecrash the VIP section, without any success. The owner of the club had taken to switching his phone off when a VIP arrived, so it was no use those wankers phoning him either. As the flashes went off, the band's security started to argue with the punters – some arguments became quite heated. One couple wanted a photo for their kids – the band had said yes but their security no. The couple started to hurl abuse at the minders, who then expected me to throw them out. In my opinion, the minders had caused the problem, so they could deal with it, and we ignored their requests to throw people out. Just to round off my terrible night, I was half expecting the band to burst into song, but thankfully that never happened.

One star I wouldn't have minded singing was Marti Pellow, former lead singer with Wet Wet Wet, as I always enjoyed their music. When he visited us, he was very low key – no minders, no entourage, just him. He was a really nice fella and not at all stage struck. I wish more stars were like him.

The Newcastle United team also became regular visitors to the club, and over time I reacquainted myself with the likes of Shay Given, Alan Shearer, Rob Lee, Warren Barton, Stephen Glass and Kevin Gallagher. I used to enjoy the *craic* about results and games – past and present – with the lads and would always share a drink or two with them when they came into the venue.

Things were going well. I was still with my girl Dawn, and life was good, but something had to give. Although I got my work on the quayside through Alan and Graham, I was actually still contracted to a security company. I had been warned about the bloke I was working for and did listen but decided to try and stick it out. I lasted just over two years until I fell out with him over holiday arrangements. I left with my reputation intact and my head held high and had Dawn to thank for keeping me going when at one point I was going to throw in the towel. He had tried to blacken my name with other door firms, but he hadn't banked on me having so much support in the town. I have since heard that he has upset a lot of other people and lost a lot of good doormen.

I eventually decided to take a bit of time off and spend some quality time with my girlfriend as well as seeing some of the lads, and it was like a new lease of life for me. It was strange not having to put on my stab-vest every weekend. I wasn't looking for work when Alan Scott called me up out of the blue to ask if I fancied a job back on my old stomping ground. He was leaving The Groat House to take over the door at a new club that was opening called Sugar. I appreciated the call and went to see him that night. After meeting the lads – Billy, Jason, George and Freddie – and the manageress Alyson, I dotted the i's and crossed the t's and was back where it all had started: the Bigg Market. It was a different cup of tea to the quay – full of locals and youngsters trying to look older, and the music was a mixture of cheesy chart tunes and the latest banging dance tracks, which was right up my street.

It was a doddle. We had a scrap there every other night – usually girls fighting each other or causing a fight between their ex-boyfriends – but it was an easy number. Alan offered me a couple of shifts, but I didn't want to go back to all work and no play, so I just took on a Thursday night for the time being.

Sugar had opened as a gay club but had flopped, so they recruited promoter Alex Lowes to pack the place out. His reputation for promoting events such as the Southport Weekender and To the Manor Born in Sedgefield meant that he duly obliged. In the first couple of weeks, I was on 'star watch' again, as Brian and Narinder, stars from the Channel Four show *Big Brother*, visited, and Olympic boxing gold medal winner Audley Harrison arrived with his family after winning his second pro-fight in Newcastle. Sugar was going to be a winner, and I was happy to be a part of it.

However, I only stayed at Sugar for a few months, as I soon got bored. I got an offer to move back to Chase on the quayside, but this time as head doorman, and I jumped at the chance. I had a great set of lads working with me there – Peter Lucy, Shaun Charlton, Mick Bradwell, Les Jackson, Freddie Suadwa, Stu the Charva – and a great gaffer in Ronnie Pagan. Life had never been so good. We had some ups and downs, but I loved them all. I was there for five years in total, but all good things eventually come to an end, and I moved on with my security boss Geoff Oughton to help out at Sam Jacks and Bar 55. I stayed there for eight months before ending up at Tiger Tiger with my old mates Buzz and Wrighty, who I started with at Masters all those years before.

I still love what I do. I wouldn't do it otherwise. I met my wife Dawn doing the job I love. As for working the doors now – as opposed to the way it was back when I started in the '90s – well, I think the SIA have a lot to answer for. We lost a lot of good doormen because of their licensing scheme, and many good lads have been replaced by mere kids who just can't do the job.

If I could give anybody any advice going into this line of work, it would be: don't take liberties and what goes around comes around. You have to earn respect. Respect does not lie in your fists. The job is so different now, but violence is still there every night you put on your Crombie and straighten your tie. You never know what's in store. For me, that was part of the enjoyment!

BIOGRAPHY OF STEVE WRAITH

Steve Wraith is now 35, lives on Tyneside and is an actor and writer. Steve's television credits include *55 Degrees North*, *Wire in the Blood* and *Byker Grove*, and his film credits include *Goal*.

His website www.thegeordieconnection.com was launched in 1998 to promote a manuscript entitled *The Krays – The Geordie Connection* written by Steve Wraith and Stuart Wheatman. The intention was for this site to help attract a publisher and then close down. However, after obtaining a publishing deal with Zymurgy Publishing, the book was a huge success, and the site became an important advertising tool. The decision was taken to keep the site up and running, and this led to a video and DVD deal with www.gangstervideos.co.uk. *The Krays – The Geordie Connection* documentary was released a year after the book and has proved to be just as successful. The site has also proved to be a useful starting point for those with an interest in the Kray family, and Steve has endeavoured to update the various sections over the years as well as answer any questions that visitors have.

The site has changed direction over time and is now dedicated to helping chart Steve Wraith's progress as an actor and writer. Steve is represented by Janet Plater Management, and any offers of work in the entertainment industry must be directed to Janet Plater on 0191 221 2490.

As well as being a published author, Steve has been the editor of two football-related magazines. *The Number Nine* fanzine ran from 1991 to 1998 and was a huge favourite on the terraces at St James's Park in the 1990s. Steve is now the editor of North East football magazine *Players Inc*. For further information on the magazine, please visit www.playersinc.org.uk

Steve has also teamed up with former Newcastle and Hartlepool striker Joe Allon to launch a successful agency hiring out former football players as after-dinner speakers. For a comprehensive list of players and prices, please email Steve or Joe at playersinc@hotmail.com

Steve is also a keen fundraiser and has dedicated a lot of his time to helping the Bubble Foundation. The annual celebrity cricket tournament The Felling Ashes has gone from strength to strength since its inaugural game in 2002, and various sportsmen's dinners and music gigs have helped raise thousands for worthy causes. For further information on charities that Steve is involved with, please visit www.bubblefoundation.org.uk, www.cancerresearch.org and www.gracehouse.co.uk

Steve has written for numerous books, including: *Survival of the*

Fattest volumes one to four (football related); *Born to Fight* by Richy Horsley; *The Guv'nor: Through the Eyes of Others* by Anthony Thomas; and *Wor Al: A Fans' Tribute to Alan Shearer* by Paul Brown and Stuart Wheatman.

8

BODYGUARD TRAINING IN THE RUSSIAN FEDERATION

BY ROBIN BARRATT

Without doubt, Iraq and Afghanistan have permanently altered the attention private security and bodyguarding has had in the media, changing forever the perception the general public has of the industry. Before the Iraq and Afghanistan wars, the public generally knew very little about bodyguarding and private security; to most people it was a twilight world, populated by thugs, gangsters and mercenaries, which they knew nothing about. However, since the US declared the end of major combat operations in Iraq in May 2003 and restructuring of the country commenced, and fuelled by recent kidnappings and assassinations – of both bodyguards and their clients – the bodyguarding industry now receives almost daily media attention and is the subject of frequent articles and editorial, as well as a fair number of top-quality television programmes. Also, with the introduction of SIA licensing in the UK, compulsory standardised training and strict vetting, bodyguarding as a career is now open to almost anyone with the aptitude and ability, the drive and the determination, and the right background. As an industry, bodyguarding has gone from strength to strength; it is no longer the sole domain of a select number of ex-Special Forces earning £500 plus per day, bonded by secrecy, mystery and silence. Bodyguarding is now big business, with corporate takeovers and multimillion-pound contracts.

But this has only been the case in some Western countries over the past few years. Prior to 2003, there were only a handful of other nations, at peace, that had such a high-profile private security industry. One such country was the Russian Federation – although many would argue that with the ongoing conflict in Chechnya, Dagestan and Ingushetia, and the occasional terrorist activity in Russia's capital, the country has never really been at peace.

Since the fall of communism, private security in Russia has grown significantly and is now a multibillion-pound industry. During the years of communism, there were no private security companies, only special military units set up and funded by the government for specific and specialised purposes. Because there was little or no crime and everything was owned by the state, there was no real need to protect anything, as there was no obvious threat. And those very few petty criminals who did exist were generally quickly caught and sent off to the Gulags of Siberia, where they usually ended their days building roads on a diet of dried bread.

During communist rule, it was the government who were the criminals, and they controlled everything anyway. But once communism fell, it was a free-for-all, and by fuck did you have to protect what you had. Without protection, a business – any business – would have had no chance whatsoever of surviving. Even a small corner shop had to have armed guards standing at the entrance, nervously eyeing up all and sundry.

I fondly remember the very first Russian nightclub I visited on one of my very first trips to Moscow. I was in the country meeting the directors of a company called Centurion VI, at that time a major player in the private security industry. I was planning a forthcoming security operation with a banker who I had been tasked to protect.

After a hearty meal at a restaurant that they said they owned on the outskirts of the city, I was invited on to a nightclub with a couple of the bodyguards whom I was going to be working with. Having already sampled the delights of Russian women, I eagerly agreed, hoping that I could at least see some wondrous female forms – even if I was in Russia on business and therefore couldn't touch . . . well, shag.

The nightclub was behind the now demolished Intourist hotel at the bottom of Tverskaya Street, a few minutes' walk from Red Square. As we approached the club, two menacing-looking doormen stood guard outside, each brandishing AK-47s. I am not easily intimidated, but even I drew a deep breath at nightclub doormen with AK-47s and asked myself why were we not allowed to work the doors with these kind of tools back in the UK – now can you imagine what that would be like!

The doormen obviously knew the people I was with, and we were quickly recognised and received a warm, enthusiastic welcome. I just smiled and nodded eagerly, not understanding a word and hoping to God that they were really being kind and welcoming and not planning to decapitate me and sell my remains for a few roubles to feed the poor beggars found on every street corner. This was one sad thing that I immediately noticed in the newly capitalist regime – there were beggars everywhere.

I spent the rest of that evening huddled in a smoky corner with four slightly insane-looking, chain-smoking, vodka-swilling, pissed Russian bodyguards, who thought it was terribly funny to unholster their weapons, swirl them around their fingers, gunslinger style, while shouting 'cowboy' at the top of their voices and pointing them at the other extremely scared customers. Needless to say, by the end of the evening we were the only ones left in the club, apart from a bevy of the most gorgeous girls, who were either dancing in front of us or cuddled up around with their tits hanging out and tight shorts up their arses. They were all so beautiful and were obviously paid to stay late and entertain us – but I never saw one rouble pass hands that evening, so I have no idea who paid for what, or if in fact anything was paid for. That was Moscow in the early 1990s.

Moscow is undoubtedly addictive; anyone who has been there will almost certainly agree. At first, you enter the country with trepidation and apprehension – after all, Moscow *is* Moscow: corrupt and criminal, crazy and callous – but you then have to be dragged screaming back to the airport a few days, or weeks, or months, or years, later. To this day, I still believe that there is nowhere like it in the world, but back then when everything was new and exciting, when you could do anything and there was little or no accountability, Moscow was simply fantastic.

Shortly after joining the Worldwide Federation of Bodyguards (WFB) as an international trainer, we decided to set up and run a training course in Moscow. After a few years of coming and going, I had developed quite an extensive network of unique contacts within the security industry. If you wanted armed bodyguards with machine guns, I could do it. If you wanted to blue-light it down the middle of major highways, I could do that for you too. If you wanted someone to disappear, no doubt that could also be arranged. Killed someone and got caught with the still-smoking gun in your hands? No worries. In fact, in societies like those, almost anything could be arranged and sorted for a fee – nothing was impossible.

Centurion VI employed mainly Russian ex-Special Forces personnel. As a Russian Special Forces soldier, when you left the army there weren't that many options available – you normally went into bodyguarding or you joined the criminal fraternity as an assassin or extortionist, earning twice the money. Paradoxically, ex-Special Forces soldiers were often protecting clients against ex-Special Forces assassins.

During my visits on contract to Moscow, I had got to know some of the bodyguards quite well, and when I mentioned that the WFB wanted to run a close protection training course in Moscow, they jumped at the chance. The WFB was growing rapidly, and its reputation was developing. I asked the ex-KGB director of Centurion if he knew a facility or base where we could run the first course. He grinned knowingly – he knew of a very good base which we could use, no problem. On my next visit to Moscow, all would be arranged.

Returning to England after even the shortest of trips to Russia was never easy. I went from running a bodyguarding operation or involving myself in a corporate and usually very interesting investigation to working back on the doors – it was the only job I could do that allowed me the time off to go to Moscow. That was one of the good things about the doors: I would just need to telephone the security company and tell them that such and such weekend or week I would not be available to work, and they would always quickly find a replacement. This was before SIA licensing, so doormen were relatively easy to find. I didn't mind working the doors, and it helped pay the bills, but I always yearned to get back to Moscow.

My next trip couldn't come fast enough, and about two months later I was on the plane back to Russia with the sole intention of finding a training camp and setting up a WFB close protection training course. I only had four or five days – it was all the money the WFB had to finance the trip – and a lot to do. I had to look for a suitable training camp, arrange a date, negotiate fees, find instructors, fit the Russian style of training into the WFB's Western style of security operations, find accommodation for the students, arrange transportation and slide myself gracefully into the knickers of at least a couple of gorgeous Russian girls – a requirement on every trip.

I made my own way from the airport to the Ukraine Hotel, a Russian hotel boasting four stars, but this meant *maybe* two stars by Western standards. I was on a tight budget, so instead of being robbed blind by the taxi drivers that hound passengers as they exit Sheremetyevo International Airport, I decided to join the hoards of Russians and take a minibus.

Unlike most other international airports worldwide, there are no trains or decent coaches from Sheremetyevo into Moscow. If you don't have a car waiting for you, you either have to pay the equivalent of at least £50 for a taxi, or squeeze onto a minibus with 12 or so other passengers for about 50p! Travelling in a minibus is definitely not for the faint-hearted. There is no room for luggage, so you sit with your bags on your lap, there is no heating, the bus is crammed and to pay you pass your money down the line of passengers to the driver while he negotiates the traffic and your change and screams back at the one poor soul who hasn't paid yet – how on earth he knows how many people are on the bus and who has or has not paid, I don't know.

The airport is about 30 minutes' drive to the outskirts of Moscow, where the minibuses stop – you then have to get a metro to your final destination. Faced with this daunting and occasionally scary journey, most Westerners on a corporate budget happily pay the taxi fare, but I was different – I wasn't on a big budget, and anyway I despised the smelly, corrupt, soliciting taxi drivers and the Mafia gangs behind them that take most of the money the drivers 'steal' from the foreigners.

The Ukraine Hotel is a colossal Stalinist building that sits on the west bank of the Moskva River at the far end of the glitzy, neon-dotted Novy Arbat street and directly opposite the Russian government's White House. It is ironic that during the cold war both the US and Russian governments had headquarters named the 'White House' – although it was the Americans who built theirs first, the Russian version not being completed until 1965. One of the 'Seven Sisters' that dot the Moscow landscape, the Ukraine Hotel was built in the 1950s to demonstrate the expertise and glory of the Soviet regime. With more than 1,000 rooms over 30 storeys, the hotel is not particularly comfortable but reasonably priced compared to Western hotels – although it is not particularly cheap, either. Although things are slowly changing, it is a big problem that there are no reasonably priced, decent Western-style hotels in Moscow. You can either stay in a Russian-style hotel for £30 to £40 a night, but with terrible service and the phone ringing consistently with strangely accented girls offering you a little extra comfort for a few extra dollars, or in a first-class Western hotel costing at least £150 to £200 a night! There is little choice in between.

Wrapped in a warm woolly scarf and thick coat, with my *shapka* (furry Russian hat) pulled tightly down over my ears, I stood on the steps of the hotel the following morning waiting for my lift. It was cold, about minus ten, and snowing heavily. Winter in Moscow is tough. It decimated the Germans during the Second World War, and before that Napoleon's army, and today it still kills many people, especially beggars, who are frequently found frozen to death in derelict buildings or huddled in doorways in the grimy backstreets far away from the splendour that is central Moscow. Unlike the West, where people on the streets tend to be alcoholics, drug addicts or the mentally ill, beggars in Russia are the old, the poor, the disabled – 'normal' people simply unable to cope.

As I watched huddled figures racing in and out of the hotel foyer, a black BMW glided into the parking area. 'Good to see you, my friend,' said Alex, jumping out of the back of the car with his outstretched hand. I had met Alex on my first-ever job with Centurion and over time had got to know him quite well. Alex had been Gorbachev's own personal bodyguard for much of his presidency and joined the Presidential Protection Team after serving as an officer in Alpha Unit – Russia's equivalent of the SAS. Alex never spoke much about his experiences in the military or by Gorbachev's side; in fact, he never spoke much at all. He was a hard, imposing-looking man with cold eyes that you just knew had witnessed some wild and probably not particularly nice things. A few years later, I was to learn that Alex had left Moscow to settle in a warm, quiet country somewhere in the Mediterranean. I was told that he *had* to leave, as he knew too much about what went on within the higher echelons of the corrupt and frequently brutal Russian government.

'Where are we going?' I asked.

'You will see. We have found a very good base for your training. Yes, very good.' He seemed pleased with himself. I really hoped that the camp was going to be OK, as we already had about seven or eight students lined up for training back in the UK, all trying to thrust their deposits into my hand. Training in Russia was definitely going to be a unique, once-in-a-lifetime experience, and we felt sure that we could find at least ten students for the first course, probably a lot more. However, I had so little time in Moscow, finding something else during that visit would have been impossible and funding other trips extremely difficult.

We drove for about two hours, first through the centre of the city towards the outer ring road, and then north-east through the suburbs, past the miles and miles of bleak, sombre-looking high-rise apartment blocks. The city turned into country, and the country turned into

113

remoteness, and we turned off down a snow-covered track between walls of thick pine trees. The place was barren and desolate except for deep tracks in the snow, where heavy tank-like vehicles had recently passed.

Then, all of a sudden, the pine forest ended, turning, it seemed, into a huge dark-green metal wall, topped with layer upon layer of barbed wire that stretched as far as the eye could see. We continued down the track with the wall on one side of us and the snow-covered pine forest on the other. After a few minutes, the car slowed and turned into a recess in the wall that had been virtually impossible to see from the road. A soldier popped his head out of a steamy cabin, looked at us, inspected the car and without even emerging from the warmth of his sanctuary pressed a buzzer, at which point large metal gates slid open sideways, allowing us to drive into the army barracks.

'This is where I trained,' Alex said to me proudly. 'This is Alpha Unit's training base. It will suit you very well for your training, no?'

I was gobsmacked. How the fuck was a non-military foreigner allowed onto a Russian Special Forces training camp? As we drove towards what looked like the offices, we passed a few soldiers darting here and there, a tank, an armoured personnel carrier, and two of the most menacing-looking gate guards holding sub-machine guns that I have ever seen in my entire life. They were obviously extremely pissed off at having to patrol the front-gate area in sub-zero temperatures, and if looks could have killed, I would have been long dead.

As we parked and got out of the car, a man dressed in winter fatigues emerged from the barracks to greet us. His name was Ivan Medvedev, and he was the commander of the base. Behind him were two more menacing-looking soldiers, who stood to attention and kept a close eye on me as we were all introduced. Ivan was friendly and smiled, while the soldiers looked as though they were going to tear me to pieces. Who on earth would think about messing with the Russian Special Forces?

After going into the office and sipping strong, black, sweet tea, Ivan proudly showed me around a few of the buildings on the base. We first went to the kennels. I didn't know that the Russian Special Forces kept dogs, but they did, mainly to guard the base, but they

114

also had a small special team to search buildings. I was introduced to Svetlana, the woman who ran the kennels, and she looked as butch and dog-like as the animals she was looking after. We then walked to the barracks where the soldiers lived. It was really basic, more like a prison than an army barracks, again confirming my initial impression that the Russian Army are a hard bunch of fuckers – you *have* to be hard to live in the conditions they lived in. Paint was peeling off the walls, the rendering was falling away, the heating and hot water, I was told, was sporadic at best. Surprisingly, though, each soldier had a small private room with bed, bedside table, wardrobe and chair. There was also a small communal area in every dormitory with tea, coffee, etc., and there was a larger communal area in the main building. There was also a rusty, antiquated gym and shower block, but it was all extremely basic.

As we wandered around, I noticed that there was only a handful of soldiers lounging around. Most, we were told, were either off base training in Chechnya or 'in your country killing spies'. Ivan laughed heartily and slapped me on the back when he said this. He was joking, right?

The main building was as basic as the dormitories, with lecture rooms, a communal area populated by worn-out, frayed chairs, an antiquated old television and little else. I couldn't imagine spending years of my life living in these conditions. It was too cold to spend long outside, so we wandered over to the indoor firing range, where the soldiers who had silently accompanied us demonstrated various fire and movement techniques with their old Russian-made Makarovs. Apparently, the Russian military and police officially stopped using these weapons in 1991 when communism collapsed but many were still kept and used for training, as they were extremely simple to operate and very reliable.

One of the unsmiling soldiers then handed me a Stechkin pistol and asked me to have a go. It was a while since I had handled a weapon, and for a few seconds I must have looked a real arse, staring at the weapon as though it was a pretty pink bow. The soldier nodded to me knowingly, and I nodded back in terror – what if I fucking missed the target completely? They stood and stared as I chambered the first round and, like a complete arse, missed the target completely! I fired off another eight rounds, double click to each target, and managed to at least hit something, although certainly not anywhere near the centre of the target, as I think everyone around me was expecting. If Alex was wondering to himself what the fuck was I doing as a close protection operative, he didn't show it; instead, he covered my embarrassment with a gruff, 'You fucking English with your fucking stupid gun laws – you really must practise a bit more!' He then turned to Ivan and said something in incomprehensible Russian, which even made the soldiers break a slight smile.

We then returned to the small office and drank some more tea, which an elderly Russian lady made and poured for us. Ivan talked to Alex, who translated. 'You can have this base and train here about four times a year, maximum. When you want to do training, you give a month's notice, and he,' Alex gestured towards Ivan, who smiled, 'will send everyone, apart from the gate guards, who will not say anything, off the base somewhere – maybe to Chechnya!' He laughed. 'You will give Ivan $2,000 each time you train, OK?'

'OK,' I immediately agreed. This was incredible. I was going to pay the camp commander of the Russian Special Forces $2,000 a week to use his camp for WFB training. This could only happen in Russia – everything is for sale, even an army military base. Alex later told me that $2,000 was more than the camp commander earned in one year! As we arranged the dates of our very first training course in the Russian Federation, I thought briefly about the poor soldiers who were to be sent off the base, no doubt to somewhere horrible, while we used their rooms and facilities and lined the commander's pockets.

Back at the hotel, I called the WFB and told them the good news: we had a base, we had weapons, we had accommodation and food, and we had instructors. It was a recipe for a very successful course.

Two months later, ten students arrived at Sheremetyevo Airport. All of them were originally from a military background: five were English, one was French, two were from Iceland, one was from Denmark and one came all the way from the USA. I had arrived a few days earlier to set everything up. I ordered a minibus, employed a translator, sorted out accommodation and paid the camp commander

116

in advance, which I am sure made our stay even better. He was like a child with a new toy, the toy being our group of naive Westerners coming into his play area.

The students were all undoubtedly hard men. The Dane and a couple of the Brits had served in Bosnia, the American was a former marine, and the Icelanders . . . well, they were Icelanders. However, nothing could have prepared them for the week ahead. Their jaws dropped in unison when the metal gates slid open and the minibus drove into the compound. They almost died with fright when they saw their living conditions and shit themselves when they were introduced to the two soldiers who were to be their instructors (alongside Alex and me). All of them wanted to turn around and go home within a few minutes of arriving, but none did, and the week was probably one of the best I have ever spent training. It was incredible, and the conditions paled into insignificance compared to the quality of the instructors and the knowledge and skill they showed.

Every evening, after an extremely tough day's training, we sat together eating and drinking vodka. The food they served was basic but plentiful and the vodka cheap and endless.

After the last day's training, we headed off into Moscow city centre and spent the evening at the Swedish-owned Night Flight on Tverskaya Street – one of the most exclusive whorehouses in the city. The team had been shocked when they had first arrived in Moscow, and I wanted to shock them – albeit in a very different way – on their last day, too. We all got pissed on expensive drinks, stared up at the knickerless podium dancers and flirted with the hugely expensive but most incredibly beautiful whores in Russia. It was a fitting end to a tough week . . .

9

A LIFE ON THE DOORS
BY BOB ETCHELLS

I started working on the doors when I was about 17 years old at a club called The Festival House in Norwich. I was in there having a drink with a friend, and I got into a fight on the stage. It was easier for the doormen to give me a job than to throw me out. I think I was too much for them. And from then on, I suppose, I just learned the tricks of the trade – I saw what went on and watched other professional doormen work, people who had been doing it for a lot longer than I had. I watched how they acted, and I quickly realised that back then in the early 1980s doormen really had no conscience.

The authorities have tried to make door security more professional, but there are no longer any professional doormen – they are now just hospitality workers or policemen of a kind. There is a big difference: if your car breaks down, you go to a good mechanic, and if you are a doorman or door agency, you should be good at what you do. You don't work the door with someone because they are your mate; you work with him because he is good at what he does and *hope* he becomes your mate. He has to be good enough to watch that you do not get hurt and visa versa. You become comrades, brothers in arms – if one person gets hurt, you all get hurt.

I also saw doormen who just didn't care what they did to people, and it made me think, 'Fucking hell.' But then I realised that those doormen hadn't been hurt themselves. The person who hesitates gets glassed or kicked in the bollocks. The doorman that doesn't hesitate doesn't *ever* get hurt, because he cares more about himself than anyone else. I learned to be dirty like everyone else and to fight for my safety. I learned not to care, because caring means getting hurt. I have been in so many situations in which the more you care, the more you have to struggle, and the dirtier you are, the less they struggle. The more you hurt them, the quicker they are taken out of the club and the quicker the situation finishes. Also, the dirtier you are, the more people look at you and think, 'Fucking hell.' And that was the idea of being a good doorman back then.

I agree with Dave Courtney when he says that there will never be the quality of fighters working the door as there was back in the 1970s and '80s, but that is also because there is not the quality of people wanting to fight the doormen. Now there is no reason to fight. You see, in my day we were fighting people from housing and council estates. For example, back then 20 to 25 blokes would come from one housing estate with the sole purpose of fighting us. You don't get that now, so doormen don't *need* to be the same class of fighters that they were 15 to 20 years ago. Also, because people now sue nightclubs and companies when doormen go over the top, the easy answer is to employ someone who doesn't really want to get into a fight, who wants to appease rather than sort it. And so, as Courtney says, there isn't the quality of fighter, because there isn't the quality of punter any more to cause problems.

Nowadays, there is a lot less violence in clubs but a lot more violence on the streets, because there are a lot more people going out. For instance, you have 10,000 people going out in Norwich, where I worked for most of my life, on a Friday or Saturday night, so you now have 10,000 chances of a fight. When I was on the doors, there were maybe only 2,000 people out on a Friday or Saturday night.

Back when I first worked The Ritzy, I would often see four or five people fighting one, but I don't think you really see that any more, either. Also, back then you would have a lot more time to have a good fight. And I really don't think people are as nasty and as dirty now as they were back then. Actually, I think people are a lot more frightened, which is why there are so many people pulling out knives on each other. That never happened back in my day. In all the years I worked the doors and got myself into fights, I only remember seeing a knife in a fight twice. There was one time in Central Park, which was the upstairs bar at The Ritzy, and I remember a bloke got killed on London Street, Norwich. But that was 15 years ago. People are now both frightened and lazy – using a knife is a lot easier than having a good bout of fisticuffs with someone.

When I was 17, I didn't think working the doors would be something I'd do for life. It was just another job. And I didn't really understand why they'd asked me. I said, 'Yeah, I'll do it,' but I didn't really understand why.

It wasn't until I was in the thick of it that I quickly realised that I couldn't just stand by and watch one of my fellow doormen get into a fight with two or three blokes. Getting stuck in and helping them out became instinctive – second nature. I didn't really care about the punters. They weren't my friends; my friends were the six or so blokes I worked with. Punters were the people who came into the club and kicked off, and they generally made for easy pickings. They were usually drunk, but you were not. You were a team, and they were not. The more ruthless you could be, the easier it was.

Violence has never frightened me. However, I must say that I have never liked violence. It has never rocked my boat, but it has never scared me either. I have never been frightened of being hurt. If anything, I think I was more worried about letting the people I worked with down, because you all rely on each other.

But it wasn't all about having fights together; it was also about having some fun. It was all about shagging girls and nicking your mate's clothes when he was upstairs with some bird. Or running up to him when he was on the job and trying to shove a carrot, which you'd stolen from the kitchen, up the bird's arse. It was even about the fun of watching other doormen get themselves into trouble, like when one of your mates tried to throw someone out and the rest of us were thinking, 'Look at the size of that punter. Fuck, you're in trouble now, buddy. You're on your own!' Of course, he was never really on his own. We would always step in sooner or later, but just watching someone else struggle for a bit could be quite funny.

As a team, we became very close to each other, which I don't think happens now. Instead of working with each other, doormen now seem to be competing with each other – who can look the best and get down the gym the most. Sadly, many doormen are now like puppets, with the manager, police, council, government and even punters pulling their strings. It is not their fault; it is just the way it is now, which I think is sad. There is no respect any more.

Back then, the manager knew you ruled by fear and respect. There was no other way to do things. I worked in the Welsh borders when the miners' strike was on. The managers there were fucking tough and knew that what you stopped at the door you wouldn't have to throw out of the pub. The front door was where you stood your ground and said, 'No, you are not coming in.' What you said to the punters and what you had ready in your hand just in case it kicked off big-time meant that they could bring it on at any time. And when you did have to show your colours, you showed your colours properly. There was no mercy. It wasn't just a case of banging someone in the mouth. You would do as much damage as possible and be as horrible as you could, because you knew that everybody watching it would never come near you again. And when you have six or so doormen all doing the same, there wasn't really much that you couldn't come up against or that would faze you. A good door team was pretty invincible back then.

I remember a bizarre incident in the foyer at Rick's Place in Norwich. A group from Great Yarmouth kicked off, and we were having a proper fight. It was a full-on brawl and getting really nasty. There was a young lad working in the cloakroom, and he was leaning out from the hatch and hitting them – and occasionally us too by mistake – with a large piece of wood. It was a free-for-all. People were trying to crawl away, getting hit by stools, strangled, bitten. And then when it was all finished, we laughed about it as we were straightening our ties and mopping up the blood from our broken noses, black eyes and knocked-out teeth – it was just our lives and our job. To us it was nothing; it was the norm for us. And that was what made a good door team a good door team.

And then, of course, there was the women side of things. Well, we could just never stop, could we? We had a little room at The Ritzy – we used to call it a 'puppy room' – which was where most of the doormen took women to shag. When I saw some girl who had just given me a blow job snogging one of my mates in the club a little later, I'd look at him and laugh to myself, thinking, 'She just had my cock in her mouth.' But, of course, I wouldn't tell him until she had finished. That kind of camaraderie also made a good door team, but sadly you really can't do those sorts of things any more. I don't know of one club that has a puppy room, and I don't know many doormen who would use one even if there was!

Doormen now stand on the doors with their earpieces and their long coats looking as 'cool' as they can, but they are not really doing the job any more. What we did back then was watch each other. We didn't stand there looking good. We would be watching each other all the time: two doormen here; two doormen there. When two people walked off, you would take their place, or when one left you would follow him to see what he was doing. Now it seems as though they just don't care about each other. The doormen outside are not concerned about the doormen inside. It seems that all they want to do is to stand at the front door, look good and just hope that no one they knock back will say, 'I'll come round your fucking house, then.' I think it would scare them shitless, but it never happens any more.

Managers also probably now no longer feel safe. Back in my day, a doorman was someone who intimidated people. If someone came to a pub and kicked off, the manager would call his doormen in, and the punter who had kicked off would generally think, 'Oh, fuck me!' But someone who weighs 11 stone and says to a punter, 'If you don't leave, I am going to call the police,' is unlikely to prompt the same reaction. Back in my day, the manager actually wanted someone who would turn up at the punter's house at four in the morning and give him a good kicking. Why would he get a kicking? Because he had been harassing the landlord, despite warning after warning. Back then, there was enormous landlord–doorman loyalty, which definitely no longer exists. Now, you are not even allowed to tell someone to fuck off. Now, managers are abused all the time, and no one does a thing about it. It is terrible.

But, as I said, it is not their fault. Being a doorman is a new game now. In our day, we did it for the fun of it. We did it for the camaraderie. We put our safety and our lives on the line for each other. We might be outnumbered five to one but would still go outside and battle with a rugby team if necessary. Doormen just don't have the opportunity to do these things any more, because now when you put someone out you have to put them in a certain arm or head lock that you have been trained to do, which is fine if the punter is prepared to let you. If not, the doorman is fucked.

In our day, we fought proper men. When I was 22, I fought blokes of my age now – 45 to 50. Hard men – men who had been fighting all their lives. I can remember when I first started at The Ritzy, I gave all the doormen heavy lead hand weights. I had spent hours making them all. Can you imagine doing that now? Can you imagine the head doorman giving his door team lead weights in case of a battle? But I bet a lot of today's doormen would secretly like them!

One time, I was working at Peppermint Park on Rose Lane. Three fucking huge Russian sailors had come into town from the docks at nearby Lowestoft and were pissed off, as we had asked them to leave because they were touching up the female customers. I am not tall, and they towered over me, looking down at me as though I was a piece of shit. We got them outside relatively calmly, and then they decided to have a go. I had to fight really dirty, probably the dirtiest I have ever fought, as I knew I would have got a real hiding otherwise. I heard one of them screaming as I shoved my fingers hard into his eyes, and I hooked my thumb into the side of another's mouth and felt it split, a bit like chicken from a bone. I think the word must have got around, as we never saw a Russian sailor at that venue again.

Another memory I have is from my second or third night on the doors at The Ritzy when I was told by the manager to throw two geezers out who were pissing around with a one-armed bandit. I knew I had to show the other doormen my colours. Billy Waters and I went up to these two fucking huge geezers and said, 'Look, it isn't my fault, but the manager wants you out.' I pointed to the manager, and when these two looked over at him we smashed them hard in the bollocks, because we knew they would be a handful. None of this nice stuff. Nowadays, doormen would say, 'Excuse me, sir, but would you mind leaving, as the manager wants you to go?' They'd reply, 'Fuck that. Tell the manager I want to see him.' And the doormen would actually go and get the manager!

Fuck me! In my day, the management didn't want to know. The manager sat in his office, and all he wanted to do was get to half-past two so that he could say, 'OK, lads, put the chains on the doors, and let's have a beer.' Things were completely different. They were a lot rougher, and there were a lot more dangerous situations. For instance, John Tansley and I were working in Central Park when three coaches of black lads turned up. We looked at each other, and I said, 'This is not going to go well, John.' Central Park was only a small function room, and they kicked off in the toilets. There was just me and John working that night, and we were the only two white guys in the building. While the manager was in his office sorting through paperwork and reading *Penthouse*, they were downstairs glassing each other. And it was all over a woman. On that occasion, I must admit that I looked at John and said, 'No, mate. Nothing to do with us. Let them sort it out between themselves.' I don't think this sort of thing happens now, either.

There are still a few 'old timers' around – a few work at the university (of East Anglia) – but not many any more. Most doormen my age gave up doing the doors years ago or were refused a licence because of a criminal record.

Obviously, because of my situation, I can't work the doors any more, but if I was, I would certainly miss the old times. Not the violence, but the fun, the one-night stands and even some of the excuses to try and get away from the one-night stands. I remember working with Robin Barratt at Rick's Place when he spent most of the final part of one evening in the cellar room because two of the birds he was shagging at the same time turned up at the club, alone, waiting for him to finish. He was fucking frozen by the end of the night. We seriously considered asking them both to wait at the bar and calling him out, but we just couldn't be that cruel.

I can remember going to some woman's house to see her after I had finished work one night, because I thought her old man was away. I looked through the window and saw her talking to someone – I couldn't see who, though. Obviously, I had been there before, and I watched her as she went into the kitchen. I rushed round the side of the house to knock on the kitchen window, but she went straight into the bathroom. A few minutes later, I heard police sirens, so I quickly hid under a hedge in the corner of the garden. The next thing I knew, I was being dragged out by my legs. Someone had reported me for looking through the window, thinking that I was a peeping Tom or something. They put me in the police car, but luckily a copper knocked on her door and she said that she was waiting for me. If she hadn't, I would have been nicked!

Another funny moment was when one of my fellow doormen was shagging some bird in the staff toilets at The Ritzy. Billy and I got a champagne bucket full of ice-cold water and threw the whole lot over the door of the cubicle just as he was doing the business. He thought it was hilarious; she almost took my head off.

I loved going to work every night, as every evening I would have a laugh and some fun, but I don't think doormen laugh as much on the doors now as we did back then. It is more serious, and everyone is trying to be more 'professional'.

Sadly, with a criminal record for a minor firearms offence I won't be returning to the doors. When I finally get out of prison, I will try and find a normal day job, but I will miss the fun of the doors – I will miss that more than anything else, really.

I am currently serving my time at Norwich Prison. It all started one day when I was driving down Drayton Road in Norwich on my motorbike from my house to the gym at the Norwich Sports Village nearby. I was pulled over by the police just a few metres from my house. I thought it was my small number plate again, as I had occasionally been pulled over for that in the past. I had been meaning to change it, but you know how things are, and I had never got round to it. Still, I thought that I would probably know the coppers and might be able to talk my way out of it – yet again. I got off my bike in my normal nonchalant manner and asked what the matter was. The copper replied by saying, 'Sorry, Bob, but we have got to arrest you for a firearms offence.'

'What?' I asked. It just didn't register.

'You have a shotgun under the stairs,' he replied.

'Don't deny it,' one of the other coppers said. 'We know where it is.'

'Yeah, but it is an antique gun. It's old,' I said. 'I was going to put it on my French dresser.' I didn't understand what was happening.

It wasn't until a few weeks after I had been arrested that I found out that one of my ex-girlfriend's teenage kids had apparently found the gun under the stairs and had told his mum, who'd decided to go to the police. Forensics tested it, and they put me away because one of the barrels worked. The minimum sentence was five years, but even the local policemen who I knew really well had said that I wouldn't get that long, not for something so trivial. I also had had no criminal convictions, apart from an occasional parking ticket.

It went to the magistrates' court, where my case was referred to the Crown court. Once at the Crown court, my lawyers and I got access to all the statements from the witnesses, and I found out that my ex's two sons had actually broken into my house, found the gun and had then given it to the police. I was on police bail, but I went looking for them almost every night once I knew what they had done. The kids realised this, and restraining orders were put in place. I wasn't allowed to pass their house on Drayton Road, where I lived, because they lived 200 yards up the road from me. It got so time consuming and difficult not knowing where I could go, what I could do and who I could speak to. It consumed my life.

After that, it was like being on a roller coaster. Every time I read the paper, I looked for crimes and sentences involving firearms – sentences ranged from eighteen months to seven years for robbing a post office. Looking at the different sentences, I thought I would never get five years – not for what I had done. I reassured myself that everything was going to be fine. I had a bit of money at that time, and I thought I would pay any fine imposed and that would be the end of it.

The fact that the police hadn't actually retrieved the gun from my house, as I had originally thought, and that it had been given to them by my ex-girlfriend's two sons, made the court case a lot longer, as my barrister tried to argue that the evidence was inadmissible. In the end, the case lasted about 11 months in total, as it kept getting put back. Because these two lads had broken into my house and had given the gun to the police, they needed me to admit that it had originally been in my possession, otherwise they would have had no proof. Me, being as honest and stupid as I was, had acknowledged from the beginning that it was my gun. Looking back, if I had never admitted this when I had been first pulled over, I would never have gone to prison. My fingerprints weren't even on the weapon.

But the judge was having none of it. He said that it was a matter of public safety. Because my house had actually been unlocked, anyone could have got access to the gun, which made me an irresponsible person. My house was never locked, but we couldn't really say in court that I had two big Alsatian dogs and no one would dare steal from me, as the judge would have certainly thought that I was a professional thug. He would have thought that I was someone who intimidated people, which was why I had the gun. I couldn't really say that I didn't need to lock my house because I had a reputation in Norwich. It was a difficult case throughout, as my barrister had to keep away from my reputation and portray me as a normal person.

As I said, it took around 11 months to finally get to sentencing, even though I had essentially pleaded guilty at the very beginning. If I had known how the courts worked and how the seasoned criminals did it, I would never have said anything at the very beginning when I had been first pulled over. But of course I hadn't known.

My barrister asked me time and time again, 'Why did you say it was your gun?'

'Because I did have an antique gun,' I would reply.

'Yes, but you don't tell the police you had one,' he would say.

'But why?' I would ask.

'Because you don't do that. Criminals don't do that!'

But I wasn't a criminal. I was just telling the truth. I didn't have a history of violence. I had been doing the doors for almost 26 years and

Charlie Bronson:
'Three cheers for the bouncers'

IBA director Jim Shortt
at his country manor in the
Republic of Ireland

Bob Etchells on the door at the Prince of Wales Pub, Norwich

Robin Barratt practising with a Glock in Sweden

Alex Powell (front row, centre) and his team protecting Iraqi votes at the warehouse in central Baghdad

Sandy Sanderson (far left) and the Hedley House door team in 1990

Paul Knight on his wedding day – 'the best day of his life'

Steve Wraith with his door-team at Chase, Newcastle

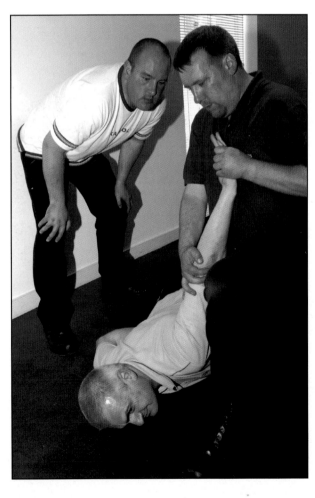

Andy Walker demonstrating
restraint techniques

Alex Powell guarding the warehouse in central Baghdad

Scott Taylor on the door at Soul, Aberdeen

Inna Zabrodskaya on a break from covert operations

Stu Cheshire (left) with Roy Shaw

Robin Barratt on the door in Bracknell

Loc19 – one of the most feared firms in the North West

A cartoon entitled 'You are Not Getting Out!' by Charlie Bronson

had a successful agency, but I had never been to court or been arrested for any violent crime. Even though the minimum sentence was five years, my barrister also thought I had a very good chance of getting away with a heavy fine and community service. He couldn't really see me getting the statutory five years.

But the judge slagged me off completely. He told me that I was a professional 'enforcer' who ran a door agency of 'bouncers' – he said there was no other way of putting it – and the only reason I had the gun was for intimidation. I felt fucked.

My mum, brothers, sister, her son and some of my friends were there to hear the judge deliver my sentence. He said, 'I am giving you five years.' The only way I can describe my reaction is to compare it to when you sometimes lose your balance and catch your breath. It was like being on a funfair ride and suddenly dropping.

'Five years for making a mistake?' I shouted. A security guard tried to grab my arm. 'No,' I shouted, shrugging him off. 'Five years?'

The judge said, 'Mr Etchells, you have nothing to say that your barrister hasn't already said. Now go downstairs.' I didn't even get to say goodbye to my mum or my family.

I was in shock. I just couldn't believe it. I had lost everything: my house, job, money, everything. It was all double Dutch to me, and I didn't really understand what was happening. It was such a numbing pain. As I sat downstairs in the cell, my barrister said that we would try to appeal. This sounded great to me, as I thought I would be released on bail until the case was reheard (just as I had been while I waited for my trial), but no. I mumbled that surely because I had pleaded guilty I should really have got a bit off, but my barrister said that I had been given the minimum sentence anyway. There wouldn't even be anything much to appeal against.

I didn't go to prison straight away. I had to wait until there were six or seven of us to fill the van. I had been sentenced at about 3.30 p.m., but I didn't end up getting to Norwich Prison until about 7.30 p.m.

My girlfriend Lisa rang my brother Andrew at about 5.30 p.m., and he told her that he was sorry but I had been given five years. She was devastated and broke down. Luckily, my family all rallied round and went round to see her as often as they could. In a way, I think I was really lucky that I wasn't there, because seeing her upset would have made things even harder.

On the way to prison, I tried to reach up to look out of the van window. I am from Norwich and know every road and turn. I saw people I knew, but they couldn't see in. I was trying to cling onto something I knew. We drove up Knox Road, through the main gates, and I heard the gates slam shut behind us.

It was a horrible, horrible feeling. I felt like a wound-up piece of string, not knowing what was ahead. I was then taken to the reception area, where the guards removed my handcuffs. 'What the fuck are you doing here, Bob?' a guard I knew asked.

'I dunno,' I said.

'What have you done?' he asked again.

'I got five years,' I replied.

'What for?'

'I dunno,' I said again, confused and stunned.

The screws who I knew started talking to me, but it was all just a blur. One minute I had been surrounded by my family and friends, and the next minute I was handcuffed and in prison. It was weird, but because I knew quite a lot of the prison officers I felt I wasn't alone. I was interviewed, and I knew the screw who was interviewing me, but I was in prison. I couldn't understand it.

After being in reception, I was then strip-searched and given my prison clothes. But I wasn't given new clothes; I was given someone else's clothes, including their boxer shorts. The clothes were all grey or mauve.

The prison was cold, damp, dirty and musky. I was put into another cell until all the other new prisoners had been processed, and then we were all taken up into the main prison – fresh meat. It was exactly like a scene from *Escape from New York*, with everyone hanging around the prison landings. I felt like a rabbit caught in headlights. I looked up at everyone staring down at me and thought, 'Who the fuck have I thrown out? Who have I beaten up? Who have I given a good hiding to?' There are a lot of drug dealers in prison, and over the years I had thrown a good few out of the pubs and clubs I had worked in or had

130

stopped them from getting in. I wondered if any of them were staring down at me.

I was lucky at the beginning, as I went straight onto the fours, which was one of the better landings, and I got my own room . . . sorry, I mean cell. I didn't come out of it for about three days. I didn't eat. I didn't do anything. The thing about prison meals is there are only three choices: crap, shit and more shit. It is disgusting, and if you don't put in your food slip, you get the vegetarian choice, which is even worse.

Because I didn't come out of my cell for three days, I didn't know about the food, about letters, about visits, about applying for work to stop the boredom or about the gym. I didn't know when I could go for a shower or about how the phone worked – that I needed to get credit and register my phone numbers – so when I did actually ask about these things I was three days behind. They had explained everything to me when I had first arrived, but because I had been in so much shock, nothing had sunk in or registered.

It is hard to explain what happens to you, but your defence mechanisms kick in, barriers go up and you go into a very basic survival mode. After three days, I came out of my cell and started to talk to people. I got chatting to a young lad whose dad had been a good mate of mine when I had a flat in Costessey. In fact, I had known the lad when he was a boy. He was in for stabbing someone and had already done four years. He obviously knew the prison routine and told me what I needed to know.

To use the phone, you had to register who you wanted to call and supply their telephone number, their full name and address, and their date of birth. However, I just didn't know that sort of information for everybody I wanted to call. So, a small problem like that suddenly became a mountain. I was given an initial £2.50 phone credit. After that had gone, I wasn't given any more. And all I wanted to do was to talk to Lisa.

Norwich Prison was exactly like the one in *Porridge*, with the same cold bleakness and brick walls and screws who don't really want to talk to you much. Everything was done by your last name: Etchells this and Etchells that. There was nothing personal.

At the very beginning of a person's stay in prison, they have to decide whether they are going to be one of the majority or one of the minority. The majority are those who know prison and the system very well and feed off the minority. If you want to be fed off, you stay in the minority; if you want to be a feeder, you stay in the majority. Most people definitely don't want to be in the minority, so they feed off others, and abuse the new arrivals. For instance, a new person is given £2.50 phone credit. Someone in the majority will offer to help him out but first ask if they can quickly phone their mum. They then use up most of the new person's credit – that's how things start. Newcomers are an easy target.

I also learned very quickly that *everyone* in prison is in on a scam. If there were, say, 700 people in Norwich Prison, I met maybe just a handful of genuine, decent people in all the time I was there. Prison is an association of criminals.

You can't have any morals in prison. If you have morals, you are nothing. For example, people will ask me if I have a stamp, but if I need a stamp, they will just say, 'Sorry, mate. Don't have any.' Even if I gave him one last week. And then I think to myself, 'Hang on. I am asking for and getting wound up over a *stamp*!' I earned £1,200 a week running my door agency in Norwich, but now I can't even buy a stamp!

When I finally settled into prison life, I really saw what was going on. I saw the bullying and the intimidation, and the threats and the fear. However, Norwich Prison doesn't have one particular hard bloke who runs the place. People generally know that no matter how hard they are they could accidentally knock into someone on the landing who has just come in, who is high on drugs and who would stab them with the pointed end of a toothbrush. He might weigh only nine stone and have never fought in his life, but he would be scared and high on drugs. Or the new prisoner might take offence at being bumped into and wait a while until the so-called hard man went into the shower and then hit him hard with a coffee cup in a sock. So, being someone who can fight doesn't count for much in prison. There are no rules, and there is nowhere to hide. For instance, if you have a fight in the middle of the street in town, you might never see that person again, but in prison you live with him 24/7. If you have a ruck with someone, you will see him again in the dinner queue and again in the queue for medication and again on the landings or in the gym. And he can stab you or throw hot water and sugar in your face at any time. So, there is not really a hard man of the prison, not like in the days of the Krays, for instance. There is no trust, and just because you might be the hardest bloke on the landing doesn't guarantee that you won't be stabbed in the shower.

Despite all of this hatred and dishonesty and intimidation, there were certain times when I was in Norwich Prison that everyone stuck together. If a member of an inmate's family died, we were sad for them; if we heard that someone who had left prison had overdosed and died, the whole landing was solemn. It didn't make sense. Two days previously, someone might have been trying to fucking stab the bloke over an argument about some speed or sleeping tablets, and yet the whole landing would go to church when he died, and we would then spend a few hours or sometimes even days talking about him. One minute it was all filth, and the next minute it was all soft. And the next day it was back to mayhem again.

Luckily for me, my cell overlooked the road, so when I got my first visit I said to Lisa that I would tie a sock to the bars so that she could see where I was. I think it made a lot of difference to her, and it made a lot of difference to me too. I wasn't frightened of getting into a fight, but there are different fears in prison. Prison can be scary, what with the noise and being next to people with hepatitis, Aids and all sorts of other diseases – you just don't know what to expect. So, the fact that I could look out of my window and see Lisa coming with the dogs and my brothers kept me human.

I never became a parasite, and I never became a bully while I was in prison. I was never in the majority. I stayed in the minority, but I wasn't bullied either. I think if I had been put in another prison to begin with, I would have got into a lot of fights and have been in danger, but not in Norwich. Because I was known and well respected, because it was known that I ran a door agency, because I didn't have anything to do with drugs and because I stayed in my cell a lot of the time, I wasn't a threat to anyone.

It is all drugs now. People smuggle in drugs up their arse. If other prisoners think that someone has smuggled in drugs, five or six guys will storm into his cell to 'spoon' his arse and get the drugs out. Pretty fucking crazy.

There was a lot of group violence as well: three or four on one. Gangs frequently went into someone's cell and made a mess of them, but you couldn't get involved, as the victim might have owed somebody something and not paid it back, despite several warnings. A lot of the time, you had to ignore what you saw – it wasn't your business. It wasn't like on the streets where you could help if someone was getting a kicking. Inside, there was always a reason. If you got involved, you were in trouble and those prisoners would turn on you.

It was all about material possessions. For instance, if you had one and a half ounces of tobacco, a half ounce of that was worth another ounce, because if you borrowed a half ounce from me, you had to give me back one ounce plus the half ounce you borrowed. This was when the majority preyed on newcomers, because the person who had just come into prison didn't have anything. This was when you got the intense intimidation and bullying. For example, some people were intimidated into pretending to have a back ache to get the doctor to give them medication. Other prisoners did little things to frighten and intimidate people, like walking into your cell and picking up your things. I told one person to fuck off when he tried to do this. He did, but many people were too frightened to tell another prisoner to fuck off, so the intimidation continued.

Prison teaches people how to improvise. Prisoners made their own 90 per cent proof alcohol. I met people who were doing their sentence brain-dead because they had drunk too much 'hooch', or 'moonshine' as it is known in the US. They just slept their prison sentence away. Prison is all about drugs and medication, and prisoners will do almost anything to get sleeping tablets, painkillers or any form of medication. They'd walk around the landings shouting down, asking who had what available. You'd then see people passing stuff up over the landings, which eventually went for four or five times its original value.

Someone can go into prison for just three months and come out a complete bastard, a liar and totally untrustworthy. You see, it is easy to lose your morals if you are intimidated, as you have to intimidate back in order to survive. For instance, you can sit and be friendly and chat to someone in his cell, before leaving a few seconds later after having stolen something that you have already sold for a few ounces of tobacco. There are no rules. The long-termers feed off the short-termers, and people who are bullied or whose stuff is stolen can't go to the staff and say they are being bullied, because then they will really get beaten up. And being a grass in prison is taboo – it's almost as bad as being a sex offender. You will be beaten, no matter what, and people will just step over you.

The regime in prison was degrading. You had to ask for everything: for shampoo, soap, toothpaste, everything. You even had to ask for an envelope. You were allowed one envelope a day. One fucking envelope! If I'd used that envelope and wanted another, I'd have to borrow one, and then I'd have to pay it back.

There are different classes of people in prison: you have the right scumbag, the lesser scumbag, the scumbag and eventually the nearly human. I struck lucky with my first cellmate, a bloke from Wymondham. He got nine months and a £55,000 fine for health-and-safety violations. He came into prison about two weeks after me and was on the same sort of moral level as I was. At first, he was on another landing, and I could see he was just a normal person in a very abnormal world. He was in complete shock. His wife was pregnant, and he was getting got at in prison. I liked him, and I took him under my wing and helped him cope a little bit. He was a nice bloke, and we became good friends.

It is amazing how people make a life for themselves in prison. Just sitting watching everything that went on was amazing. As well as physical violence, intimidation was rife. The fours intimidated the threes, the threes intimidated the twos and the twos intimidated the ones. Each landing had their little crew running all the scams, but I managed to make friends with other prisoners without joining their ranks.

Nobody wanted a job as a landing cleaner, because you'd be used to move drugs around. So you'd refuse the job, which then gave the pushers and dealers an opportunity to get someone they wanted. It was important to pick and choose your jobs because of the wider implications of what each entailed. I was lucky, as I worked in the printing shop, where I was treated a little bit better and more like a human being than in many of the other jobs. But even in the printing shop, I saw people take the pots of glue used to join the pages together and sell them as solvents.

The prison authorities tried to move me twice: once to Wayland and once to Highpoint. However, I refused to go, because I knew that if I could stay in Norwich I would eventually be sent to Britannia House, an open prison that was a lot more comfortable. It was just a matter of time, and I was eventually transferred. However, I was sent to Peterborough Prison for a week while I was at Britannia House, as I broke my bail conditions. By then, I was working at the YMCA on day release. I left work, went to ASDA and drove down Drayton Road, which I wasn't meant to do – I still wasn't allowed to go past my ex-girlfriend's house. I was seen, arrested later that evening and sent off to Peterborough Prison for a week. Peterborough was very different – it was private and run like an American prison with gangs. I wasn't there long enough to judge, but people did say that the facilities there were much better than at Norwich and that the food was much better.

Norwich was such a cold prison. Visits lasted only an hour, whereas in most prisons visiting times are two hours minimum and sometimes up to four hours. Norwich was not a nice prison to be in. For instance, if you had to make an appointment to see the dentist, it might take three weeks or more to see him. You could have an abscess and a horrendous toothache and be in pain for weeks.

Eventually, I went on a course and became a 'listener' – somebody people could call at any time for a talk. I made friends with John, a lifer who'd killed someone and been given 15 years. He'd then stabbed his cellmate and been given life. He'd served 27 years. His skin was sallow and grey, he had prison tattoos on his neck and arms, he was covered in scars, and his eyes were dead – there was no sparkle or life left in them. He was never getting out. He looked a bit like Robert De Niro in *Cape Fear*.

One day, we were chatting when a black man came into the cell and interrupted us, asking if we had any 'burn' (dope). From his sock, John took out a blade he had made from two toothbrushes melted together with a lighter and told the guy to fuck off or he would stab him there and then and leave him to bleed. We then returned to our discussion as though nothing had happened. He would have killed him just because he'd interrupted our conversation. John had nothing to lose. That is what it is like in prison.

Lifers who will never get out, who have no family, who no one writes to, who have nothing and who have nothing to lose make their life a little better by intimidation and running the prison as best they can. Their only home is prison, which is why they are the way they are.

Lisa wrote to me every single day while I was inside. I could not have done it without her. A lot of problems with prisoners is that they don't have anyone to keep them strong. They get depressed and try to hang themselves. They self-harm. They don't wash. They stink.

Compared to Norwich Prison, Britannia House is brilliant. It is really for people who have only made one mistake and shouldn't have been put in prison in the first place. In Britannia House, you eventually become a human being again, and after a while you can do charity work or get a day job. However, you have to work hard to get to Britannia House – you have to be a listener or a Samaritan, you have to keep out of trouble and you have to be seen to be a bit of a mentor to other people. It was a little bit easier for me, because I was well known around Norwich and well respected, and I became a mentor to a lot of young people coming into prison. Usually, if you do all of these things, you can get to Britannia House after about half of your sentence, but I was transferred in just ten months, mainly because I stayed in Norwich and used my reputation and the people I knew.

At Britannia House, you are allowed out every day, but you have to report back every night for the duration of your sentence. It is still prison, and if you don't return one night or are late, or if you do something wrong, you are sent straight back to Norwich Prison. You can lose your place in Britannia House just like that. There could be an argument in which someone gets hurt and you get sent back to proper prison just for being a witness. Or if you get stopped when on day release for not wearing a seat belt or for not having a tax disc on your car – in fact, if you have any kind of run-in with the police at all – that will be it.

I sometimes stop at The Prince of Wales, the last venue I worked at, on my way back to Britannia House. If there has been an argument, part of me wants to sort it out, but the other part says, 'I am invisible. I am not here.' Because of who I am, I could so easily get dragged in. While I am in Britannia House, I have to be whiter than white.

One of the most moving and emotional experiences I had while in prison was on my first New Year's Eve inside. Because I could see into the car park, Lisa told me she would come and visit me. I kept looking for her and eventually saw her waving up at me. On the stroke of midnight, and just as the fireworks exploded nearby, she shouted, 'I love you, Bob.' Suddenly, one of the other prisoners shouted, 'She loves you, Bob.' A few seconds later, the whole prison was filled with the noise of inmates banging their mugs on the railings and shouting, 'She loves you, Bob. She loves you, Bob.'

I would never be allowed to work the doors any more, but, to be honest, I don't think I want to. Prison has allowed me to get out of the door game. I did almost 27 years and left the industry with my reputation and more importantly my dignity intact.

BIOGRAPHY OF BOB ETCHELLS

Bob Etchells started working the doors when he was just 17 years old at The Festival House, one of the toughest pubs in Norwich at that time. He ended his career in 2005 when he was charged and found guilty of possessing a firearm. For almost 27 years, Bob ran some of the toughest and busiest clubs and pubs in Norwich, as well as following his managers to work the doors with them in Plymouth and the Welsh borders. However, Norwich was his home, and he always came back.

Bob ran a number of door companies, at one time employing over 50 doormen throughout the region, as well as providing debt-collecting and other security-related services. He has never applied for his SIA badge, nor is he ever likely to.

Bob will soon be due for parole.

10

LETTER FROM IRAQ
BY ALEX POWELL

It was mid-December. Christmas decorations sparkled annoyingly in every shop window and on every street corner. Stupid-looking Santas stood in shopping malls and on high streets, ringing their irritating bells and demanding money for some good cause or other but probably pocketing half of it themselves and spending the rest in the pub at the end of their shift. People raced around frantically, looking morose and stressed, worried that they wouldn't be able to do all their shopping on time or that the gift they'd bought their uncle's cousin's first nephew's fucking sister wasn't expensive enough.

Don't get me wrong, I love Christmas ... really. I love waking up on Christmas morning next to my gorgeous wife and presenting her with a gift I have tried – although admittedly not always successfully – to think carefully about buying. I love the Christmas morning shag and a hearty English breakfast – although not always in that order. And I do love vegging out in front of the TV after an excessive Christmas dinner, trying to keep my eyes open but never quite managing it.

I just hate all the crap that goes with Christmas and the obscene commerciality of it all. It drives me mad, and every Christmas since leaving the Foreign Legion I have vowed to escape to somewhere better, sunnier and infinitely more exciting.

But I didn't really expect to be going to bloody Iraq again!

After my first stint in the hellhole of the universe, I was told many times, by many people, that one tour would never be enough. Like a virus, the bug of war wiggles its wretched way into the soul of a true soldier and embeds itself for all eternity – or at least until the nagging wife really does pack her bags and leave. Even then, I have met many soldiers who have endured failed marriages and relationships just to get back to the front line, listening to the sweet sound of bullets whizzing by their heads and the thud and mayhem of the mortar shell. After my first spell in the 'sandpit', I half-heartedly said I wouldn't be going back – that one tour was enough – but I think deep inside I knew I would. Just one more trip, and it *would* help with the bills and go towards a nice car. It might even pay off a bit of the mortgage.

I am a former French Foreign Legion soldier, or a Legionnaire as we are usually more affectionately called. For some reason, I didn't fancy joining the British Army and joined the Legion in 1992 when I was just 18 years old – I was young, incredibly foolish and most definitely off my tiny trolley. One evening, while getting high on grass and drunk on cheap Tesco lager, I had watched a fascinating documentary on the National Geographic Channel about the French Foreign Legion and decided there and then that a Legionnaire's life was definitely the life for me. Surprisingly, I thought the same the very next day when I had a blinding hangover and had to clear up my vomit-stained carpet. And the day after, I still wanted to join. As days turned into weeks and weeks into months, I made my plans to escape the mindless teenage world of grass, cheap beer and puke and do something constructive with my life. And one day, I just woke up, packed my bags and headed to Marseilles.

After the initial basic instruction and tests, I trained to be a medic, as that almost guaranteed a posting to some god-forsaken hellhole where the action really was. It was just kicking off in Somalia at that time, and I knew they wanted as many medics as they could muster, so I was first in the queue. If you finish high in the rankings, you get to choose which regiment you go to, and if you finish low, you go wherever you are sent! I finished 12th out of 65, which I was surprised at. I chose to go to the 13th DBLE (*Demi-Brigade de Légion Étrangère*) based in Djibouti on the Somalia border. It was a fucking crazy hellhole. I was in Djibouti for just three weeks before I was sent into Somalia, and I ended up doing two tours there altogether – out of my two years in Djibouti, I spent nearly eighteen months in Somalia. There were bad bits, of course, and war had a huge impact on me mentally, as I witnessed a lot of really bad things when I was still very young. Africa was, and still is, fucked – life there is worth shit. Also, having to learn a foreign language and being away from family and friends at that age was also sometimes very hard, and losing friends in accidents or incidents had a profound effect on me.

As well as the action, there were other reasons I chose Djibouti: the sunshine and the higher wages!

I had some great moments in the Legion. One time, during basic training, there were really severe floods in Avignon, very similar to those in the UK in 2007, and the Legion was sent to help out. We spent days rescuing people, saving lives and belongings, and cleaning up. Afterwards, when the floods had receded and the city was almost back to normal, we were asked to parade through the town centre, and we all received commendations for the work we had done to help the local community. It was a proud moment.

Then, while on leave in Marseilles, I managed to be in the right place at the right time and prevented two girls from being robbed at knife-point. I was 21 years old at the time and on leave after returning from Djibouti. It had been a tough two years, and I was settling back into life in France. I had met a French girl while on leave previously; she had fallen pregnant and had just given birth to a baby girl. We had a little apartment in the town and had just moved in together. I went out to the local hypermarket to buy milk, a few fluffy toys and a couple of cans of lager for my own private celebratory drink, as I didn't know anyone locally whom I could get pissed with. I was standing at the bus stop waiting to return home to the weird smell of nappies and to my girlfriend's pretty puffed up face, brought on by a lack of sleep. I was

143

in my own little world, enjoying a precious few minutes of 'peace and quiet', listening to Metallica on my Walkman. Metallica deafens me and helps to take my mind off things. There must have been at least 40 to 50 people standing at the bus stop: little old biddies with their trolleys on wheels, pumped-up guys returning from the gym, and the token single mother with three kids and a pushchair with at least a dozen carrier bags of crisps and sweets hanging from every corner.

There was also a couple of girls sitting on a little wall just a few feet away from the bus stop chatting happily to each other. From the corner of my eye, I noticed a group of about nine young Algerian lads walking towards them. They were a typical bunch of street lads, aged around 20 to 23ish, kicking Coke cans, spitting on the floor, larking about and pushing each other into the road. I assumed that the two girls knew them, because they started talking to each other. Metallica was bursting my eardrums, so I couldn't make out what was being said, but then one of the lads grabbed one of the girls' handbags. Because no one else said or did anything, I didn't realise anything was wrong for a few seconds, but then the girl lunged to get her bag back, and once she did that the other lads started to severely punch and kick the pair of them and grab at the second girl's handbag. Even though there were several guys who were a lot bigger than me standing at the bus stop nearer to the group, no one reacted or did anything. It was obvious to me that these Algerian cunts were prepared to do whatever it took to get these poor young girls' handbags, and it seemed that no one at all was prepared to stop them. Big mistake! I quickly took off my Walkman, shoved it into my carrier bag and hurriedly gave it to an old woman standing next to me to hold while I went to work.

I went straight for the biggest and nutted him hard. He fell. As soon as I did that, the rest turned and were stunned for a second. This gave me a few seconds to unleash a torrent of punches and kicks, and I had managed to down five of them before they knew what was going on. I noticed a couple of them were already gone; they were halfway up the road. The two who remained gave me a couple of quick digs. I kicked one of them in the chest, and he collapsed like a bag of shit. His mate quickly followed the others up the road. As I was standing over the scumbags on the floor, looking down at them deciding whether to kick them in the ribs or the stomach, a screeching of tyres broke my concentration.

Next, I felt the hot metal of a police car bonnet as my face was slammed into it. I was handcuffed and put into the back of the car. Over the pounding of my heart, I could hear one of the officers calling on his radio for an ambulance. As I stared out of the window, I noticed several people at the bus stop rushing over to the policemen, obviously explaining to them what had actually happened. Thankfully, one of the officers immediately came over to the car, took me out and removed my handcuffs. He was babbling away to me in French, but even though I spoke the language fluently and had a French girlfriend whom I only spoke French to, I was bizarrely oblivious to what he was saying. I could see his lips jabbering away, but my mind was elsewhere, and I couldn't understand a word he was saying. For a few seconds, it was as though I didn't speak a word of French. Rage? Anger? Mental breakdown? Stress? I don't know.

I was taken to the police station to make a statement, and once I had identified myself as a Legionnaire I was immediately treated in a more respectful and courteous manner. Once I had made my statement and had calmed down a bit, a high-ranking police officer walked in and introduced himself. I guess he would have been the equivalent of a British superintendent. He told me that one of the girls attacked at the bus stop was actually his daughter. He shook my hand so hard it seemed as though he was going to cut off my circulation. He said he owed me and would do everything he could to make sure that what I had done would not go unrecognised.

My leave lasted 93 days, and upon returning to the regiment I saw my name on the notice board telling me to report immediately to the base commander. Everyone in the regiment knows that if you get nicked when on leave, you are going down big time, and doing time in a Legion nick is not something that anyone wants to do.

So there I was in my parade uniform, in a long line of guys who were all reporting to the base commander to be punished. My shoes were shining in the roasting summer sun, sweat was streaming down my neck and back, and my trusty white *képi* was keeping the sun off my worried head and out of my eyes. One by one, the colonel and his assistant worked their way down the line of soldiers, dishing out various punishments for stupid things like drunkenness, crashing a jeep, coming back from leave a day late. They all got prison time. Harsh? Yes, but (in theory) they would think twice before making the same mistakes again. Then they reached me. Fuck. The colonel stared at me for what felt like ages, and then in a harsh tone said, 'You know what happens to people who get arrested outside of the regiment, don't you?' Of course I fucking did. 'This is really unfair,' I thought to myself, but what was I supposed to do? Let those girls get mugged and beaten?

As I stared at the colonel, I wondered what he would have done? Probably fuck all. He was half my size, in his late 50s and French. I stared straight at him and unkindly thought to myself, 'Not the bravest chap in the world, are you? Weren't so fucking brave in both the world wars, were you? Isn't that why you have Legionnaires? You need a foreign army because the fucking French Army are a bunch of cowards.'

Fuck it. In a similar situation, I would have done the same again. 'Fuck all those pussies at the bus stop who didn't help, and fuck you,' I almost shouted at the colonel.

'While you prats were crashing jeeps and getting pissed,' he said, turning to rant at the other guys who were being punished, 'this crazy bastard fought off a gang of nine Algerians who were mugging two girls with no regard for his own safety.' I wasn't going to be punished after all. 'Damn right I'm not,' I happily thought to myself. The colonel didn't seem so bad after all. 'This is why I want to see Legionnaires standing here in front of me,' he shouted. He then pulled out a sheet of paper and told me he was presenting me with a citation. He read out loud, embarrassing me, 'It is with great pleasure . . .' Blah blah blah. My citation looks great framed, but I didn't really want it and didn't really need it – it is something I think I would have done any time, anywhere, and it certainly didn't merit a fuss.

I served five years in the Legion altogether, and ten years later I am still immensely proud of what I achieved personally and what the Legion achieved as a unit. We did some good work in Somalia: we

146

delivered tons of food, managed a massive vaccination campaign, and escorted a large number of medical convoys throughout the region and into some of the worst places in the world.

I certainly missed the Legion when I left. Five years were enough, but for a few years after I left I pined to see some action again and was chomping at the bit for an adrenalin rush and to smell the smell of war. It is an experience unlike any other: gruesome yet compulsive; exhausting yet exhilarating; exciting yet fucking scary.

I first decided I wanted to go to Iraq when the war ended and reconstruction of the country began. I knew then that private security would be big business, as many of the major security providers were already in discussions with both the British and American governments with regard to tendering for security contracts. Most of the large private security companies are run by high-ranking ex-military officers, who have all the contacts to be able to secure the ripest contracts, and discreet nods were already being given to the likes of Olive Group, CRG, ArmorGroup, etc. I had just started close protection training and had attended a three-day course run by Robin Barratt in Norwich. Robin had just returned from Moscow and was eager to start instructing again, both in the UK and abroad. He ran a three-day course entitled 'Introduction to Close Protection' for those of us who were keen to enter the industry but wanted to know more before committing a lot more money and time. After that, I went on to join Robin in Iceland for three weeks of intensive training and then went back to Iceland once more on a course for instructors.

It was while I was on the initial three-day course that I decided to qualify and go to Iraq. I was given a list of contractors, and a friend of mine called Craig Hales, who was also on the course, heard that a company called Hart Security had just secured a major contract. They were a lot smaller than the other major players setting up in Iraq and probably a lot better to work for as a result. Hart was a fairly new company, originally founded in 1999 by Richard Westbury, who had previously been the chief executive of Defence Systems, so they seemed to have a good commercial manager. I sent off my application and was called down to London a week later for an interview. I thought the interview went well, and the fact I was a Legionnaire seemed to help – 95 per cent of their staff, they said, were ex-military or ex-Special Forces.

I was expecting to hear back from them pretty quickly, but days turned into a couple of weeks, then a month, then six weeks. Then early one morning, and almost exactly six weeks after my initial interview, the telephone suddenly rang. It was just past 9 a.m. I had had a late night and was still half asleep, so I initially thought about letting it ring, but curiosity took hold, and I sleepily picked up the receiver. Did I still want a job? 'Fuck, yes,' I almost shouted. I was told to be at Heathrow airport in 48 hours. The first contract was for ten weeks.

After returning home, I decided to go out one more time. Hart had called to say that they had one of the most important and dangerous contracts in post-war Iraq and to ask whether I would be interested. Again, it was a case of, 'Fuck, yes!' And again, I was given 48 hours' notice and told to pick up my tickets to Kuwait from the Emirates desk at the airport. I have to say that my wife was not pleased. It was Christmas, after all, and a time for family and friends and log fires and 'Jingle Bells', not for scrambling frantically through the sand, being chased by a deranged fanatical Iraqi who believes his God would welcome him with open arms if he blew the arms and legs off a British non-believer. Of course, Iraq is not really like that – we never once scrambled through the sand.

After collecting my tickets, checking in and making my way through Customs, I met up with a few other guys who were also on their way out into the field – it was good to not have to sit alone, thinking of the missus waiting for me back at home and the heat and dust and shit to come. Like me, most of the guys had been out before, so we had a lot to talk about.

Just before we boarded, I called my wife, but she didn't answer. Maybe she was on the toilet, or doing her hair, or maybe she just didn't want to answer, but I left a short, cheerful message, telling her that I loved her, that I would be back soon and not to worry, because everything would be fine – as if that would make a difference. For me, this was much better than actually speaking to her, as I was never any good at saying goodbyes.

After what seemed a fairly quick six-hour flight, we arrived and were met by a Hart representative holding up a big placard. Once we had all gathered together and were checked off his list, we were ushered to a waiting minibus. Leaving the airport terminal and chilly England and entering the searing, oppressive heat of the Middle East is a complete shock. It is hard to imagine a wall of heat, but that is exactly what it is like – like being slammed up against an invisible brick. Immediately, you start to sweat. I was used to the feeling, as I had already been out to Iraq and had lived and worked in hot climes with the Legion, but for the newcomers it was a shock. Thankfully, the minibus was air-conditioned.

We drove through the centre of Kuwait City to a rented safe house, where we were to spend the night before going into Iraq the following morning. Most of us hadn't yet signed a contract for the trip, as recruitment had been rushed due to the large number of personnel needed for the job. Therefore, we didn't know anything about the job – we just knew it was going to be fucking dangerous. I signed a nine-week contract, visas and permits were sorted, insurance and waiver forms were signed, and the rest of the administration associated with sending Westerners into a war zone was hastily completed.

While this was all being sorted out by the guy who had picked us up from the airport and a couple of his administrative assistants, we were allowed to go into town for an evening stroll and a bit of shopping. I spent most of the money I had, just in case something happened to me and I ended up coming home in a body bag.

That night, I was restless. It was hard to sleep, as memories of my previous tour kept creeping into my mind: the few contact situations I had experienced; a round slamming into the side of our vehicle; the adrenalin rush I felt as we reversed our vehicle out of a contact zone and sprayed the building that we thought the hostile fire had come from. Was I really going back? Damn right I was!

The next day, we were taken in a convoy to the Iraqi border, where we passed quickly through a Kuwaiti checkpoint then on to an American checkpoint. The Americans seemed to take for ever to check our documents and papers. The lads manning the checkpoint were a great bunch but paranoid as fuck, even though no Iraqis have yet blown themselves up on the Iraq–Kuwait border. I bet they were as happy as could be when they were told they would be on that post as opposed to working on streets in the centre of Baghdad.

After passing through both checkpoints, we were in Iraq, where we were met by two more Hart close protection teams. We were each handed an AK-47 and two magazines, which we all hastily checked. The nerves of the previous evening had all but disappeared, and with the AK in my hand I felt back at home. My wife always said that I had a stupid grin on my face whenever I had my weapon in my hand, and I knew what she meant – it felt good. Weapons are compulsive and addictive, and absolutely necessary in a place like Iraq – you simply would not survive as a Westerner without a weapon.

Once we had checked and signed for our weapons, we were driven to the Hart compound inside Basra Airport complex, where the British Forces were based. Basra Airport is the second-largest airport in Iraq and located south of the city. On my first tour, Hart had based themselves in and operated from a large villa in the city itself, but due to the elevated risk, coupled with the number of times they were mortared, they wisely decided that it was a lot more logical, and infinitely safer, to move into the airport complex and nearer to the British Army.

We had a few minutes to arrange ourselves and settle into our dorms, then we were all mustered to the courtyard. There were over 90 personnel altogether; there were 20 or so in the team that had just come in from Kuwait with me, and the rest had arrived over the previous 48 hours. We were the last of the batch, which was why we were mustered so quickly after we arrived. Apparently, everyone had been eagerly awaiting the last batch of fresh meat from the UK.

Because of the extremely important, high-risk contract Hart had just won, they'd embarked on a massive recruitment drive, signing up almost anyone with a security-related background, including lots of doormen from the UK. I have worked the clubs and pubs myself on and off for many years, so I know the job well, and I can usually spot a doorman a mile away. Standing outside in the searing 40°C heat, it was easy to spot the nightclub bouncers amongst the many ex-soldiers. I fondly remembered the story Robin had told me during the initial three-day course I'd attended. He'd worked in Bosnia during the conflict and had secured a contract to pick up mercenaries from Zagreb Airport and take them to the *Hrvatska Vojska* (Croatian Army) camp near the front line, where they would be put through their paces before being sent into action. They were not really mercenaries, as they didn't get paid – the Croatian Army always fervently maintained that they never employed mercenaries during that particular conflict. Instead, they were unpaid volunteers, and many of them were from the UK. Robin told me that those who were full of bravado, boasting and bragging and doing their best to look hard, would shit themselves at the first sound of a mortar shell or the first live round whizzing past their ears. They would literally crap their pants, and it seemed to me that a few of the guys who looked very much like nightclub doormen standing amongst the rest of us might have been doing the same thing.

Sam, the project manager, stood on a small podium in front of us all and told us that some of the team would be working in Basra, while the rest would be sent to central Baghdad on an extremely high-risk operation. Before we had even been allocated our assignments, and to my utter amazement, about six of the guys who looked as though their pants were a lot stickier than they had been a few minutes previously put up their hands and said that they had changed their minds and felt they didn't have what it took to go to Baghdad, and could they please stay in Basra. What a bunch of utter cunts. The rest of the team almost collapsed with laughter. Sam screamed at them, telling them to fuck off, and within the hour they were back on the bus towards the border, where they were left to make their own way home. There was no room for people who didn't have the bottle for the job, and for the life of me I could not understand how some cunts could come so far and then lose their bottle at the last minute – surely they knew what they were there for? It is 'virtual' bravado. Being a big man in a small pond somehow makes some people believe that they could be a big man in a fucking huge pond somewhere else, but the reality is very different. These people are only brave in the small, insignificant world of their own nightclub door – anywhere else, they are cowards and cunts. The sad fact is that I have heard that some of those wankers who were sent home actually went on to tell other people that they'd served in Iraq in private security!

151

Sam explained to the rest of us who weren't packing our bags and changing our trousers back in the dorm that the job in Baghdad was far more dangerous than any other job the company had taken on, and only those who were completely right for the assignment would be asked to go. As he said this, I smiled to myself, because I realised that the cunts who didn't want to go to Baghdad probably wouldn't have been chosen anyway.

Sam asked for volunteers, and I was probably the first to put my hand up. I couldn't wait. I hadn't come all the way to Iraq not to see some real action and not to get involved in something risky and dangerous. There was only a handful of us who had been with Hart before, and as Sam counted the hands he recognised me from my last tour. 'This is your second time out with Hart, isn't it?' he said.

'Yes, sir,' I replied casually in army mode. He told me that because it was my second time with the company, I didn't have to go on that particular mission – there were other less dangerous jobs he could assign me to. 'But I want this job, sir,' was my swift reply. He nodded his acceptance, and the job was mine.

The next day, we were split into two groups, consisting of four or five teams each. Because I was bilingual, I was put into a half-English, half-French team; astonishingly, it even included a couple of guys whom I'd served with in the Legion. The first group were driving up to Baghdad in convoy with all our equipment, baggage, etc., while the rest of us were being sent to the capital by helicopter. I really didn't fancy going all that way in convoy; it was a long, arduous and uncomfortable journey, and I was therefore really pleased when my name was called in the group travelling by helicopter.

We regrouped at Baghdad Airport that same evening and were given the exact details of the task. I must be honest that it did come as a bit of a shock when I realised just how high profile the job was.

Each team consisted of eight 'internationals' – the foreign contingent – and sixteen 'nationals' – Iraqi guards who were employed by Hart. The vehicles for the assignment were to be totally standard local cars with local plates – no armour or markings or anything out of the ordinary. At first, I was horrified, but it proved to be a stroke of good thinking, as throughout the assignment we could travel freely around town and on the motorways without anyone giving us so much as a second glance – unlike American security companies, such as Blackwater, who used huge white Ford pickups that stood out a mile and made wonderfully massive targets. 'Typical Americans,' I thought whenever I heard of another white pickup coming under fire, whereas we never once had someone even look our way, let alone fire a gun at us.

Each team was to be holed up in a warehouse in the centre of the city. Our job was to drive from the warehouse to the airport two to three times a day. Once there, we would form up a new convoy with six to seven forty-feet trailers, containing portable voting stations, ballot boxes and all the necessary equipment and materials for setting up polling stations for the upcoming elections to select a new Iraqi government. We were then to escort the convoys back to the warehouses so that the electoral equipment could be securely stored until the elections were ready to be held. With the political mayhem and social turmoil in Iraq, these convoys made much bigger and more important targets than the American soldiers patrolling the streets.

We were taken in convoy to the warehouse. To our complete horror, we discovered that not only was the warehouse in the middle of Baghdad, but it was in constant daily use by local traders and businessmen – it was used for storing wheat, sugar, oil and other foodstuffs, and trucks and lorries would come and go, delivering and collecting, all day, every day. We were told in any one day that there could be anything up to 200 trucks and possibly up to 1,000 workers coming and going. And we only had control of about a third of the warehouse. It was a complete and utter fucking nightmare.

As we settled in and surveyed our temporary new home, the Americans turned up with two or three heavy trailers, containing concrete blocks and giant sandbags, which we used to try and form some kind of last line of defence should we come under heavy and sustained attack.

The plan was for half of the international close protection team to go backwards and forwards to the airport with all of the Iraqi nationals, leaving just four of us to guard the warehouse and equipment until the team returned. It took about a week to escort the convoys with all of

153

the ballot boxes and polling stations from the airport. Once all the materials and equipment had been collected, we spent a further week looking after them before the Iraqi national guard turned up with the election committee officials to organise, separate and despatch the stuff out so that polling stations could be constructed around the country.

After the election, all the votes were brought back to the warehouse for us to guard until they were ready to be taken to the airport for counting. Things heated up for us once we had the votes in our dirty, grubby little hands. We all felt like we were protecting Fort Knox and then some. We had the future of the country under our noses, and it seemed as though everyone in Iraq knew it – especially the fanatics and extremists. As we patrolled the dim exterior of the warehouse, there was an almost constant sound of gunfire in the air – the city sounded like bonfire night on steroids. Nights were worse – the bastard Iraqis just would not let us get a minute's sleep, and the heavens were filled with the thuds and tremors of an almost constant barrage of mortar shells, which felt as though they were being aimed directly at our tired little heads.

Life in the warehouse was completely shit. It was a big unit divided into three sections; my team had the third section, furthest from the main gate. Because the warehouse was in daily use, we had to quickly build a makeshift defence barrier between us and the rest of the yard. The lorries that were coming and going and the hundreds of fucking workers walking around were supposed to be controlled and guarded by the local Iraqi guards based at the main gate – but these Iraqi guards were about as useful as a chocolate coffee mug. We also had to man the corridor area leading to our part of the warehouse and make sure that no one wandered, accidentally or otherwise, into our area. We were instructed to shoot anyone who even remotely looked like a threat – the consequences of destroying even a small part of the material we were guarding was immensely grave, both politically and socially. To lose votes from the first so-called Iraqi democratic free election could bring the civil unrest in Iraq to even greater heights.

Our part of the warehouse was about 200 feet by 75 feet and had previously been used to store sugar. There was sugar all over the floor, and during the night, in the pitch black between the volleys of mortars and the near constant sound of gunfire, the only noise you could hear – apart from the occasional snores of our team leader – was the steady scurrying of rats below our beds. We needed the warehouse to be in blackout during the night, as we didn't want to highlight our position within the unit.

On our first evening in the warehouse, we made makeshift beds by laying a couple of wooden pallets together on the floor with our sleeping bags on top. However, after trying to kip for one night on an uncomfortable wooden pallet with the sound of gunfire and mortars keeping us awake and fat rats scuttling all around, we were supplied with some slightly more comfortable US camp beds. Our kitchen area was in the same room and consisted of a simple gas stove balanced on a pile of pallets. Our dining table was a piece of wood on . . . guess what? Yep, a fucking pile of pallets. I am sure that I even tried to shag a pallet in a dream one night.

The only thing we couldn't do with pallets was eat them, so at the start of our assignment we were given a few boxes of US Army rations, which kept us going. Now and then, the US Army popped in with an occasional warm lunch when they were passing on patrol. But this didn't happen that often, as it wasn't very safe for the US Army to patrol in our area.

We passed our time by sitting on the roof of the warehouse, counting the clouds of smoke from explosions around the city or by trying to identify where the shooting was coming from. We also tried to sleep a lot and played many games of chess. Other than me, there were a couple of strong characters in the team, including a couple of Bosnians who spoke very little English, which was fun, especially as I thrashed them time and time again at chess. There were also a couple of French ex-soldiers, which was good, as we could have one or two decent conversations.

After many sleepless, nervous nights, the instruction came for us to escort all the votes back to the relative safety of the airport, where they would be guarded by military personnel and counted. The trucks for the votes were escorted to us at the warehouse by another close protection team, and we guarded them with our weapons at the ready, as they were being loaded with the containers of votes we had protected with our lives. The Iraqi forklift operators were completely useless and kept bashing into the boxes we had carefully guarded. I lost my patience, kicked one of them off and loaded many of the crates myself. I felt like shooting the bloke in question, but that might have been a little extreme.

Before we left, my team sat down with the drivers and explained how we were going to set up the convoy back to the airport, with the votes tightly protected by our vehicles and weapons. This meant that when we hit the motorway, I was in the rear car. My main task was to make sure that no one overtook us or got in between the vehicles in the convoy. I constantly swept the area from side to side all the way to the airport, making sure that no one got too close. A few times, vehicles did get too close, not really knowing who or what we were, or perhaps they were just trying their luck, and I leaned precariously out of the window, aiming my AK at them, showing them that we were armed and dangerous and that they'd better back off. I waved my hand in an up-and-down motion to show them to slow down. If they were stupid enough to ignore me, I fired a couple of rounds into the ground in front of them to indicate that we meant business. Thankfully, everyone in Baghdad is now used to a high-profile military and private security presence, and when someone points a weapon at them or their vehicles, they know precisely what to do . . . they back off!

At the end of that particular job, most of the guys were sent home, but a few, including me, were kept back to help out on another job – to guard the new court house, which was under construction for the trial of Saddam Hussein. Our job was to control the entrance, patrol the perimeter, and check vehicles and personnel coming in and going out, making sure that no one took any photos or 'souvenirs' or blew themselves up! But that is a story for another day.

AUTOBIOGRAPHY OF ALEX POWELL

I was born in North Wales in 1974. Due to a change in my old man's job, I moved to Birmingham when I was four years old. I grew up there and went to a Church of England school in Highgate – I was the only white kid in my whole year, which wasn't easy. My parents got divorced when I was about 11 – I suppose my life changed at that point. It was no fault of my mother's, but discipline lessened, and I realised I was able to push her boundaries a lot more than when my old man had been around. Boys will be boys.

I started to get into trouble with the police around the time I left school – petty little things, such as smashing windows, joyriding, drunk and disorderly behaviour and plenty of fighting. I ended up on a supervision order for three years, which is like a junior version of a probation order. One day, I woke up and decided enough was enough – I had to straighten myself out. I knew that if I carried on in the same vein, I was going to end up going down – and that scared the shit out of me.

I was just an 18-year-old kid when I took my sorry ass down to the army careers office. To my amazement, as soon as they found out about the supervision order, they told me to fuck off and come back in three years' time. There was me trying to straighten myself out and the army shoved me back into the life I was trying to get away from. So I gathered some money together and went off to France to join the Legion. It was much easier than I expected. I arrived in France on 13 July. I secured a bed in a youth hostel in Lille for the night and got pissed with a couple of young Aussie birds who were also staying there – luckily for me, they were both gagging for it, which was nice!

In the morning, I went into the town centre looking for a McDonald's, as I was starving. To my amazement, there was a huge military parade through the town centre. I hadn't realised that it was 14 July – Bastille Day! There were soldiers and tanks everywhere, and at the end of the parade I approached a soldier who seemed to be in charge of a unit and asked him if he knew anything about joining the Legion. Surprisingly, he spoke very good English, and after initially looking at me as if I wasn't right in the head (I wasn't), he gave me a sympathetic smile and told me to go down the road to La Citadelle, a large military base with a Legion recruitment office.

After answering a few questions and passing a basic medical, I said goodbye to all my personal belongings and was put in a minibus with a few other recruits and sent to Marseilles. It was as simple as that, and for the following five years I was a Legionnaire.

157

11

AN EXTRAORDINARY TALE ABOUT A COVERT SECURITY OPERATION AND A SNOOPING RUSSIAN BABUSHKA

BY INNA ZABRODSKAYA

You might be intrigued to learn about a strange and somewhat bizarre connection between the security industry and a Russian *babushka* – for those of you who don't know, *babushka* is Russian for 'grandmother' – and you may or may not be surprised if I told you that as long as we have inquisitive, interfering *babushkas* on guard night and day, no spy, secret agent or terrorist will ever be able to infiltrate and penetrate Russian soil unnoticed! You might also ask yourself what on earth have these sweet little old ladies to do with the security industry in the turbulent and dangerous Russian Federation? You wouldn't believe it, but one of these sweet, innocent old ladies actually ruined my first-ever covert security operation . . .

All day long, these elderly ladies sit on the benches that can be found near almost every high-rise apartment block in Moscow, gossiping to each other about this and that. If you are new to an area, you don't ever have to go to the local information bureau – just ask a *babushka* what's what. They are the best neighbourhood watch you could ever imagine, and they know everything: who went to the market in the morning and exactly what shopping they came back with; who had a quarrel with their partner or lover or friend; who left the water running and flooded the apartment below; who got engaged to whom; and who is pregnant – frequently before they know it themselves! That is our lovely Russian *babushkas* for you.

After graduating from Moscow State Linguistic University in the summer of 1998, I had a part-time job as a translator and became acquainted with a former KGB officer by the name of Lev – a very experienced, educated and intelligent man. I must say that to serve and protect the interests of the Soviet Union, the KGB never failed to employ the 'best of the best'. And these high-ranking KGB officials enjoyed good rewards for their undying and faithful service to the Soviet state – they were often deployed abroad during the Cold War when most of the Soviet citizens never went any further than the Black Sea in the south of the country. These KGB agents were probably some of the very first Russians since 1917, and the beginning of the Soviet Union, allowed to shop at the likes of Marks & Spencer. Lev would later joke that the KGB officials who operated in the UK often referred to Marks & Spencer as 'Marx & Lenin'. And obviously these KGB officials earned good money compared with the rest of society!

After the Soviet Union collapsed, most ex-KGB employees used their experience, intelligence, connections and knowledge of one or more foreign languages to reinvent themselves as private security consultants. And it wasn't difficult to see that they quite quickly found a niche in a new Russia entering the capitalist era, which, ironically, they had previously fought against all their lives. Like many ex-KGB officers, Lev also started a private security company, which operated from the office next to where I worked.

Although Lev spoke good English, he would occasionally pop into the offices of the company I worked for and ask me to help out with some administration and translation work. This was normally while he was away from the office, and occasionally the country, on business trips. He would set me certain tasks and translations for when he returned, which I always managed to complete. After carrying out a few tasks for him, he invited me into his office one day, and in a typically abrupt KGB fashion asked me what I intended to do with my life. I must admit that his question took me aback – how can a naive, inexperienced 22 year old, more or less fresh from university, know what she intends to do with her life? I had only just graduated and didn't know what I was going to do the next day, let alone for the rest of my life. So, I stupidly gave him the only answer I could – I didn't know.

At the back of my mind, I realised that I had probably blown my chances of a job, as I had deduced that his question had something to do with an offer of employment. He was an old-school army officer and would have probably liked me to have been more ideologically prepared, but he gave me a satisfactory smile and confirmed that he did indeed want to offer me a job. His business was expanding, and it was no longer possible for him to manage it on his own. He needed someone with good language skills to assist him full time with his increasing workload, as he was dealing with Western clients on a more frequent basis.

Despite being fresh from university and totally inexperienced in the security industry, I did have a fairly good command of the English language, as well as a smattering of French, which I also studied at degree level, and sufficient administration skills to run a small office, so I found myself saying 'yes' almost immediately. I had read all of Ian Fleming's James Bond stories and, like most teenagers, had imagined myself as one of the gorgeous Bond girls. 'Now,' I thought, 'I will actually have a chance to be one!' On my way home that day, I was on cloud nine, and my imagination went wild . . .

And so my career in the security and investigation industry had begun. During my years with the company, we did a lot of private and corporate investigations, as well as many security operations. The first few years of Russia entering the market economy were very difficult, but as the years passed foreign investors started flooding into the country, and they needed everything from preliminary intelligence reports and data collection to interpreting and translation services and personal protection. At that time, Russia was not really safe for most foreigners but many risked their lives and welfare, as they could build enormous wealth in a relatively short period of time if they were brave and clever enough to come and set up business in the country. My boss, using his ex-KGB friends and his vast network of foreign connections, built a sound database of blue-chip foreign clientele who wanted his security and investigation services.

I always craved action, being out in the field, undercover, spying on somebody, like those gorgeous Bond girls, making men weak at the knees with just a flutter of their eyelashes, but sadly I didn't have very long eyelashes, and I spent the first couple of years mostly doing office work and basic administration, as well as occasionally collecting and analysing data, translating documents for Western clients and typing up report after report. It was not the glamorous, exciting industry that I had anticipated and dreamed of.

The company continued to expand, and after two years we were employing two more ex-KGB staff, a part-time accountant and a part-time IT man. Finally, after two years of patience and frustration, my big day of field operations finally came.

One of our clients, the deputy director of a large multinational oil company with an office in the centre of Moscow, contacted us with a suspicion that he was being followed. He was quite frightened. Back in those early days of democracy, it was not unusual for businessmen, entrepreneurs and managers of big companies – both Russian and foreign – to be targeted by the Mafia or other business rivals, with the intention of frightening and extorting money from them or forcing them out of business. There were many cases of kidnapping, torturing and even the assassination of businessmen and members of their family.

One of the more famous cases was that of American hotelier Paul Tatum, who was shot in cold blood with an automatic Kalashnikov in front of several passers-by at around 5 p.m. as he and two of his bodyguards left the Slavyanskaya Hotel and headed towards Kievskaya metro station, where he had arranged to meet somebody.

162

Kievskaya metro is integrated within the mainline railway station and is situated right next to the hotel. In the underground passageway leading through to the mainline station, Tatum's killer walked up to him and shot him 11 times at point-blank range in full view of everyone passing by. The killer then calmly laid down his gun on the passageway steps and walked away while Tatum's bodyguards stood silently by. Had they also been paid by the person responsible for the hotelier's death? The assassination ended Tatum's long dispute with the Moscow City Government as well as with his so-called business partner, a Chechen who jointly owned the hotel with him. An American–Chechen business partnership was probably doomed to failure from the very start – with the odds considerably stacked against the American.

Apparently, it later transpired that the dispute involved Tatum's refusal to pay a bribe of $1 million to cover up an original earlier bribe he had made of $500,000. He was being extorted in typical Russian Mafia style: pay a second bigger bribe to cover up the first bribe.

The Mafia's torture methods were sometimes even more barbaric and horrific than those of the KGB. There was a famous case of the telephone receivers in the office of a wealthy Russian businessman being poisoned – half an hour after he spoke to a colleague on the phone, he died of chemical poisoning, as did his secretary some time later. The girlfriend of another wealthy Russian businessman was tortured when the kidnappers placed an iron on her stomach and slowly cooked her to death by increasing the temperature. Also, the hand of a bank manager who had been kidnapped and held to ransom was sent in an envelope to his wife – the kidnappers promised to send more body parts if she did not raise enough money to pay up.

In most cases, kidnappers initially carry out comprehensive surveillance of their victims, following them everywhere and recording their comings and goings, changes in routines, and how often they use bodyguards and how many, with the fundamental objective of finding a few weak points . . . and then bang! They close in when the victim least expects it.

After the initial briefing from the client, we sat down to work out a plan of action to identify whether or not our client was being followed, and if so, by whom. Because of the sensitivity of the operation, we decided not to involve any outside people and just use those who worked within our company, including me! This was my 'Moment of Truth', my 'Ultimate Test'; if I did well, I knew that this would be the first covert James Bond-like spy mission of many – and I just knew I was going to do a great job!

We worked out a route for our client to take the following day. It was going to be a similar route to that which he would normally take, but with a few slight diversions and alterations. My colleagues and I would be strategically placed along the route. Obviously, we knew the model, colour and number plate of our client's car, so the only thing we needed to do was to take note of the number plates of all the vehicles that followed our client's within a few minutes of it passing by. Afterwards, using a method of cross reference, we would quickly establish whether or not our client had been followed. If he had been followed, we would use our connections with the police and security services to identify who it was and have him quickly arrested. It was such a simple plan – what could go wrong?

We could not afford to arouse the suspicion of pedestrians, passers-by or, more importantly, the potential kidnappers, so we had to hide ourselves in such a way that we could clearly see the road and all the cars passing by but nobody could see us. In my new role of covert surveillance operative, I found what I thought was the perfect spot – an enclosed patch of bushy greenery.

I got there nice and early, crawled into the bushes and made myself comfortable. I had my sandwich on my knee (after all, a spy can't go hungry, can she?) and my notebook and pen in hand, and I prepared to wait. Before I got into the bush, I had a good look around to make sure nobody could see me. Apart from ruining the whole operation, it would have been quite embarrassing to hear somebody laugh (or scream) at what they thought was me attempting to have a wee! Muscovites often use these lovely hiding places to do their business, because although there are quite a few public toilets in the city, the state of them is so horrific that going there once is enough to put you off for life. (Public toilets cost five roubles, which you pay to some horrible-looking hag, chain-smoking stale, cheap cigarettes and smelling worse than the loo she supposedly cleans but hasn't used herself for years.)

Excited about my first big assignment, I made myself snug in the bushes and was all set for the task in hand. If only I had known that in an apartment block not far from my 'secret' spot, an elderly woman, whose name I'll never know, had looked out of her window at precisely the same time as I had slipped between the bushes. From above, she must have seen me crawl into the undergrowth and, as all Russian grandmothers would, thought to herself, 'What on earth is that pretty young woman wearing a smart office suit doing squatting in the bushes?' Or something like that, anyway.

I had arrived well in advance of the arranged time to make sure I was not late and that I was well prepared. I had planned to spend about half an hour watching the cars pass by to make sure that I was quick enough to write down the number plates. I started practising, ever so slightly squeezing my head through the thicket at every car that passed, then back in as I frantically scribbled down the number plate, all the while thinking about telling my friends and family about Inna 'Super-duper Spy' Bond!

Right in the middle of my daydreaming, I suddenly heard a rustling sound behind me, followed by the angry voice of an elderly woman: 'Hey you! What are you doing there? Get out immediately. I have been watching you for a while. We have had enough of people pissing in our bushes. You wait. I have called the police already. They are on their way. They will take you to their quarters. You will have to pay a fine for spoiling our park area, and then you'll have to come back and clean up after yourself!'

I froze with fear and utter embarrassment, and wondered how it was possible to clean up pee from the ground. What could I do? I couldn't tell her that I was on a covert surveillance operation, but I also couldn't admit that I was peeing in the bushes! Right at that moment, my eye caught our client's car passing by. I quickly decided that it was better to lose face than ruin the whole operation and said in a timid voice, 'Just give me a minute and I'll be out.' After that, I started frantically writing down the numbers of the cars that followed the client's silver Mercedes SLK, as I didn't really believe that the angry *babushka* had called the police about someone peeing in the bushes.

A few seconds later, I heard a man's voice shout, 'Stand up with your hands in the air!' This, I must admit, I did not see coming. I automatically put the list in my mouth, chewed it and swallowed, as the last thing I needed was to end up in the police department with a list of number plates in my possession. And anyway, that is what I had read in the James Bond books: if spies were caught red-handed, they ate the evidence.

Swallowing the last remains of the paper, I meekly edged my way out of the bushes, my face scratched by sharp thorns, my legs weak from sitting in one position for such a long time and my whole body shaking with fear. Never in my short life had I been in any kind of trouble with the police, and to find myself in this horrible situation was beyond my wildest imagination. As soon as the policeman saw me and my pitiful appearance, he understood that I was no threat. Standing next to him, shaking her wrinkly old fist at me, was the *babushka*.

The policeman asked for my passport and demanded an explanation. I needed to find an excuse for why I had been sitting in the bushes. Saying that I had been having a shit was right out of the question, and the only thing I could immediately think of was that on my way to work I had been followed by a stranger. I had been scared and decided to hide in the bushes. I wasn't sure whether they believed me or not. Frankly, I didn't care – I just wanted the whole thing to end. After a stern warning, the policeman finally let me go.

When I got home, I kept wondering how I was going to tell everybody at work what had happened and why I had so miserably failed on my very first security operation. I would have to think of something to tell my boss, so I decided to make up car number plates and hope for the best.

The next day, when we all compared our lists, it turned out that the client's car had not been followed after all . . . or maybe it had been? Thankfully, he went on to spend many more happy years in Russia.

The moral of the story is never to piss or shit in the bushes, as there will always be a *babushka* on guard! And so much for my covert surveillance skills!

Biography of Inna Zabrodskaya

Originally from Moscow, Inna moved to England in 2003. She has worked in the security industry on and off since 1998, first for BLM Security Management Consultants, where she was the personal assistant to the ex-KGB director, and then for a short time as the assistant to the director of the Russian branch of the Olive Group. Inna has spent many years researching and compiling business intelligence reports for foreign clients on the Russian Federation, as well as being involved in a large number of security and investigative operations. However, she has refrained from doing any operation that might include bushes and number plates, and always tries to use public toilets, despite their horrendous state.

Inna currently provides Russian translation services for the security and investigation industry, and runs the membership section of the British Bodyguard Association. She can be contacted at www. russotranslationservices.com

12

So, Who Wants to Be a Bouncer?

By Andy Walker

Just before I left school in west London in 1980, my contemporaries and I all had to suffer a visit to the careers officer. 'And what do you plan to do with the rest of your life?' I was asked. Luckily, I already had a cunning plan: I was going to join the army, get a trade and see the world – hopefully at the same time as drinking lots of beer and meeting pretty girls! Other mates wanted a career in law, banking or industry, while others still hoped to earn their fortunes with a trade such as carpentry or plumbing. Obviously, we all discussed our career plans, but I don't remember anyone ever saying, 'I want to be a bouncer when I leave school.' Not even the 'big boys' amongst us ever considered working the doors as a possible career path, and it was certainly never mentioned as a possibility by the careers officer.

It wasn't until I was well and truly ensconced in basic training up in sunny North Yorkshire and was finally let loose at the weekends on the unsuspecting northern pub and club scene that I first came across a bouncer. Remember, this was in 1980, before we had ever heard of such a thing as a 'door supervisor'. There was no training, no registration or licensing system, and most doormen in those days were what we would now call old school. They were normally large, strong men, very rarely with a neck or any hair to speak of, and they usually gave off a menacing air of authority that definitely helped ensure that young bucks like me behaved themselves on their premises. The uniform was pretty standard, too: shiny black shoes, black dinner suit, white shirt and black dicky bow. In the winter, this would all be neatly hidden under a long Crombie-style black overcoat and a pair of black leather gloves.

These were not men to mess with. I still remember the distinct feeling of nervous trepidation on a Friday and a Saturday night as I approached the black-and-white guardians of the door, never certain whether I would be able to convince them I was such a nice guy that they simply *had* to let me in. Sometimes I got in; other times I was made to skulk off into the night to try to find somewhere more accommodating to drink.

WHAT IS A BOUNCER?

Twenty-five years ago, bouncers were usually only found outside the larger nightclubs and dance halls. Today, however, they can be found outside most pubs and clubs in our major towns and cities, and are now even used to protect late-night restaurants, takeaways and shops. Some local-council crime-prevention schemes even use bouncers to patrol town centres and taxi ranks, and there are a couple of schemes that use them to travel on late-night buses to prevent disorder and protect clubbers on their way home.

Door supervisors, as bouncers are now called, are usually hired to protect the staff and property of licensed premises and to look after the safety of the customers who use them. They now fulfil many of the general functions that you would expect to be carried out by uniformed security staff in shopping centres. The main difference between these two sectors of the private security industry is the type of people who tend to do the job. Door supervisors, as a rule, have to deal with potentially far more violent confrontations with the public than most uniformed security guards will ever have to in the

170

normal course of their duties, so the physical and mental attributes of bouncers tend to reflect their ability to deal with such situations. Therefore, door supervisors are usually well built and physically fit, attributes not always seen in the uniformed sector.

As the result of the confrontations that inevitably occur at premises that supply alcohol, door supervisors generally have to exercise their statutory and common-law rights to use force more regularly than security workers in other sectors. This is why bouncers have unfortunately acquired a bad reputation in the past, with allegations of unwarranted or excessive force being applied to customers.

An academic study in 1998 explained that the stereotype of a bouncer was perpetuated by the media. In some newspapers, they had been described as 'gorillas in suits' and 'Rottweilers in bow ties', and various television programmes reinforced the perception of bouncers being men of enormous proportions, low intelligence and a propensity for violence. The author of that work also reported that studies and observations made in 1988 and 1989 described the typical characteristics of a doorman as being 'masculine, of large stature, aged 26–35 years, has non-verbal control in antagonistic encounters, exerts anger-threat controls against persistent individuals, has fighting ability, a reputation for viciousness, and forms a visible coalition with other doormen when threatened'.

In 1995, a Home Office circular, giving advice to local authorities wishing to set up door supervisor registration schemes in their areas, defined a door supervisor as 'a person employed on premises which have a music and dancing licence in operation, with authority from the owner or landlord exclusively or mainly to decide upon the suitability of customers to be allowed on those premises; and/or to maintain order on those premises'. This definition was widely used by council- and police-run registration schemes throughout the 1990s until it was superseded by the definition provided by the Private Security Industry Act, 2001.

WHAT DO BOUNCERS DO?

Thankfully, in most areas, the days when doormen were hired at only the most unruly of pubs and clubs to stop fights, to protect the licensee and to administer their own brand of summary justice to customers who dared to breach the rules of the house are long gone. Professional door supervisors are now considered an essential part of many well-run establishments, ensuring a safer environment in which customers are free to enjoy themselves. Their duties now extend far beyond simply ejecting drunks and preventing disorder, although these elements are still essential to the proper management of any licensed premises. Today's door supervisors are the eyes and the ears of the licensee, and, as such, are expected to become involved in the many different aspects of running premises designed for entertainment. They are expected to properly welcome customers onto the premises, whilst at the same time enforcing the venue's entry conditions in a firm but fair manner. Once those customers are inside the premises, door staff are expected to ensure that the evening runs according to everyone's expectations, at the same time maintaining order and preventing breaches of criminal and licensing laws and house rules. If any of those laws or rules are breached, they need to act within the guidelines of the law and company policy to resolve the situation.

Occasionally, as part of the customer services element of the job, door supervisors may be required to administer first aid to anyone who becomes ill or injured on the premises before medical help arrives. They are also required to patrol the premises and to look out for fire hazards or suspicious packages, and need to be able to carry out basic emergency procedures if problems occur. They now have to be aware of basic heath-and-safety rules and must help the licensee to ensure that the venue is safe enough to be open to the public. Whilst fulfilling all of these functions, door supervisors are also required to be pleasant and polite so that the customers feel welcome. They therefore need to use effective communication and social skills in everything that they do.

The basic job requirements of modern-day door supervisors are much more than they were only twenty years ago, a point reflected in the four-day basic training programme that all entrants to the game need to complete prior to applying for their licence to work in the industry. Door supervisors basically 'police' a venue on behalf of its management.

How many door supervisors are there?

Some door supervisors work for large leisure organisations, some for leisure security companies and others are classed as in-house, meaning that they are hired or employed directly by the licensee of the premises. Some work at pubs or in wine bars, some at clubs and others at restaurants, casinos, amusement arcades and even cinemas. Some door supervisors work part time, some full time and others only occasionally at one-off events. Some of this work is done legitimately with the appropriate tax and national insurance being paid to the treasury; some of it is still done cash in hand and without the proper declaration of earnings.

It is difficult to give an accurate figure of how many door supervisors there are working in the UK at present. Back in 1999, I carried out some research for the Home Office on the subject and from that estimated that there were about 100,000. However, under the current national licensing system, only 86,000 door supervisors have been granted an SIA licence (statistic dated August 2007), although double that figure have sat for the qualifications required to gain a licence.

What type of person works the doors?

In 1999, I carried out a nationwide survey on the door supervision sector, interviewing 500 door supervisors. That research showed that 93 per cent of door supervisors were male and covered a fairly wide age range. About 75 per cent of door supervisors at that time classed themselves as 'white European', with 49 per cent of them educated to just O Level standard.

As local registration schemes had already come into force in about two-thirds of England and Wales, we asked the candidates what they preferred to call themselves. Over half (54 per cent) called themselves 'door supervisors', with 31 per cent preferring the term 'doorman'. Only 3 per cent used the term 'bouncer'. One interviewee described himself as an 'ejection technician' and two called themselves 'in-house behavioural therapists'! Only 27 per cent said that they worked full time as a door supervisor, 72 per cent claiming part time only (1 per cent failed to answer the question).

When asked why they worked the doors, 27 per cent said they did

173

so as their primary source of income, 52 per cent explained that they did so to supplement their day job, 7 per cent to supplement state benefits and 10 per cent to help pay them through further education. When asked how long they had been working as a door supervisor, 21 per cent said for less than a year, 45 per cent for between one and five years, 16 per cent for six to ten years and only 6 per cent said that they had been in the door game for more than 15 years. Of those surveyed, 36 per cent said that they were employed in-house by the venue, and 62 per cent said that they worked for a leisure security company.

At the time of the survey, 76 per cent were registered with one or more of the local-authority door-supervisor registration schemes, and 71 per cent of those surveyed said that they thought that such schemes were a good idea. Out of the 500 door supervisors surveyed, 90 per cent wanted to see a national registration or licensing scheme brought in. It would be interesting to see whether the SIA national licensing system has changed people's opinions.

THE OLD REGISTRATION SCHEMES

In the late 1980s and early '90s, various forward-thinking local authorities and police forces started their own door-supervisor registration schemes. These schemes enabled them to vet, train and monitor the activities of their local pub and club doormen. These schemes were set up with the intention of:

- securing and maintaining a degree of legal controls over door supervisors
- having some control over who was employed as a door supervisor in that area
- changing a general feeling of dissatisfaction with the attitude and behaviour of some door supervisors
- reducing the number of complaints by customers about door supervisors
- reducing incidents of violence and disorderly behaviour in and around licensed premises
- reducing the rates of assault allegations against door supervisors

- deterring door supervisors from acting aggressively and/or illegally
- preventing incidents of door supervisors dealing in controlled drugs
- reducing underage drinking and drug abuse on licensed premises
- enhancing the status of door supervisors through vetting, training and making them more accountable
- reducing problems of security agency cartels, intimidation of licensees and inter-agency violence
- promoting better relations between the police and door supervisors
- reassuring customers that action was being taken to control the actions and behaviour of door supervisors
- improving the safety of persons attending the premises for entertainment.

About 65 per cent of England and Wales was covered by one registration scheme or another by the year 2000, and these schemes were hailed as a great success. Areas that had initiated such schemes saw a reduction in problems on licensed premises, particularly those involving door staff, with police forces all over the UK boasting impressive reductions in relevant crimes in those districts.

The only problem with these local registration schemes was that each area decided on its own vetting criteria, training criteria, licensing system and costs. For example, in London many door supervisors who worked for leisure security companies found themselves in the situation that they had to apply and pay for several different licences to cover them to work in several different areas. I once met a doorman in London who was the proud owner of 17 local authority licences!

NATIONAL LICENSING

As the result of calls from the press, the public and the industry itself, the government decided to regulate the whole of the UK private security industry, and in 2001 the Private Security Industry Act was passed, which allowed the Home Office to form a new independent body to bring about a national licensing system for people and companies in

175

the security sector. As well as issuing licences, that body also became responsible for raising standards of training and professionalism across the industry and to reassure the public by preventing unsuitable people from carrying out security work. That body is called the SIA.

In March 2004, the SIA opened its doors for business. Door supervisors were now able to apply for a licence, and the initial requirement was that every single doorman, whether they worked in-house or for a security company, was to be licensed by April 2005. That deadline was extended several times, but it is now illegal for anyone to work in a security role without a licence on licensed premises anywhere in England and Wales. (Licensing has recently been launched in Scotland and will be followed up in the years to come in Northern Ireland.)

To get an SIA licence, applicants have to attend the national four-day basic training programme, which must be held by an awarding-body-approved training centre, leading to the national Level 2 qualification in door supervision. Once applicants have received their formal training qualification certificate, they can submit their application form to the SIA with a payment of £245 and an accompanying identification document. A criminal record check is then conducted and 'suitable' applicants are issued with their three-year SIA door supervisors' licence. This licence allows them to work legally on any licensed premises in the UK until such time as that licence either runs out or is suspended or revoked.

WHAT DOES THE TRAINING INVOLVE?

The basic licence-to-practice qualification is run over four days. The SIA does not run training courses, give qualifications or provide funding. Instead, it has endorsed awarding bodies who offer the qualifications linked to SIA licensing, and those awarding bodies approve the training providers. The awarding bodies currently overseeing door supervisor qualifications include NOCN, BIIAB, ASET, City and Guilds, Edexcel and the SQA (in Scotland). Awarding body details can be found on the SIA's website, as can a list of regionally based training providers. The basic door course costs between £150 and £250, depending on the area and the training provider.

The four-day course is split into two parts. Part one (two days) is all about a door supervisor's responsibilities and duties in the workplace. The second part (two days) covers communication skills and conflict management. There is a multiple-choice exam at the end of each part, and you have to pass both parts to get the full qualification.

The subjects covered in the training include: introducing door supervisors to the leisure and security industries; defining the role of the door supervisor and identifying the qualities required to be one; discussing the behaviour appropriate for individual door supervisors using the SIA standards of behaviour; and discussing and identifying civil and criminal law relevant to door supervision, e.g. what is meant by 'reasonable' and 'necessary force', the requirements relating to the use of force, types of assault, etc. Also, door supervisors' powers of arrest, offences, procedures following an arrest and search procedures are covered, as is drugs awareness, recording incidents, crime scene preservation, licensing law, equal opportunities and discrimination, health and safety at work, emergency procedures, communication skills, and conflict management.

CONCLUSION

There has been much debate over the last few years as to how well the new national licensing system is working. Some people complain that the licence application process is difficult and takes too long, while others complain that it is too expensive. Many people are disappointed at how the new laws are being enforced, with many questioning why there are still so many unlicensed doormen working in pubs and clubs. Some leisure security companies complain that there are not enough decent, experienced doormen available to fulfil their contracts. Others say that the industry is being overtaken by inexperienced 'jacket fillers' who simply can't do the job properly.

The SIA, on the other hand, will tell us that there is broad compliance with the new regulations, that the system has turned away many unsuitable characters from the industry and that it has raised standards of competence and professionalism thanks to the new training regime.

I personally spent a lot of my own time many years ago campaigning for a national registration scheme for door supervisors. We have one now – it's not ideal, and there are many things that need to be changed before it 'does what it says on the tin', but things will hopefully improve. In the meantime, just remember, 'If your name's not down, you're not coming in!'

BIOGRAPHY OF ANDY WALKER

Andy Walker, a former police officer, has nearly 20 years' experience in the world of door supervision. In 1990, whilst a 'moonlighting' policeman, Andy worked the doors in London's Notting Hill. At the same time, he started London's first police-run door-supervisors registration scheme. He was invited to help write the first set of national occupational standards for the sector and trained hundreds of doormen for various schemes in and around London.

In 2001, Andy published the well-known *Safer Doors*, a 356-page training handbook for doormen, which has sold 10,000 copies to date. He is currently busy writing the second edition. Also that year, he ran the first 'Safer Doors Conference', a national conference specifically for the door game.

In 2002, Andy left the police force to work for a national door company as their training director, and in 2003 he became a consultant for the newly formed SIA, specifically advising on door supervisors. At the same time, he was still working the doors in East Yorkshire and various other parts of northern England.

Andy now runs his own security training company, teaching not only the SIA qualifications but several bespoke accredited training courses aimed at keeping front-line security operatives safe in the workplace. These include the only accredited plastic handcuffing course for security personnel and the new Offender ID Spray training programme.

You can contact Andy, or find out more about his training, via his website at www.fedstraining.co.uk or go to www.workingthedoors. co.uk, where he is regularly found discussing the industry with fellow doormen around the country.

He has never said, "'ello, 'ello, 'ello, what's going on 'ere, then?'

13

CELEBRITY PROTECTION
BY JOHN BADLY

Before the story starts, I must stress that just because my name happens to be Badly, it doesn't mean that I have lived up to it in my professional life. But I hesitate somewhat when it comes to categorising my personal life in a similar vein, as it has not always been good; in fact, 'badly' is probably quite a good word for how my personal life has unfolded since entering the business of celebrity protection 15 years ago. You see, celebrity protection is very different to corporate protection. The challenges are different, as are, of course, the risks, but mainly it is the environment in which we work that makes family life and long-term relationships almost impossible.

I first started in close protection as a bouncer in a nightclub in London. I had just left the army, where I'd served in the Parachute Regiment, and I really didn't know where I was going or what I was going to do. I thought about truck driving – lots of ex-Paras obtained their HGV licence as part of the resettlement programme and drove trucks for the rest of their lives. Driving is good because it gives a sense of freedom that many ex-soldiers crave, plus if you are an international driver it takes you to the Continent for days, sometimes weeks at a time, which is another thing ex-soldiers tend to like and are used to.

A good friend of mine and fellow Para gained his HGV licence and ended up transporting goods for a charity – aid, medicines, etc. – in and out of Bosnia during the first couple of years of the conflict, which he thoroughly enjoyed. It would take him three or four days to get to his destination, followed by a couple of days turnaround and, strangely, a seemingly quicker journey back home. He would then rest in the UK for a couple of days before going back out to Bosnia. Although he didn't go directly into the war zone, he loved the job, as he felt he was doing some good whilst getting a little bit of adventure at the same time. He would take his truck almost anywhere that the aid was needed, from a warehouse on the Italian–Croatian border, where it was then unloaded and distributed into the war zone by the Red Cross, to towns and villages recently bombed and desperate for aid.

I was lucky enough to join him on one trip. He called me and asked if I wanted to sit with him for a week or so while he took his truck to a place called Lipik in northern Croatia. He said it would be good to have some company, and I agreed. The bombardment of Lipik, along with the nearby village of Pakrac, was started by the Serbian forces at 5.30 a.m. on 19 August 1991. The first building to be destroyed was the orphanage, which was home to around eighty children between the ages of three and sixteen. For seven days, the children cowered in the cellars while the building above them, as well as most of the rest of the town, was shelled. In a lull in the fighting, the children were quickly evacuated to the coast.

My friend and I were one of the first convoys of private humanitarian aid into the town. The charity my colleague was working for had arranged for us to be met in Lipik by their local representative. We had a map and were able to find the town, although finding the warehouse that we were supposed to deliver to was a bit of a problem. However, an English truck in the middle of war-torn Lipik caused a great deal of interest, and we were soon found by the charity worker and directed to a shelled-out warehouse, where the aid would be fairly divided between the town's inhabitants. Half the truck was filled with baby food donated by Cow & Gate, and the other half was clothing, toiletries, bedding, blankets and other much-needed sundries. Many people who survived the shelling remained in their burned-out homes, and the aid was a godsend to the majority of people who had found themselves with nothing.

As a Para, I had been to some very interesting places and had met some wonderful people, but nothing had quite prepared me for the destruction a continuous mortar bombardment can bring to a town and its inhabitants. Every single building, without exception, was in ruins, and it amazed me how people could have survived it.

After we had unloaded the supplies, we found a small bar in the centre of Lipik that had been hastily set up once the Serbs had moved on to destroy another village. It was an improvised establishment, using the living room and garden of a partly bombed house next to the original bar, which had been completely destroyed. Although makeshift, it was nevertheless somewhere for the locals to meet and relax.

As foreigners, we attracted a lot of attention, and the evening was spent listening to the countless stories of atrocities and carnage perpetrated by the Serbian Army. We were also introduced to Colonel Mark Cook. He was the commander of the British contingent of the United Nations Protection Force. He vowed to the mayor of Lipik that he would help rebuild the orphanage. Mark went on to raise over £1 million and a few years later rebuilt the orphanage as he'd promised. He asked us if we could bring in our next container some children's clothing for the orphans who were now living safely on the coast. The children got their clothing a few weeks later, and Mark Cook went on to form the charity Hopes and Homes for Children, which has helped thousands of children worldwide.

Having experienced the conflict, albeit in a very small way, I felt I had been part of it and wanted to do something more to help. But, sadly, I knew that unless I could quickly find a job with a charity based out there, I wouldn't be coming back. It was just a one-trip deal for me.

Although the experience was wonderful in many ways, I knew I couldn't drive trucks for a living. I needed to be more active. Sitting down all day, every day would have sent me crazy. It was also very unhealthy. I have kept fit for most of my life and have trained every day more or less without fail, but truck driving, whether in the UK or abroad, affords you little chance of keeping in shape.

Spending over a week in the same cab as someone gives you the opportunity to talk about anything and everything. My friend and I spoke mostly about trivial things but with the occasional gem thrown in. At one point, he mentioned that he knew another ex-Para who had gone into personal protection. I didn't know much about the industry, except that it was a business populated mainly by ex-SAS and RMPs (Royal Military Police). However, the idea was a good one, and once I got home I made some enquiries about training.

At that time, there was no standardised training and no SIA licence. You had to shop around, make lots of enquiries and find the best privately run course you could find. There were a few training companies run by ex-SAS, but not many, and they were quite hard to find. Of course, the Internet was up and running, but many companies still did not have websites, so my research was mainly via word of mouth and advertising.

I looked at a few companies but eventually chose to train with the WFB. Back then, the organisation was based just outside Manchester, near to where I lived, so it was a simple task to visit them and get all the relevant details. The WFB had not been going long but were accredited as a training provider by Manchester College of Arts and Technology, an accreditation most other training companies didn't have.

A month or so later, I paid a deposit, and a month after that I was on my way to Wales for my first-ever close protection training course. Luckily, my resettlement grant covered most of the training fees, so I really had nothing much to lose, apart from a hundred or so pounds of my own money and my time, and I had loads of that.

We met in a car park in the village of Llandrindod Wells, mid Wales, which I thought was a bit bizarre. According to the organisers, the reason for this was that the training camp was almost impossible to find, and it was far easier for everyone to meet at a specific location at a specific time, rather than us all arriving in dribs and drabs or getting lost. There were supposed to be ten of us on the course altogether, although only eight arrived at the car park. Maybe two pulled out, or perhaps they couldn't even find their way to the town centre! We nervously waited in more or less silence for thirty minutes after the arranged time, then the eight of us made our way in convoy behind the instructors to the training camp – a huge farmhouse down a tiny, muddy lane in the middle of nowhere.

On arrival, we were given 30 minutes to find a bed, unpack and pour ourselves a cuppa. Then we all met downstairs in the living area, where we were introduced to our instructors and talked through the days ahead.

In the army, we did some crazy things and went to some crazy places. The training was tough, and I thought I was fairly hard, but, fuck me, the training these guys put us through over the following ten days was definitely some of the best I have ever had. Initially, I think we all questioned what was going on, as sharing a room and training in a farmhouse was not what any of us had really expected, but realism was the name of the game, and everything we did during those ten days was based upon us being out in the field – literally – and on real operations.

One of the instructors was a Russian ex-Special Forces officer, the other was an instructor with the Lebanese forces, and our fitness and martial arts instructor was an ex-Scottish boxing champion. I have never seen a pair of fists move so quickly.

Every day started at 6 a.m. with a three-mile run and an hour of unarmed combat. We then showered and had breakfast, and the rest of the day was meticulously planned: 9 a.m. to 10.30 a.m. – theory of convoy driving; 10.30 a.m. to 11.30 a.m. – planning a convoy; 11.30 a.m. to 1 p.m. – first convoy practice; 1 p.m. to 2 p.m. – lunch; 2 p.m. to 3.30 p.m. – building search theory; and so on throughout the course. After the first six days, we used what we had learned and put it into practice with a 'real' operation. The WFB team had arranged for someone to fly into Cardiff International Airport, and we were to look after him as if he was a real client for two days and two nights.

Those two days were probably even more difficult than the training we had all just gone through, as everything was thrown at us. But I believe we learned more during those two days than we had done during the previous six.

Going to meet the principal (the person who we would be looking after) was easy, but coming back was one of the most fraught and difficult situations I have ever found myself in. We were all nervous but didn't expect what followed. First, the principal was with his girlfriend, which was not part of the plan, so we had to adapt to looking after two clients instead of just one. And then he fell ill, so we had to divert to the hospital. On the way, we had a call from the operations room to tell us that the route to the hospital had become compromised, so we had to frantically work out a secondary route. Then his girlfriend wanted to buy a new pair of tights, so we had to stop and find her some. Finally, after the principal miraculously recovered a few hundred yards from the hospital entrance, our communications were compromised, and we were told we could no longer use our radios.

Of course, all of this had been planned by the instructors, but what hadn't been planned was that once our communications were out of action we lost the rear vehicle and had to embarrassingly drive back to the base individually and not as a convoy. Luckily, the instructors were fairly patient with us, as it was our first client pickup, and we were bound to make some mistakes. However, as the course continued, we were allowed less and less leeway, and we were bollocked more and more if we made fuck-ups. We had been told at the beginning of the course that if we made the same fuck-up twice, we would be on our way home, which only increased our stress levels.

While the client was in our care, none of us slept, which made battling our way through the plethora of planned emergency situations and events even more demanding. The principal went for a walk and got shot; he and his girlfriend had a major bust-up and darted off in different directions; he became ill; a fire started in the house; he wanted to go out for an unplanned evening drink at a minute's notice; and in the middle of the night we had to arrange residential patrols while infiltrators tried to breach the building and attack the principal.

Packages were delivered, improvised explosive devices were found on the premises and a team member crashed one of the vehicles.

Those two days looking after the principal were definitely among the longest and hardest two days of my entire life – not because of the lack of sleep or intense physical and mental stress we were under, but mainly because of the knowledge that if we got it wrong out in the field as a protection officer, we would not have a second chance and could be coming home in a body bag. It was a great way to learn.

The last two days of the course consisted of a complete debrief with long conversations and discussions about the mistakes we'd made, specific operations, protocol and operational procedures. But we still started each morning with a run and unarmed combat training.

It was a shame that the WFB was later sold and disbanded, as the systems they used and the standards of training were certainly pioneering and original within the close protection industry at that time. Now I believe it is all namby-pamby theory. I have seen overweight, unfit muppets pass close protection courses. Back in my day, the industry was for the elite.

After the course, we all went our separate ways, although many long-term friendships were made. Two of the students went on to work for the United Nations, and many years later I actually saw one of them on television standing behind Slobodan Milošević in The Hague, where the former president of Serbia was on trial for crimes against humanity. Apparently, after a time spent taking judges to Kosovo to investigate war crimes and looking after them while they were there, he was tasked to keep an eye on Milošević during his court appearances – a boring but steady job! Another of the students went to Australia, where I heard he was arrested for supplying drugs. At the time of writing, he is still in prison! I didn't hear from a few of the students again, but a couple of the others are still working in the protection industry and currently serving in Iraq.

After the course, I went back to working the doors in London and found myself a cushy little number at a club with nice clientele. For six months, it was great, but it became a bit boring, and after having been in the army and doing the close protection course I knew that I liked excitement and not comfy stability. I also thought that it would be a waste of time and money if I didn't do anything with my protection training. One night as I stood pondering these things, Errol Brown, the lead singer of the band Hot Chocolate, came into the club. Surprisingly, he stood making idle conversation with me for a few minutes, although I was not sure why, as he had a small entourage with him. It was then that I made a decision: I would use my new-found skills to look after celebrities.

I first applied for a job with a famous bodyguard called Jerry Judge, who looked after many of the celebrities in London. Although getting on a bit now, his face was often seen on TV behind someone famous, and he was (and I think still is) responsible for the security at most of the London film premieres. I started off ushering vehicles at these one-off events, and I progressed to actually opening the car doors for celebrities and keeping a close eye on the crowd as the film stars wandered around signing autographs. To be honest, we were all pretty insignificant in the grand scale of things, but it was certainly great fun.

I did this for a couple of years and continued to work the doors before I was asked to work full time with a very well-known male pop star. What a life I found myself leading! I was surrounded by glamour and beauty, and thoroughly enjoyed every single minute of it. I really didn't mind that my client was a complete nob at times and frequently drunk. However, although it could be great fun, looking after a celebrity could also be really hard work, especially when my client was drunk or high on drugs, which sadly was often. He would go from one extreme to the other. One day, he would be the life and soul of the party; the next day he would be sobbing to himself that his life was worthless, that he was crap at what he did, that no one liked him and that he was a failure. They say patience is a virtue, and that was certainly the case when I provided security for this client. It was sometimes very hard work.

The pop star's manager would plan events or appearances, and my job was to get him to the locations safely, look after him while he was there and get him home again. It was a full-time position, but there were days when he didn't leave his house and I did nothing, and there were other days when he would go from studio to studio, from

TV and radio station to TV and radio station and from gig to gig, so over the course of the year it generally evened itself out to around 100 hours a week – or so it sometimes seemed!

Much of the time, though, it wasn't really work. I went to the Caribbean with him about four times, where I spent my time sitting in a speedboat or cooking burgers on the barbecue. I would patrol the grounds of his rented villa while he had long and noisy parties, trying to keep my eyes on the area in front of the house and not the naked arses and tits happily bobbing about in the pool behind me.

Over time, we became quite good friends. Some people say that it is not professional to become friends with the person you are tasked to protect, but I disagree. It is human nature to protect more the ones we care most about, even in the security industry, in which we are supposed to guard everyone in the same manner and with our life if need be. I was always dismayed and saddened by my client's occasional despair, when in fact he had millions of adoring fans. I was also saddened by his loneliness. Being famous but lonely is an appalling way for anyone to live.

A couple of years ago, he moved out of the UK, seeking a better and more settled life in an environment in which fame is more accepted and expected. Although I was asked to accompany him, I couldn't. Not because I didn't want to, but because it would have been very hard for a Brit to get the licences required to provide proper security and personal protection and because after many years working for someone else in an amazing and unique environment I needed a life of my own. With two failed marriages and hundreds of one-night-stands behind me, I found myself in the same situation as the person I was protecting: in a wonderful place but desperately lonely – and I didn't have the consolation of vast amounts of money!

Over the years, I earned enough money in celebrity protection to buy a nice place for cash somewhere warm. I met some great people, including many big names from the pop world and other celebrities, and I had some very good times. Although there were a few unfortunate minor incidents – which were all resolved very quickly – nothing major ever happened to my client on my watch. I still speak to him, and he often asks me to work for him again, perhaps as part of his management team rather than in a security role – I don't think he really sees me as his protector any more.

A life in celebrity protection can be a great life, but be warned: it can also be a lonely and difficult life. A life protecting a pop star can be amazing and luxurious, but it can also be exhausting and uncompromising, and a life protecting a drunk and drug user can be fraught and infuriating. But would I do it all again? Too fucking right!

BIOGRAPHY OF JOHN BADLY

John Badly can be found at his small villa on the Costa Blanca with a whisky bottle in one hand and a gorgeous girl half his age in the other. He occasionally has holidays to the USA to see his old client and friend.

14

Journey to Baghdad – 2004
Anonymous

I have a basic military paramedic background and was a member of 23 SAS regiment, a Territorial Army reserve unit, also known as Special Air Service (Reserve). There are three squadrons in 23 SAS: A squadron, based in Glasgow; B squadron, based in Leeds; and C squadron, based in Newcastle and Manchester. As I lived just outside Manchester, I was in C squadron.

Once I left 23 SAS, I got into close protection and did a few small contracts as a bodyguard in the UK and abroad, including Russia. When I wasn't working in close protection, I normally worked the doors. It helped pay the bills between operations, and door work gave me time off as and when I needed it. Being a member of 23 SAS and a qualified paramedic, I was privileged to be invited to many of the regiment's training courses and asked to instruct, which also required time off. That was the beauty of door work; I doubt any other job would have been so accommodating. I loved working in the protection industry. It is what I always wanted to do. It is a great industry.

Once the war in Iraq came to an end and investment and rebuilding programmes started, more and more bodyguards I knew applied and were accepted on security contracts protecting foreigners throughout the country. I heard stories of three- to six-month contracts paying upwards of £350 a day. A year or two of this would allow me to pay off my mortgage and be financially stable. I'd be able to buy the things I needed, pay off my car loan and give my girlfriend a few nice gifts. Plus, I would be doing a job I could previously only have dreamed about.

There will never be anywhere else quite like Iraq – there will simply never be any comparable opportunities for bodyguards anywhere else in the world. Iraq has brought the world of the bodyguard into the spotlight. There are thousands of bodyguards working in Iraq – if not tens of thousands – and almost every major foreign company with contracts in the country employs teams of security personnel to protect its employees and assets. I wanted to work within one of those teams.

I had heard that Control Risk Group (CRG) was one of the biggest and probably one of the best security companies operating in Iraq at that time. CRG is a truly international company with offices in almost every major country around the world. They didn't pay as much as some of the other companies, but their structure, equipment, facilities and logistical support seemed much better, and this was much more important to me than a few extra pounds in my weekly wage packet. It was my first real high-risk assignment, and I wanted the extra security of a well-established international company behind me.

I had a contact within the recruitment section at their head office in London, to whom I sent my CV. I had heard that CRG received hundreds of CVs each and every day, so I followed up my letter with a telephone call a week or so later. I was told that the company was not currently recruiting and to call back in a month. I persevered and called them a few more times over the following couple of months, until one Friday afternoon when they confirmed that they were recruiting again. I was told to attend a special recruitment day at a hotel near Victoria Station on the following Tuesday.

Living in Manchester, I made arrangements to stay with a friend on the outskirts of London on the Monday night so that I would be fresh for the interview on the Tuesday morning. I was allocated a one-hour spot, along with hundreds of other hopefuls. The interviews began at 8 a.m. and finished at 7 p.m., and there were about 50 applicants being seen each and every hour. After spending the first 45 minutes filling out application forms and listening to the company history and profile, I was ushered into a small office, where I was interviewed. Most of the applicants didn't get an interview – they were turned away just on the weakness of their application forms. One of the interviewers asked me a few questions about my background and experience, while the other listened and took notes. The interview only lasted about 15 minutes. I was told that I would be contacted within three days.

I think those were the slowest three days of my life. I waited beside my phone, praying that I'd been successful, but it didn't ring. On the fourth day, I called them and was told that I'd got the job and would shortly be going to Iraq. I was put on standby, which meant that I could be called at any time and given 24 hours' notice that I was leaving. I didn't know where to start to get everything organised. I was given a kit list, and I spent a day and a lot of money buying each and every item, but I soon realised once I got to Iraq that I would never need most of it.

My girlfriend and family were not at all happy. They didn't want me to go and tried their hardest to talk me out of it. But I needed the money, and it was what I wanted to do. No one could stop me.

The call finally came on the following Friday morning. I was told to be at the CRG offices in London the next day, at which time I would sign the contracts and complete the final paperwork before being taken by minibus to RAF Brize Norton in Oxfordshire, about 50 miles west of London. From Brize Norton, we would fly via Hercules to Cyprus, where we would stay overnight before flying on to Basra. Once in Basra, we would then make the brief flight to Baghdad International Airport, formerly known as Saddam International Airport. Apparently, Saddam had contracted the French to help build the airport, at a cost of over $900 million, which was never repaid.

Although each and every one of us was very nervous and scared, we were all in complete awe as we arrived in Baghdad. We were met by a team of veterans, each fully armed. We were given body armour and AK-47s and told that if a contact occurred on the route out from the airport, we should stick together and listen to the instructions.

The road from the airport into Baghdad is probably one of the most dangerous in the world. The route – sometimes referred to as 'Route Irish' – is almost eight miles long and links the airport to the Green Zone – the heavily guarded area of central Baghdad where the UK and US embassies and most foreigners are based. Passengers from the airport are ferried along the route in armoured buses called 'Rhino Runners', because they look a bit like big grey rhinoceroses. A great many bodyguards, journalists, businessmen and military personnel have lost their lives along this route, and I was praying I wouldn't lose mine on my first day in Iraq. Along with the rest of the team, I snapped madly at everything I saw with my new digital camera. It was surreal looking around me at the burned-out cars, bullet-ridden buildings and smoke swirling into the air – I had seen it on the news but had never imagined that one day I would be experiencing it for real.

Before we were allowed onto a team, every new recruit had to undertake an intensive assessment. This comprised driving skills, weapons handling and knowledge, and advanced first aid. You had to pass all three to be allowed onto a team, otherwise you would be sent straight home. This rule was not compromised, and many new recruits were sent home after the first or second day because they had failed one or more of the modules. The only exception was if you had a particular skill and excelled at two of the disciplines, in which case you might be allowed to fail the other, but this was rare. I passed all three and was accepted onto my first team. My wages were £280 per day, paid directly into my UK bank account, and I worked six weeks on with three weeks off.

Among its many contracts, CRG had been tasked to protect dignitaries from the Foreign and Commonwealth Office (FCO). Our job was to escort FCO personnel around Iraq, visiting schools, hospitals, government buildings, charities, organisations, etc. We almost always used three-car convoys.

When we were not working, we spent our time training and

practising our emergency drills so that every possible scenario we might encounter was covered. I enjoyed driving and was particularly good at it, so I was increasingly tasked to drive the principal vehicle. The good thing about CRG was that almost all of the vehicles they used were armoured, whereas many other security companies only had armoured vehicles for the client – the rest of the team had to put up with soft-skins.

We were soon to realise the importance of armoured vehicles when we had our first live contact about two weeks after I arrived. Our convoy came under fire as we were making our way back to the Green Zone. The client's vehicle, which I was driving, was targeted. A number of rounds went into the side of the vehicle. As the sound of the first shot hit the car, the client cowered on the floor while I slammed my foot down on the accelerator. A round had gone into the radiator, and we had to evacuate the vehicle about six kilometres further up the road, just before the temperature gauge went off the scale. We locked the bullet-ridden vehicle and evacuated the client into one of the convoy cars.

When we came back to retrieve the vehicle, it was evident that someone had tried to break the window – probably to steal the high-frequency radio – without any luck. It would have been easier for them to have broken the lock rather than to have tried to pickaxe the window.

I had been in Iraq for about eight months, and I knew the country as well as anyone, but still things changed dramatically and quickly, and we always had to be prepared for the unexpected. For this reason, all operations had to be meticulously coordinated and planned. Iraq is the bodyguard's dream job, but it can also be his or her last-ever assignment, and many have died in the field. The Iraqis learn very quickly and are getting more and more sophisticated. When I first went out, improvised explosive devices were easily spotted and generally very crude, but as time passed everything and anything was utilised. A good example of this was a dead dog by the side of the road. It had been there for a couple of days, but no one had taken any notice of it. However, one day a convoy passed it and it exploded. The Iraqis had gutted it one night and packed it full of explosives. Another time, a box that had been left at the side of the road for a few days was suddenly filled with explosives and detonated.

Tunnels were always a problem, as you never knew who or what was waiting for you at the other end. Whenever a convoy was just about to enter a tunnel, the local Iraqi vehicles behind would suddenly slow right down to leave as much distance as possible between themselves and the convoy – just in case.

CRG lost one of their bodyguards while I was out there. He wasn't on my team, but I knew him well. He was a team leader and was in a two-car convoy with the principal when his vehicle exploded. It had either gone over a landmine or someone had slipped an improvised explosive device under it at a junction. When it exploded, it threw the team leader through the front window. He lay dead on the ground with the left side of his face, his left arm and shoulders on fire. The rear vehicle pulled alongside to evacuate the principal. When the second in command looked into the rear of the exploded car, he saw the principal engulfed in flames, waving his arms frantically and screaming. The second in command didn't know whether he should put him out of his misery with a single bullet to the head, but the principal soon stopped screaming and died. There was nothing left of the driver apart from a piece of leg and a bit of torso.

Texts and emails relating to the incident flew around the British bodyguard community. Some new recruits waiting in Jordan for their onward flight to Iraq turned around and went home and others who had been planning to come over never left the UK. Most of us were in Iraq for the money, but many of us had families, children, girlfriends and wives, and many people realised that the job simply wasn't worth it.

Most bodyguards working for CRG now arrive on scheduled flights via Jordan. Iraqi Airways and Royal Jordanian Airways were two of the first airlines to operate regular international flights, and it was quite surreal sitting on a flight going into Baghdad and being served sandwiches and coffee by a pretty flight attendant. The 'hosties' were also in Iraq for the money. It is said that they earn hundreds of pounds per flight.

Take-off and landing from Baghdad is not for the faint-hearted.

Flights use a 'corkscrew manoeuvre' to avoid coming into the range of small-arms fire and ground missiles, forcing you to hold on to your seat and hope for the best. The take-off is quick and the climb steep and dramatic – the objective is to get as high as possible as quickly as possible, and the reverse is true for landing, except it is even scarier.

I have since been offered contracts with other security companies, but from my experience CRG is still one of the best. They charge a lot to their clients, but the equipment they supply is excellent. CRG's employees stay alive because of the money the company spends – many teams in non-armoured vehicles are dead now because a company refused to invest. Some bodyguard companies seem to lose more personnel than others, and the American companies seem to lose more than most. Blackwater, probably one of the biggest employers of bodyguards in Iraq, seem to lose personnel every week. It was even rumoured that one of their teams was found hanging from a bridge. Custer Battles – or 'Cluster Fucks' as they were nicknamed by the security community in Iraq – was another US firm that seemed to lose many of its personnel.

Contracts are ongoing and continuous until you resign. You are staggered with your team – on and off at the same time; rest and recreation at the same time – so you really form a close working relationship with your colleagues. Some companies don't do this. They chop and change teams, and you never know who you might be working with from one contract to another, but CRG do their best to keep you in the same teams until your resignation.

After one more tour, I will have enough to pay my mortgage off and will come back to the UK and to my girlfriend and look for another job. The trouble is: what is there to do after the excitement of Iraq?

15

WORKING AT WIMBLEDON – WHAT A FARCE!
ANONYMOUS

A pair of bright eyes beneath an ill-fitting, wide-brimmed cap poked sheepishly out of a frosted-glass door. Autograph hunters of all ages and nationalities began to gather outside the door, situated beneath the walkway to the new Millennium Building, which replaced the old No. 1 Court and was officially opened by the Duke of Kent. The rumour of a big name's imminent appearance was being eagerly passed around. Suddenly, the door burst open, and a stream of blue-and-yellow uniforms with a streak of white in their midst poured through. The lady in white was Maria Sharapova, who immediately set off a strobe effect of camera flashes, a surge from the crowd and an eruption of ecstatic cheering as the uniformed group barged their way through the throng and out to the main concourse. With the walkways between courts at Wimbledon being barely wide enough for single file, there were another two or three claustrophobic encounters

197

with the excitable fans before the group finally made it to the assigned drop zone at Court 13.

Once Sharapova's feet had touched the turf, the uniformed guards disappeared, fading into the background. They were scheduled to return to pick her up an hour later. In the meantime, you might have expected that they would keep a watchful eye on the crowd, attempting to identify potential threats to their charge. Not likely; instead, they sloped off to watch the tennis, sleep off the heavy night before or go hunting for food in the hospitality tents. If they remembered to get in position when Sharapova was ready to leave, she could count herself lucky.

When the threat to the biggest tennis stars (particularly female) was never so great, the protection that they could expect at the sport's premier tournament was provided by lazy, opportunistic and untrained students looking to earn some pocket money during the summer. I know, because for two years I was one of them.

While I worked at Wimbledon, a security company was contracted with ensuring the highlight of the tennis calendar passed off safely. Along with the more typical responsibilities associated with a sporting event, including ensuring spectators got in and out of the complex as quickly and safely as possible, the company was charged with providing security for the players on their journeys between changing room and court. That meant that the positions filled by the company ranged from bag searchers and security guards to the job that I did: player escort.

Efficient and intelligent application of human resources should have made the staffing of these diverse roles a fairly straightforward task. Anyone with a brain and bit of training can perform basic crowd control or keep an eye open for sharp objects in picnic hampers. However, when it came to the protection of the players as they made their way around the complex, you might have thought that more would have been asked of the guards, especially in a job that required 'access all areas' security clearance, and that security professionals with bodyguard training would have been brought in to manage the potentially dangerous interface between the stars and their fans. You would have been wrong.

The shocking truth was that the recruitment process for these highly sensitive positions was arbitrary, unvetted and completely open to abuse. Amid an unprecedented climate of fear of terrorist attack, coupled with the ever-present danger of stalkers, people wandered in off the street and were given jobs – jobs that granted unfettered access to some of the biggest names in sport. My story is neither exceptional nor exaggerated.

Having applied for the job of security guard through a website, I received a tip-off from a friend who had worked at The Championships before. He claimed that if I followed up my application with a phone call stating that I was taller than six foot, I would be considered to join the player escort team. I was dubious, but given the stories I had heard about guards spending two weeks minding fire extinguishers or endlessly burrowing through hampers I made the call. It worked like a charm. On the first of our two induction days, both my friend and I were immediately informed that we had been selected to be player escorts.

Although I was pleased, I was slightly apprehensive about the prospect of extra training and perhaps having to go through a short course in the technicalities of guarding. I needn't have worried. The only consequence of my new status was to be in a group that undertook the same generic training as all the other guards – a tour of the grounds, a lecture in basic customer satisfaction, and a pep talk on discipline and presentation by the self-appointed ringmaster of this 'circus'.

So, with my references unchecked, completely bereft of experience and having just set foot on the Wimbledon turf for the very first time, I landed one of the top guarding jobs in the business solely on my physical appearance: six feet four and sixteen stone. The way in which I had eased my way from student to sentry came as a rather worrying surprise.

Fortunately, on the first day on the job, my fears were put at ease. 'Remember, you are only getting £7 an hour for this. If someone comes at you with something nasty, then get out of the fucking way!' The instructions from one of our managers left no room for interpretation. Having reputedly come by the job (also with no experience) after meeting one of the senior managers in a notorious Sunday drinking hole, he was neither willing nor able to offer any further guidance. Although I could see his point, this advice to abandon ship at the first sight of trouble was yet another twist to an already bizarre story. It was becoming clear that the job we were being asked to perform was purely role play. It was an act. With an access-all-areas pass and a lot of time on our hands, it was not long before the actors turned to clowns.

During the two years I worked as a player escort, there were countless incidents of incompetence, negligence and wilful disregard for the risks to players that we were supposed to eliminate. Having been informed by managers that we were a sham, and in many cases proving to be nothing more than a hindrance to the minor players who could otherwise move around without attracting attention, it was inevitable that liberties would be taken. First, there was the almost constant attempt to forage for food. The media centre was usually the place to begin in the mornings. A plentiful supply of coffee and croissants on the roof terrace made it an excellent alternative to the staff canteen. Sue Barker, John Inverdale and Alistair McGowan would routinely share our choice of venue, once more highlighting the limitless possibilities for a huge security incident that our all-area passes had given us.

Once play began, we would return to the escorts' base, conveniently situated next to the female seeds' changing room, to receive our list of jobs for the day. For me and my star-struck colleagues, the most important issue to be resolved at this stage was who would get the big-ticket escorts. Who would be accompanying the matches most likely to get us on TV or our face in the paper? Offers such as 'I'll swap you a Davenport for an Agassi' could regularly be heard deep in the bowels of the players' area. Occasionally, our boss would have an input, insisting on the 'big meat' being used to escort Anna Kournikova, who caused our only problems when she began to progress in both doubles competitions. This success resulted in regular visits to the outer courts through large excitable crowds. Unsurprisingly, there were no shortage of takers for this assignment, resulting in a chaotic scene of six or seven burly students trying to

200

march a rather frightened young woman through throngs of people whilst paying most attention to trying to get noticed by nearby TV cameras. Jonas Björkman, her partner, would trot unaccompanied behind in tranquil amusement.

The other most interesting escorts were those of the Williams sisters, Venus and Serena. Serena was the only player to have her own permanent bodyguard, Darios, and it did not take a genius to work out what this ex-boxer from Brooklyn made of the spotty students charged with assisting him. 'Amateurs!' he raged after one escort back from a practice session had taken the Wimbledon champion on a five-minute detour of the hospitality tents. 'Anything could have happened out there! If you guys don't get the next one straight, then I might have to give you some training of my own!' No one was under any illusions that this would be an hour's study of the map of the complex.

Venus, on the other hand, was more than happy to let the escorts take care of her safety, and on one occasion she appeared in our waiting room and said, 'So, which one of y'all is going to take me and my mom shopping?' I was lucky enough to be conscious and uniformed at the right time and took on the task with another couple of eager opportunists. Sadly, the expedition was not as glamorous as we first imagined. In fact, the former champion just wanted to make an unscheduled visit to the Wimbledon shop, a ridiculous idea in itself, but made all the more farcical by three uniformed bumblers trying to force a path through what is one of the busiest spots on site at the best of times. Whilst Venus and her mum shopped for videos of herself (I kid you not), the shop eventually had to be shut to prevent a crush incident that a riot squad of fully trained personnel would have failed to control. The whole episode could so easily have ended in disaster.

It was not only the players who suffered as a result of our play-acting. All-areas pass aside, it is surprising what an unsuspecting public will let you get away with if you are wearing a uniform, walkie-talkie and earpiece. In teams of two, we would frequently amuse ourselves by heading down to the morning queue to pull people out and 'scan' them with our walkie-talkies. (We'd remove the aerial to make the device look more like a magnetic scanner.) Pushing the button to make the handset beep at unlikely places around the body, the challenge was to see what state of undress or distress you could get the unfortunate punter into before they cried foul.

Another classic ruse was to play out the *Trigger Happy TV* sketch by sending one guard over towards a distinctively dressed member of the public with his radio on full volume. The second guard would then put out a call over the escort signal to apprehend someone for beating up old ladies on the North Concourse, for example, describing the offender standing next to the first guard. Meanwhile, the poor victim would be listening in on the transmission in confused horror. In one case, an escort who was not in on the joke replied with a transmission saying that he had the described felon in his view. A cruel but inevitable reply to 'take him down and ask questions later' resulted in an ill-fated attempt at a citizen's arrest and the end of one escort's summer of fun.

These moments of crisis and amusement, along with witnessing such things as Richard Krajicek smashing up three rackets in succession in the tunnel and Elena Dementieva in a towel, helped hold off the urge to simply sleep off the night before. When play was suspended, there was time to gloat at the court coverers, whom we often competed with for the title of easiest job in Wimbledon. Meanwhile, the real scandals took place in the little nooks and crannies around the complex. I knew of at least one incident of escorts having sex in the No. 1 Court players' waiting room, and it became standard practice for escorts to use their all-areas privileges to dupe guards into letting mates in for free through the less well signposted gates. I could go on.

For any security professional, there is nothing worse than seeing your work undertaken by amateurs. Not only does the employment of underqualified people reduce the number of positions available for those fit for the job, but when those without adequate training or experience take up roles they are unprepared for there will inevitably be a devaluation of the profession as a whole. This is what made the situation at Wimbledon even more tragic.

Despite all of the above being revealed to managers over a pint every evening, I was offered the job of escort team manager a year later. This fact alone suggested that policies and practices were unlikely to change any time soon, making the All England Championship a high-profile accident waiting to happen. However, the introduction of SIA licensing meant that within a couple of years the approach to security at Wimbledon was completely revamped and thoroughly professionalised. Just as well, really.

16

WHAT THE BLOODY HELL AM I DOING HERE?
BY DAMIEN BUCKWELL

How many times had I asked myself the question, 'What the bloody hell am I doing here?' God only knows. These days, however, I don't need to ask that question as much as I used to. Going from operations to administration and then into training over a 12-year period means that I now have something of a luxury ride. Monday-to-Friday hours, holidays with the kids and only the occasional weekend interruption when courses are on or we are undertaking professional development with our trainers, clients, etc.

My venture into the world of security and close personal protection has been an eventful one – nothing spectacular or heroic, but a steep learning curve nonetheless. And my experience in a multitude of security activities over 12 years has led me to where I am today. I give lectures, write training materials, design e-learning content and undertake a whole host of educational tasks related to delivering training for the purposes of being issued a security licence in New South Wales, Australia.

Twelve years ago, you probably wouldn't have bet two bob on me making it through in one piece, let alone getting to where I am today. Well, I am here to tell you that you should have bet the farm on me – you'd be filthy fucking rich by now!

It all started in 1995. I had just finished a stint working as a pathology courier, driving around to doctors' surgeries, picking up pathology materials and taking them back to the labs. On the return trip, I would drop off the results. Anyway, long story short, shit happened, and I took my then employer to court for allowing me to be potentially exposed to pathogens. The union was as weak as piss and didn't defend me, even though I had photographic evidence. I went on stress leave and eventually left the job, and the missus and I ended up moving from the sunny northern beaches of Sydney to a place two hours north on a lake. It was a beautiful spot, but there was one big problem: I had no fucking job. Great!

I applied for roughly 300 jobs of varying types: delivery driver, office clerk, sales rep – hell, I even applied to sell bloody cars! No takers what so bloody ever. Not a single call back. The arseholes didn't understand common decency.

By that point, I was pretty much all at sea, and I decided to try an advert for security-officer training. If only I had known then what I know now. I rocked up keen as mustard, ready to be the best I could be – sound familiar, anyone? – but I was dismayed to find that I had to fill out reams of paperwork over the course of two days and then sit an exam. Struth, I had been charged up to throw people around and be all Starsky and Hutch on a brother's ass, but instead I found that I had to do schoolwork. I mumbled under my breath as I found a seat near to someone whom I considered to have equivalent bodily hygiene and prepared myself to be dazzled by the lecturer's renditions of cop-type stories.

It turned out that the lecturers were in fact actual cops, from the robbery squad of all places, moonlighting at the weekends as instructors. It also became apparent that it was an open-book exam in which you could check the answers. If you could read, you would pass, so to speak – unless you were a complete stargazer!

After passing the exam, I was given a serious-looking certificate that I took to the cop shop, where I filled out some more forms, and, *voilà*, I was licensed to work. I had a choice of licensed categories I could apply for: static guard, armed guard, bodyguard or bouncer. I figured what the hell and ticked all the boxes. And that was that. I was licensed after just two days' textbook training. I had no practical instruction and no experience, yet I could legally offer my services to provide the licensed activities listed above! Luckily for me (and for the rest of the free world), I wasn't satisfied with just two days' theory and began a quest to find mentors in the business to teach me how the job should really be done.

My search wasn't always successful. Being something of a rabbit caught in headlights, I was taken for a ride by some bastards, but overall I met and learned from some very switched-on people, many of whom I am honoured to have known, let alone worked with.

At one point, it got to the stage that I had six different uniforms in my car, and I seemed to be continuously wearing a duty belt (fully equipped with holsters, handcuffs and all the 'works and jerks'), a firearm, dark blue pants, black shoes and a T-shirt. I'd get a phone call and be told what uniform to put on, and off I'd go into the blue yonder. Seven days a week, twenty-four hours a day, day in, day out. I loved it. I was doing everything a boy could wish for: working with 'stars', doing all sorts of covert stuff, getting mentored by the best of the best and loving it. However, there were many occasions when I thought I was centre stage in a Frank Spencer show but still managed to walk away as the 'hero'.

I remember my first cash-in-transit job. It was a typical day. I was at my boss's house, all tarted up but with no place to go, when another guard dropped round. We started to have a chinwag, as you do, when lo and behold the phone rang. It was a job: two armed guards were required to transport a consignment of cash from a vault in one bank to another vault in another bank. It sounded simple enough. So, after taking no notes during the briefing, my newly acquired buddy and I jumped into his car and made our way to the job, which was about 40 minutes' drive away.

As we were driving along, we got into some serious chinwagging, and it turned out that we shared the same birthday and had similar hobbies. (He was a pom, but I didn't hold that against him.) Anyway, while we were gasbagging away, both of us forgot what we had been told in the briefing – neither of us could remember the name of the bank we were supposed to go to. The only thing I could remember was the letter of the alphabet that the name of the bank started with. So, when we arrived in the town, we went to the first bank we saw that started with that letter.

Let me set the scene for you: it was 5.45 p.m. on a Friday afternoon, and the bank was closed but the staff were still on site. We knocked on the door. We were dressed in full uniform, complete with ID and guns, looking a million dollars. A member of the staff asked if they could help us, and we responded by saying that we were there for the 'job'. The woman looked at us in a puzzled fashion and then said, 'Come in and we'll sort this out.' The bank was an old one with no screened counters, and the vault was open. There was money as far as the eye could see. The woman told us to wait and went off to speak to someone. When she returned, she told us that no one knew anything about our job. 'It's all right, love,' I said. 'I'll call the boss and see who stuffed up.' We were then escorted out of the front door and back onto the footpath, where I got on my mobile and rang my boss.

'Boss, we are here at Bank X, and they reckon they know nothing about our job.'

'No fucking wonder, brainiac. You're at the wrong fucking bank.'

I experienced a sudden constriction of my bowel muscles as I anticipated my boss jumping out of my phone and kicking me in the arse. An abrupt disconnection awoke me from my stupor, and we both hurried to the correct bank to start the real job, which was now behind schedule by 45 minutes after we had dicked around in the wrong location to begin with. It could only get better, right? Wrong.

We arrived at the correct bank this time and walked into a branch that was obviously moving, given the boxes and packing material lying around. A very attractive young lady (or so I thought) was on the other side of the counter, folding perforated cardboard packing boxes into shape. 'I see you have spent time working at McDonald's,'

I said, trying to be all that. It was then that I noticed her lapel badge: 'Branch Manager'. Aw shit, not again. How many more screw-ups could I make? Plenty, as it turned out.

The branch manager gave me a stern look and said, 'Where's the strongbox?'

'And what strongbox is that?' I replied.

'The one you are going to use to carry the contents of our safe up the street to the other bank?'

'Oh, that strongbox.' Nobody had told me anything about a fucking strongbox. 'We'll simply use one of your McDonald's folding boxes,' I said, suddenly realising what was coming out of my mouth.

'OK,' she replied.

The safe was then opened and its contents piled into a box. Anyone who tells you money isn't heavy is a liar. About $400,000 in cash, cheques and other valuables was to be transferred, and we got ready to walk to the other bank, which was about 800 metres up the street.

'How are we going to do this?' the manager asked.

'Well, we'll go first, and you can follow at a safe distance.'

'OK.'

I looked at my partner, and his face told me that he had never done this before either! As we walked out of the front door of the bank, some space opened up between us and the manager, and I said to my mate, 'If anyone comes within 20 metres, give 'em the stare. If they come within ten metres, rest your hand on the butt of your firearm and give 'em the stare. If, after all that, they are still coming towards us on a mission, shoot the fuckers.'

He agreed that my suggestion sounded reasonable, and we continued on our way. As luck would have it, we arrived at the other branch without any issues whatsoever and surrendered the box to the new safe for storage. Job completed, we both exited stage left and returned to the car. The ride home was somewhat quieter than the ride up. Eventually, we both looked at each other and burst out laughing.

As a footnote to that tragedy, the branch manager actually rang my boss and raved on about how cool, calm and collected we were and that we'd done the most professional job she had ever witnessed from security guards. If only she knew.

My next big adventure brought me into contact with the dizzy heights of stardom and arguably the biggest celebrity of them all: Tom Cruise. It was during the filming of *Mission: Impossible II* in Sydney that I had one of the funniest cock-ups of my career, although it actually turned out brilliantly. In fact, there were several cock-ups, and not all of them turned out too brilliantly, come to think of it.

I received a call from a guy I knew who told me to get my sorry ass down to Sydney for some high-paying work doing crowd control on a movie set. I grabbed another mate, and we ended up working on the periphery of a shoot in The Rocks precinct of the city.

During the filming, Tom and Nicole were apparently splitting up or something, but don't quote me on that – I ain't a columnist. Anyway, word came down that no paparazzi were allowed anywhere near the shoot. My mate and I were at our assigned posts when we heard the head bodyguard screaming on the radio about a 'pap' photographer with a telephoto lens, taking shots from the hill just above us. The guard assigned to that location said that there was nothing he could do, as it was public space. The head bodyguard was seething. We decided to head up and see what was happening. My mate was tall – about six feet seven inches or more – and when we arrived on the spot he walked in front, around and underneath the camera to block the photographer's view – it was hilarious. The photographer sure as shit pissed his pants, because he took off at a great rate of knots. Victory was ours.

Shortly after that, the bosses started to migrate towards us to see who we were and what our story was. We then started to get the cushier jobs and better hours, including overtime rates, because it was obvious that we could do the job effectively and legally. This was uppermost in the film people's minds, what with the publicity and all.

My first fuck-up happened out the front of a government building they were filming in. They had a movie prop in the form of a sculpture out in front. It was fenced off, and my job was to look after it. One morning, a police security officer from the government building came wandering down to have a look at the sculpture. 'Excuse me, officer,' I said. 'I can't allow you past this point.'

'You what?' she growled.

'I am sorry, but I cannot allow you past this point,' I replied. I have never seen such a shade of purple and red before, and the steam coming out of her ears was breathtaking.

'Do you know who I am?' she screamed.

'Yes. It says on your badge that you are a police security officer,' I replied without emotion.

Out of nowhere, the set manager arrived. 'What seems to be the problem here?' she asked sweetly. I was lucky she'd shown up, because in another second I reckon the police security officer would have probably shot me or eaten me whole.

'I am sorry,' the set manager cooed, 'but he is following very strict instructions.' The police security officer mumbled something or other under her breath as she wandered off, escorted by the set manager to the café cart that had just appeared. This thing was a fucking cake shop on a trolley with everything you could wish for. But we weren't allowed to touch it, as security was not catered for.

Later that night, the feeling of us versus them (us being security and them being the 'filmies', the people wearing tool bags and carrying gaffer tape, running around madly making Hollywood happen) was broken down a little. A filmie was struggling to push a trolley full of stuff up a steep street, and I saw him and gave him a hand. Apparently, up until that point the guards hadn't lifted a finger to help, so this guy was very grateful, and he introduced me to the people I needed to know. As a result, I soon got to know who was who as far as the filmies went. In terms of food, water, coffee, toilets, etc., I went straight to the head of each queue and got permission for security to have access rights to catering and the like. In exchange, we made arrangements for lines of communication to be set up to assist the caterers and the other site suppliers with access issues and deliveries. I had gone from a guard standing next to a generator five miles from the action to a 'get things done' guy who knew all the right people. However, I still got rotated through shitty locations and posts, mainly because none of the others could do the job properly, and the job still had to be done.

One night, I was standing at a shitty position doing access control. It was cold, exposed and I had been dealing all day with bloody tourists with cameras asking, 'Where Tom Clooooze?' I was tired and feeling a tad flat. Out of the blue, the head bodyguard came down and said to me, 'Tom is driving himself to the set and will be coming through here shortly. Don't cause him any grief. Just let him through without any fuss or hoo-ha. Understand?'

'Righto. No problem,' I said.

One of the filmies came rushing past with his ID badge out, and I gave him a wave. A bit later, a couple of lost tourists asked me what was going on, and I told them to move over the road to the viewing area. Then, another filmie came past, so I gave him a wave, too. I then noticed a guy at the bottom of the hill walking towards me. He was wearing a baseball cap, which was partially covering his face. Alarm bells started going off in my head, because he was exhibiting signs of being some dodgy bastard out to knock something off or steal anything not nailed down. To make matters worse, he was sticking to the shadows. Taking into consideration my earlier briefing, perhaps it wasn't a surprise that I saw a dodgy bastard – not a megastar trying to be low key.

The dodgy-looking bloke finally made it up to the checkpoint and tried to come past. I asked him where he thought he was going, and he told me that he was going onto the film set. I moved in front of him. 'Excuse me, sir. Do you have your Photo ID handy?' I asked.

'They didn't give me one,' he replied.

People will try anything to get into a movie set, so I wasn't buying this guy's story for a second. 'Well, mate, you'll have to move over there to the visitors' viewing gallery. Thanks.' I pointed in the direction of the viewing gallery and was just about to say, 'What part of "fuck off over there" don't you understand?' when the guy tilted his face a little, allowing the light to shine on it. Fuck me. It was Tom Cruise, mega fucking star, known the world over, and I was giving him fucking attitude because he didn't have a photo ID badge. In my defence, he was considerably shorter in the flesh than his publicity photos suggested.

About 20 minutes later, the head bodyguard came down to my position. 'Was it you?' he asked. Considering I was the only fucker at the post, I couldn't lie. 'Um, yes, it was.' I had visions of receiving my DTUM (don't turn up Monday) notice. But the head bodyguard was pissing himself laughing. I presumed he was some sort of sadistic prick, getting his kicks from sacking me. 'What's so funny?' I asked.

'Well, Tom appreciates the fact that with almost 50 grand a day being spent on this film, security is so tight that even he can't get in without photo ID.' I was waiting for the punchline, but it didn't seem to be coming. 'We'll talk some more tomorrow, but well done.' Say What? Well done? It turned out that Tom was happy not to be recognised and had a chuckle over it.

That incident meant that I went from doing menial jobs to being responsible for coordinating set lockdowns during filming. I would rush around with two headsets on separate channels and another mike pinned to the lapel of my jacket on another channel. The two headsets were tuned to security and the filmies, and the lapel one was for my 'response squad', which would deal with shit if and when it happened. This position gave me the opportunity to talk to the crew, including John Woo, the director of the movie, and I loved every minute of it. At the same time, I always ensured that the guards got fed, rotated and looked after as best as could be expected on such a job. The hours were long, and you were on your feet all day. It could be very boring, but you still had to do your job.

I got some offers of further movie work at the end of the filming, which I was very grateful for, but I declined because of the distance I would need to travel. Nonetheless, I did have fun on that movie set!

Not every job I did was like a scene out of the *Keystone Cops*, and one in particular will stay with me for the rest of my life. I was sitting in my boss's office one day when a call came in requesting two armed guards as soon as possible. It wasn't often that we were told to expedite our arrival at a site, but this was no ordinary job. My boss and I responded to the call and made our way over to the Department of Community Services building. Upon arrival, we were greeted by people who looked very relieved to see us. As we sat down for a briefing, a senior police officer arrived with a folder. What I was about to become involved in would change my whole outlook on life.

The police officer asked us about our firearms and what our status was. I had a Smith and Wesson 9 mm semi-automatic handgun, which held sixteen rounds, and two spare clips, which held fifteen rounds each. It was a beautiful piece of equipment. My boss was old fashioned in his tastes: his was a Smith and Wesson .357 Magnum with two spare speed-loaders. I had seen him empty that beast faster than a guy with a Glock semi-automatic and have good grouping at distance. The policeman expressed satisfaction with the equipment and our abilities – we were both members of a pistol club and practised after work on mock buildings with man targets and training rounds. It was the best we could do, given the lack of access to more sophisticated facilities as civilians. I'd always figured that if I was going to carry a gun, I had better be damn sure I knew what, when, how and why . . . and then some. I'd trained with blockages until I knew the motions like clockwork, improved my draw motions and learned the value of maintenance. I was confident and knew that I could face a situation and rely on muscle memory as a natural reflex. I'd grown up with my dad's old .22 bolt-action rifle and knew what constituted responsible behaviour around firearms, so I guess this was just further training with a different type of tool.

The police officer then told us the reason for our attendance. In a nutshell, a guy with a drug habit who lived with his missus and three kiddies had run up a lot of bad debts, and no one would sell to him. His particular choice of slow death was amphetamines, more commonly known as 'speed'. He'd told his missus to go out and get some for him, but she'd said no, so the gutless freak had poured lawnmower fuel over the three kiddies and threatened to set them on fire unless she did what he'd told her. Somehow, calm had been restored, and the kiddies had survived. It was at that point that Community Services had got involved, rescuing the kids and sending them to a safe house. The gutless freak had then rung up the Community Services office and told them he was going to kill everyone in the office. That's when we'd been called.

The policeman continued with the briefing by informing us of the following:

1. Of all the local nutters, scumbags and criminal trash, this guy would actually carry out his threats and possibly take hostages.

2. He was making serious attempts to get his hands on firearms.

3. Given his drug addiction and increased paranoia, he would not back down should a confrontation involving 'use of force' arise.

4. He had a large knife and machete collection.

The policeman then added that if this psycho entered the premises and had any objects in his hand we were to 'aim for centre body mass'.

'What the bloody hell am I doing here?' I thought. 'Fuck, I knew I should have done the lunch run.'

We spent several weeks playing cat and mouse with this freak, and we ended up having to get vests, as he'd apparently acquired a shotgun and bragged about it to someone who'd spilled to the police, who then told us. The situation was becoming more dangerous, but complacency was starting to set in with the office staff we were protecting. They would congregate in the car park in full view, making them easy targets. One day, I lost my patience with one group who were having a laugh and completely forgetting what was going on. I asked them several times to move into the safety of the building, but they didn't pay any attention to me. I was getting pissed off, as I didn't want them to be exposed like this, given what I knew. In the end, I politely advised them that I wasn't wearing a bulletproof vest as a fashion accessory but because a nasty man was threatening to kill them all. As much as it may have been harsh, I achieved what I needed: them out of the line of fire.

After approximately six weeks, we had a meeting to discuss whether we should stand down, as nothing had happened and the enormous cost of having us there was impacting on the department's budget. This meeting took place on a Wednesday night. It was decided on the Thursday morning that we would stand down on the Friday night and simply be on call if required. On Thursday afternoon at about 5.45 p.m., freak boy was arrested five blocks from the site. He had consumed numerous grams of speed, armed himself with countless knives and was on his way to the office to carry out his threat of killing all the community workers. Two things led to his arrest. One of his friends had seen us at the office, kitted up and looking the biz. When he'd asked someone about us, he'd been told that we were under orders to 'shoot to kill' and we had laser sights and stun grenades – pure shit, really. The friend then went back to freak boy and told him all this bullshit in front of freak boy's mother. When freak boy tooled up and headed for the office, his mother rang the cops, because she figured that we would kill him outright, based on the bullshit she'd heard from the friend.

It took five police officers to take him down and restrain him. When they got him back to the police station, he raved like Charles Manson about how he was going to do this and that. He ended up doing time and getting his comeuppance in jail for the drug debts and for what he had done to his kiddies. Scumbag.

I have one final story to put another grin on your dial. I once did a close protection job for a gay businessman who owned a nightclub and had lots of money. Now, I don't really care which side of the bed your slippers are on – just don't think you can put them on mine. Only Mrs Buckwell gets to shag me, lucky thing, or maybe some nymphet who has come backstage for autographs. However, each to their own is my point of view.

My brief was simple: if he picked someone up, I was to go back to the hotel (I had a separate room!) and make sure his wallet wasn't rolled. Anyway, we were in a nightclub, and there was very little smoke around, as most gay people are health freaks of some kind. My client decided that he was going to light up his pipe. The stuff stank – and I smoke! He was in the middle of the dance floor, trying to be a 20-something in a 50-something body, and started puffing out his rancid pipe stench everywhere. I knew it wasn't going to be a pretty ending, and sure enough a massive cross-dresser walked up and knocked the pipe flying. The client grabbed me and said, 'What are you going to do about that?' He stank of alcohol and tobacco.

'We're leaving,' I said.

'Why?'

'Because you've made a lot of people unhappy, and there is only one of me.'

With that, he sheepishly walked outside, hailed a cab and handed me a wad of notes. 'I won't need you any further tonight. I am going home to grow up.' His cab took off, and I never saw him again. I reckon I spent at least the following 20 minutes pissing myself laughing.

BIOGRAPHY OF DAMIEN BUCKWELL

Damien Buckwell, based in New South Wales, Australia, has been in the security industry more years than he cares to remember. He has been a part of the Intercept team since mid 2004, providing a complete range of training services for the security industry. He is currently studying for a Bachelor of Arts in security, terrorism and counter-terrorism. Contrary to what he has led you to believe, he really does like the English and sings 'God Save the Queen' every night before going to bed.

You can contact Damien via www.intercepttraining.com

17

DOING THE DOORS –
A GENTLEMAN'S GAME
BY SANDY SANDERSON

I started working the doors back in the 1980s when I was a crane driver by day. One evening, my wife said to me, 'Why don't you take up a hobby?' Around the same time, a doorman job was advertised in the *Lowestoft Journal*. I had some fighting experience – I'd boxed for my school and then for the Isle of Wight, where I grew up – so I popped along for an interview for the position. I got the job. Karen Shaw, who owned Snaps nightclub in Lowestoft, said I was to start that Friday evening. I was thirty years of age, about ten stone and had never worked the doors before. When I went to the club on the Friday night, the other doormen looked down on me. I will never forget that first night; they all looked down on me because I was small.

The first and second weeks went by without incident. There were no problems, but I felt a bit humiliated, as none of the other doormen spoke to me – not one. Then, during the third week, there was an incident at the bar. I don't really know what happened, but one lad in a group of three threw a pint mug against the wall. I went racing in and got him outside onto the Lowestoft seafront. We got the other lads out, too, but one of them then punched the door, causing the glass to cave in. I kicked the door open and went back out. I punched one of the lads – he went down. I hit the second lad – he went down, too. And the third one ran away, which I was glad about. An ambulance then came and took one of the lads away. And that was the end of that; in those days, the police didn't really get involved. They didn't want to know.

The next day, Karen Shaw said that she needed to speak to me urgently. 'Here we go,' I thought. 'I'm getting the sack.' But I was really desperate for the money. I was only getting £7.50 a night, but I had just got married and had a small child. Times were hard, but instead of getting the sack I got a pay rise! She said I had done a great job, and from that day onward I got a little more respect from the other doormen. Word quickly went round that I knew how to handle myself, and I was left alone. I stayed on that door for about a year and was then offered a job as a crane driver in Angola, which I accepted.

I stayed in Angola for two years. It was interesting, but at that time there was a war going on. We'd fly into Kinshasa and from there across to Kabinda, a province of Angola where groups would often kidnap foreigners for money and goods. From Kabinda, we would then follow the coastline down to Luanda in Zaire. We stuck to the coast because of the high risk of getting shot at – not by the army firing at Western civilians not involved in the conflict, but by some lunatic seeing a helicopter and deciding to shoot at it. It happened all the time.

I saw and witnessed some good things in Angola, but I also witnessed some really terrible things. Many of the crew members on the rigs were very prejudiced against black people. We had an incident when a Kelly hose – a large-diameter high-pressure flexible line used to connect the standpipe to the swivel – came off the crane and hit one of the Angolan boys. His injuries were quite severe, but the Americans who managed the rig would not have him flown to hospital on *their* helicopter. They made him go on the boat. His ribs had pierced his lungs, and the boat was bashing about on the waves. By the time he got ashore, he was dead. As compensation, his wife got a food parcel every month. That was how it was. Life was very cheap in Angola.

On another occasion, I gave an Angolan some cigarettes for two small black ivory statues. Unbeknown to me, you were not allowed to take them out of the country, because the Angolans thought that Westerners laughed at these effigies. We didn't laugh at them, of course; we saw them as works of art. But the Angolans had some very strange beliefs. When I got to the airport for my flight home, the statues were taken off me, mainly because they thought I was American, and they didn't much like the Americans. In fact, no one out there much liked the Americans. (At that time, the Soviet Union was arming one side of the conflict and America the other.) I was pushed along the corridors of the airport by armed soldiers. Most of the soldiers had their weapons loaded with the safety catches off, which I wasn't too happy about, but when they realised I was English and not American I was released. I never got the statues back, though.

The choppers we used out there had originally come over from the Vietnam War, as had a lot of the pilots who worked for us. It was the early 1980s, and it wasn't really that long since the Vietnam War had ended. The pilots were really nice people but shot to pieces and really off their heads. They used to do crazy stunts with their choppers when we were in them, but we were young and foolish and thought it was a laugh.

On one occasion when we were due to return to the UK, we took a chopper from the rig and landed in Luanda. We were then going to take a small twin-engine Otter plane – apparently one of the safest we had – from Luanda to the capital Kinshasa for the scheduled flight to Belgium and then home. When we were in Luanda, we waited in a bar, and I got chatting to three Dutch mercenaries – they were man-mountains. I had a couple of beers with them, and they were really nice guys but completely off their heads.

Very often when we had a crew change, half of the Angolans wouldn't turn up, because the army trucks had come round to their village and had taken most of the young men to fight at the front. These Angolan crew members were used to being on the rigs, where they were fed steaks, eggs, orange juice, and all of a sudden they were put on the front line with no food, no uniform and no life. Some of them would run away from the army and walk through the jungle back to the rig. It was incredible to see them turn up for work, a week or so late.

After two years in Angola, I returned to the UK. I was still doing the doors and went to work at a big hotel. There was a very successful nightclub attached to the hotel. It was a good place to work, because the people were nice, and if you are good to people, people are good to you. However, the owner's two sons did cause them a lot of problems. Most evenings, I would have to go jogging with one of the sons, because he couldn't go out alone. He couldn't go anywhere on his own, because he had so many enemies. At the time, he had a Porsche and lots of money, and women were throwing themselves at him. Because of this, he made a lot of enemies, although I always found him to be a good guy. Basically, if he jogged, I jogged; if he went somewhere, I went with him; whatever he did, I did too.

One particular incident involving the son that springs to mind was when I was working the doors one night. A Mercedes pulled into the drive with five big men sitting quietly inside. One of them wound down a window and told me to go and get the owner's son. I asked him if he had a problem. He told me that the son had been a very naughty man and had shagged his girlfriend. I then asked the bloke if the man in question had tied her down and forced her to have sex with him. He said no, so I then said that it seemed consensual to me and that he needed to get his arse back home and sort things out with his girlfriend rather than causing problems at my club. He said that I was either a very stupid man – there were five guys in the car – or a good man. I said, 'Well, you boys are in the car, and there are five of you, so it is entirely up to you what you decide to do.' Thankfully, we talked some more, and they eventually drove off.

There were a lot of incidents like that when people tried to get to the owners of the club. It was all mainly personal stuff that I didn't much care for. However, there was one funny incident when a right ding-dong started up – it was like something out of a cowboy movie. People were fighting everywhere, and the son's £10,000 Rolex came off. We shouted 'stop, stop, stop' and everyone helped search for the watch. Once it was found, everything started up again. It was bizarre.

The doormen caused a few problems themselves. They would bring other people's wives and girlfriends to the club to shag. Numerous husbands would come down to the venue looking for their wives. Although I had a lot of opportunities, like most doormen, I had a wife whom I treasured and would never let down, so I never got involved – a couple of the other doormen were the same.

In some respects, I think my wife was proud of the fact that I worked as a doorman, and I met some really nice people on the doors. But don't get me wrong, I also did some things that I really regret. I put people in hospital and knocked people's teeth out – things like that. At the time, it was probably the macho thing to do, but now that I am 55 I look back at some of these things with regret and think maybe I could have handled them differently. However, doormen were different in those days. You didn't have the police hounding you as you do now, there was no licensing or accountability and the management rewarded you for being tough.

I was involved in a really terrible incident when I worked the doors at a venue called Hedley House in Oulton Broad, near Lowestoft. The doormen were not allowed to go into the ladies' toilets on their own; they always had to go in with another doorman. One evening, I was called into the ladies' toilets because a young girl had collapsed, so I took another doorman in with me. The young girl was lying on the floor, and I just knew she wasn't well. I just knew it. I lifted her head up, stroked her hair, spoke to her and asked the other doorman to go quickly and phone an ambulance. The young girl's friend was with me, so I wasn't left alone with her. The doorman shot off but almost immediately came back again and said that he didn't want to call an ambulance, as he didn't think there was anything wrong with her. I told him that the girl needed an ambulance. The owner of the club then came in and agreed that she was not well but he would put her in a taxi instead. I said to the manager, 'No, you don't need a taxi. You need an ambulance.' But because he was the boss and paid the wages, he took over, and although I continued to protest they put her in a taxi and sent her home. The next day, I got a call from John Beckett, the head doorman of the club, saying that she had passed away. It was her 18th birthday.

There were many other times on the doors when I put a drunk young girl into a taxi and was happy that I was doing my best, both as a gentleman and as a professional doorman, to make sure that she was safe. But there were lots of other times when I had arseholes coming into my establishments and causing trouble, and because I was small I had to be really hard. I actually lost my job when I went too far confronting someone outside one of the clubs I worked at in full view of the punters. We were full, and there was a queue. One chap asked me how long it would be to get in, and I said that I didn't know – it was one out, one in, so it depended on how many people came out as to how many people I could let in. The first time he asked, he was as good as gold. The second time he came up to the door, he was a little more aggressive, calling me an arsehole and a twat. The third time he came up, he was getting very loud and out of hand. He was getting far too confident for my liking, so when he came up for the fourth time I let him have it. I realise now that I probably should not have done what I did, but he had wound me up so much that for the first and only time in my life I gave a man a good kick when he was down. I should not have done it, but in my reckoning I was only small, he was a big guy and he would have probably strangled me if he had got up.

At that time, I was on £60 a night as head doorman, but by the end of the night I was sacked and told in no uncertain terms that no one would touch me again. As far as they were concerned, I would never work the doors again. But I think that there was a lot of stuff going on behind the scenes with the other doormen who wanted to get me out and get their friends in.

Doing the door has been an amazing journey, and being a good doorman really does make you a better person. You look at life differently. When you speak to most doormen, there is this comradeship between them, which you rarely find in other industries. But, of course, as in all walks of life, there are some bad doormen out there as well.

Even though I continued to work on the rigs, I always went back to door work when I was on leave. My wife used to ask me if I was tired of bouncing, but I was never tired of it. I loved it. When I first started, I needed the money. We were really desperate for the cash, which was one reason I never let anyone beat me up – I was so desperate not to lose my job. However, as time passed and I worked offshore, I didn't need the money as much. I'd put all the money I earned on the doors over the year into a sock. When it had mounted up, it would pay for a holiday or some other luxury.

After being dismissed from Hedley House, I did quite a long spell on the rigs in the hellhole that was Nigeria. When I was there, I worked with a guy who was a doorman in the Gorbals, Glasgow. As soon as he mentioned where he worked, the hairs on the back of my neck stood up. I immediately thought that he must be tasty. It was one of the roughest areas not just in Glasgow but in the whole of the UK. He was basically a good guy but very noisy, and he wanted to let everyone know he was the boss. However, an incident made me seriously doubt him.

We were working in Warri, one of the ten most dangerous places in the world at that time. Pirates operated on the Warri River, but being ordinary crew we had to travel up and down the snake-and-crocodile-infested waters in large motorised canoes without any armed guards before meeting up with the barges that were towed down from Eket. Management travelled separately with armed guards with machine guns – that was the difference between management and ordinary crew. It was only once we got onto the barges that we had armed guards protecting us from the pirates.

On one occasion, we were kidnapped by the Nigerian crew, who locked us up in the barge. They then doused the vessel with diesel and threatened to set us on fire if the company we worked for didn't give them what they wanted. There were two main tribes working on board, and they just didn't mix – although they hated us even more! The chief wanted a generator, lights, enough diesel for about six months, some goal posts for the children of his village, a football and some money.

When we heard that the crew were threatening to set us on fire, the so-called 'handy' doorman from Glasgow went to pieces. He started to blubber, saying that he couldn't understand what was going on or why the crew would want to do such a thing. I told him that there was

225

nothing to worry about. They just wanted money and would not set us on fire. However, this tough doorman from the Gorbals in Glasgow could not get it into his head that he was not going to die. And when I then tried to explain to him that if they did set fire to the barge, we wouldn't feel anything anyway, as we would fall unconscious with the heat and the fumes, it made him even worse! Needless to say, the company did negotiate, and we survived, but I saw the doorman in a totally different light from that time onwards. People had seen his weaknesses when they had been looking for leadership.

On another occasion, I was on a different rig in Nigeria when a Dutch guy decided to insult the chef. For 11 days afterwards, we were all ill – and I mean very, very ill. We had sickness and diarrhoea, and lost an incredible amount of weight, all because someone had bad-mouthed the chef.

In April 1998, I began working with Mark Davey. Mark had been a regular at The Wherry Hotel. When I first met him, I thought he was a complete arsehole. He'd come into the club and pinch beer, and I was always throwing him out or barring him. And then, lo and behold, I met him thousands of miles away on a barge in Nigeria! It was a small world. The odd thing was that out there we hit it off straight away.

We were both on the barge for a month at a time – it was one month on, one month off. There was a bar on board. Nigerian beer was obviously not brewed to the same standards as in the UK; for example, one bottle might be 5 per cent alcohol and another bottle 19 per cent. You could have one bottle one night and it would be nice and refreshing, and another bottle another night and it would knock you out!

More and more Scottish lads were coming out to the country to work. Like most Scotsmen, they liked to have a few beers, and the ones I worked with were quite loud. One night, they had a few too many and had a go at the few of us who were English. Things got out of hand, and Mark and I ended up scrapping with them on the helipad. It was sad. We were all away from home, and they just wanted to fight us.

I came back to Britain slightly earlier than Mark, and we arranged to meet for a meal once he got home. Before I'd left, we had been working on a contract with an engineering company. On one of his leave periods, Mark went back to Eket, where the company owned some houses that were supposed to be guarded. In Nigeria, it is common for robbers to take the tiles off the roof of your house and drop down through the hole. Apparently, one morning a group of thieves came down through the roof of the house Mark was staying in at about 2.30 a.m. and started rummaging through his personal belongings. Mark was a pretty big guy, and when he confronted the thieves they shot him. He died in Nigeria, and his body was flown home. Bob Blizzard, the MP for Waveney, went out to the country with Mark's brother to try and find out what had actually gone on, as there were lots of conflicting reports, one of which said that he had been shot while he slept. In Nigeria, there is always more to things than meets the eye. The company promised to step up security after that incident, but we didn't notice any change. When you employ Nigerians, you get what you pay for.

There were two types of police in Nigeria. The kind that wore black berets could more or less do whatever they wanted with no questions asked. One such policeman, whom we called Magnum, guarded our barge. He took great delight in being very sadistic – not to Europeans, but to other Nigerians. I bought him a beer one night and was talking to him near the back of the barge when one of the crew members went by and accidentally stood on his foot. I couldn't believe it, but Magnum took out his pistol and beat the poor crew member with it. I had never seen anything like it. All this poor guy had done was step on Magnum's foot. It is how things are over there, and they will probably never change.

In Nigeria, you tend to go around on motorcycles, so one night a guy called Steve and I hired a couple of motorcycles and went to a nightclub by the name of Cinderella's. We were the only white people with money there that night, and I think we were the focal point of the evening. Everyone stared at us. I said to Steve, 'I'm going to show you a little trick.' I went outside, jumped on my bike and rode straight through the entrance, into the nightclub and around the dance floor. The police were called and came with batons drawn, but when they saw that we were white we started to chat. I bought them a few beers and gave them some money, and they left extremely happy.

On the way home later that night, we were stopped by a group of vigilantes at a roadblock. There are a lot of vigilante groups in Nigeria, each responsible for a specific neighbourhood or district. I asked the vigilante his name, and he said it was Patrick – they all adopt Western names. I said to Patrick, 'We have heard of you on the rig. We have heard about you. You are a great warrior.' After that, he was like putty in our hands. We sat on our bikes chatting to him for ages, and after a while he said we could go on our way and that they would keep an eye on us as we travelled through their neighbourhood.

Working on the doors with people from all walks of life actually gave me self-confidence in these terrible places. Having been a doorman, I definitely felt that I could handle most situations. It was not about being a thug or hard, but about being wise and working around difficult things – doing things in a sensible manner.

In the clubs I worked in, I had very attractive women try to hit me over the head with a shoe or try to glass me, and in the ten years I worked the doors I was involved in lots of incidents with people who came into the club as complete ladies and gentlemen, but who suddenly changed after a few Cinzanos and wanted to pull my eyes out or give me a good kicking. I had to be on my guard at all times.

I almost always found that people who could really handle themselves were generally very nice people, and I also found that people who had a reputation were generally very modest. It was the people who felt they needed to prove something who were the real arseholes. However, no matter who they were or where they came from or what they said, I always tried to bear in mind that they were someone's son or daughter, mother or father, and were therefore very precious, and I would take great pride in looking after them and making sure they had a safe time under my roof. That was my main reason for working as a doorman.

In August 2006, I was walking to work in London early one morning. An Asian guy came towards me, and when we got level, he turned and said something to me. I didn't hear him and said, 'I beg your pardon?' With that, I was called a white fucking arsehole and told to mind my own fucking business. I said that there was no need to be like that, bearing in mind that I was 54 years old and he was probably in his early 20s. He just saw an old guy and started insulting me. I backed off, as all I was doing was going to work, and I didn't really want any trouble at that time in the morning – or at that time in my life, come to think of it. However, it got out of hand, so I gave him a good hiding. I then immediately phoned the police and told them what had happened. I knew they would believe an old man like me before a big Asian guy in his early 20s. I still don't know what that situation was all about, but he probably had some hang-up, or maybe I caught him in a bad mood. I just don't know. But working away from home has made me very wary of people, and I have discovered that they are not always what they seem.

If I could live my life again, I wouldn't change much. I was brought up in a children's home and used to hear my brother screaming in the room next door. Because of that, I grew up abhorring bullying of any kind. I think what I have lacked in my childhood, I have gained in my adult life. People have always commented on what a bad childhood I had, but I never thought my upbringing was particularly bad, just a learning experience. Handling a lot of difficult situations has made me a stronger and better person. Each life is a book, and it is up to you what you choose to fill it with. Will it be full and interesting, or empty and dull? When I go to my grave, I would rather have had lots of different experiences, met lots of interesting people and done things that really mattered.

Many years ago, I'd walk through Lowestoft and Great Yarmouth and people knew me. I had quite a reputation – not as a bully, but as a good guy and a good doorman. But now I am 55, and no ones knows me any more, which can be annoying! If I go into a pub now, people push me out of the way. And you can tell I am getting old, because when I walk past nightclubs and look at the doormen I think they are not old enough to be doing the job. But I always have a chat with them, and I have found that most of them are pretty good guys. If I speak to them for long enough, they almost always ask if I want to come in, but I am far too old for all of that nonsense – nightclubs are not my scene any more.

I was walking along Lowestoft seafront about three years ago when a doorman called out my name and asked if I wanted a job! I was 52 at the time. It was a lovely thought, and I was very tempted, but I was a bit too old – you have to know when to call it a day.

BIOGRAPHY OF SANDY SANDERSON

Sandy still lives in Lowestoft and still drives a crane. He hasn't worked the doors for many years, as he now considers himself to be far too old, but he readily admits that he misses the excitement and comradeship of his old career.

18

FROM LANDLORD TO TRAINER OF BODYGUARDS
BY MOLLY PRINCE

The question I always get asked is, 'How do you go from licensee and landlord to trainer of doormen and bodyguards?' But a good licensee or venue manager is not so different to a good doorman or doorwoman. If you've had interesting life experiences and good training, the transition is not such a difficult one.

Over the years, I had some tasty experiences in the various venues I managed before I entered the world of security training, doormen and bodyguards. Many incidents occurred without the assistance of door staff, and looking back I certainly wish I had had some back-up on occasion.

After I divorced my first husband, I wanted a fresh start, so I moved to a sleepy (or so I thought) village in Yorkshire. Milnsbridge, a lovely picturesque mill town, is on the outskirts of Huddersfield. I took over a pub called The Post Office, which my good friend Mandy used to call 'The Slaughtered Lamb'. But I thought it was great . . . at first.

There were two prominent families in the village: one of Irish descent, the other of Fijian, would you believe? A few of the Fijians were rugby players, and they were the biggest, meanest-looking blokes I had ever seen. The two families weren't supposed to be friends, but it seemed that they were all shagging each other, and it was as though everyone in the village came from one family or the other. I could just imagine the teacher reading out a name from the school register and half the kids answering at once.

I quickly sussed it all out and recruited a very attractive barmaid, who looked and sang like Whitney Houston (no prizes for guessing which family she belonged to). My karaoke nights were fantastic, the pub was rocking and I was making a decent living. One night – or should I say early morning? – four of us were left at the bar: me, my boyfriend, a nice lad from Bury who lived in the village (I never did find out why he was there) and a local lad who was quite hard but belonged to neither family. There was a frantic knock at the door, and my badly beaten star barmaid came in. We cleaned her up and settled down to listen to what had happened. It transpired that it was her boyfriend who had done this to her, and I invited her to stay the night, being the mumsy person that I am. She refused and wanted to go home, saying that he wasn't going to chase her out of her own home. I then suggested that I could go home with her and stay the night – my thinking was that domestic bullies don't usually like an audience.

So, off we went in my car, minus my boyfriend, who went to bed. The two lads said that they would come with us to make sure that the boyfriend wasn't waiting for us. When we arrived, they found him hiding down the alleyway at the side of the house, and he got the beating of his life after they had chased him for miles. The lads eventually returned, reassuring us that he wouldn't be back, and they asked me to give them a lift home.

Whitney went to bed, and I gave the lads a lift. Little was said in the car but our adrenalin was high. When we got back to the pub, the coal fire was still burning, and one of the lads tossed in a big stick, explaining that my fella had given it to him for my protection. 'Oh fuck,' I thought. 'I am really in the shit here.' And I was.

The following morning, we found out that the arsehole who had beaten up Whitney was in a coma. She was in love with him again, and he had just managed to say that it was my friends who had beaten him up. I was arrested, my car was impounded and I gave a bit of a woolly statement. Worse, her boyfriend played rugby with her brothers, and they all thought I had had him nearly killed. I had only been in the village about six weeks – what had I got myself into? (This episode taught me to not get involved in domestics, as they inevitably bite you on the arse, and I have since walked away from many situations when I was tempted to intervene.)

The eldest brother came into the pub first. I spoke with him quietly and respectfully and gave him my version of events. He told me that his sister had said that it was me who had got the boyfriend beaten up because of an incident in the pub – she had only got caught in the crossfire. Bitch. I was then told that I would be dealt with if I did not leave the village. I had my sister take my son, who was around two at the time, back to Manchester, and I got on with the day's business. To say it was an arse-twitching moment is an understatement – and it went on for a day and a half.

As Sunday night fell, I was in the fucking twilight zone. I was without my car, I was short-staffed and without my karaoke singer, and I was nervous. But it was busy all day and night. There is nothing like the gossip of someone being nearly beaten to death to keep a boozer like The Slaughtered Lamb busy.

Whitney's family arrived in force at around 9 p.m. I'm no coward, so I tried to deal with them, but I soon realised that it was personal and these guys had no manners with ladies. One spunky little blonde barmaid – I am ashamed to say I can't remember her name, but I probably owe my life to her – told me to go upstairs and out of the way. I didn't want to, because it was my pub, but, hey, instinct took me upstairs. (She explained that her dad was at the end of the bar and that she had grown up with these nutters – she was safe, but I wasn't.)

I was upstairs for the longest 40 minutes of my life. As they helped themselves to beer and frightened all my customers away, I dialled 999 four times and explained what was going on. I was shitting myself when I made the last 999 call, as one of the animals downstairs picked up the bar extension, and I heard him shout that the police could come if they fucking dared. 'I am out of here,' I thought.

My spineless boyfriend didn't do much to defend my honour – nor did our relationship last long after that – so the fire escape seemed the best option. I thought I could go out the back and get in my car – but the police had impounded it. I was surely dead. As I was about to leave, I realised I might never return, so I thought I had better bring the weekend's takings with me. They were duly stuffed down the front of my leather jeans.

I got out just as the mob were breaking into the flat, and for the first and last time in my life I ran about two miles (I couldn't normally manage two hundred yards) down the canal towards Golcar. The thugs, who had picked up cricket bats and stumps that my tit of a boyfriend had left in the hall, were nearly catching me up. In the pitch black, I climbed over a canal lock and started banging doors in an adjacent street. As soon as someone answered their door, I dived inside. I then phoned the police again, but they didn't come. Eventually, the owner gave me a lift to a hotel on the M62, a few miles away.

Daylight broke and decisions had to be made. I called the police again and told them where I was. Later that morning, there was a knock on the door of my room. It was two guys from CID. Hooray, the police. I was livid and started ranting and raving about what time did they call this and where were they a few hours earlier. They said that they knew nothing about the night before. They also explained that mentioning the names of the thugs might have stopped the police from coming into the village at night! Fucking marvellous. I was then arrested for committing GBH on the arsehole who had beaten up the barmaid.

I was interviewed in one of those rooms that you see on *The Bill* and bailed to return to The Slaughtered Lamb. 'I'd rather be in the nick,' I thought. The police explained that my car had been returned to the pub. 'Fan-bloody-tastic,' I thought, as I wasn't going back there. But I did.

That's when the scary 'gangster' thing happened. I was met on the street by the barmaid who had saved my life. She gave me the keys to the pub and said the eldest brother wanted to see me. I met him in a café, and he apologised, saying that they had got it wrong. Whitney had told them the truth. However, she hadn't passed that information onto the police for fear of being charged, and her boyfriend was still in a coma. The brother also said that he wanted me to come back and run the pub. 'No fucking way,' I thought.

I believe he never fully recovered, and the two lads got five years, but they did not implicate me or my dickhead boyfriend who had handed them the stick. I refused to give evidence against them and thought that the whole thing would be thrown out of the magistrates' court. But it wasn't, and my bottle truly went when the case was heard in the Crown court some 11 months later. Although there was no real evidence against me, Mandy came with me so that she could drive my car home – just in case. The two lads had been inside on remand since being arrested. They looked shocking, and one of them had deliberately dropped three or four stone so he wouldn't look 'hard'. I copped a plea of perverting the course of justice and was given a 12-month suspended sentence. I was out of there in a shot and never looked back. I sold the tenancy of the pub to the gay barber in the village and headed home.

Not long after, I was asked to infiltrate a restaurant called Fat Pigs in Eccles, a not-so-lovely suburb of Manchester, for the owners of Hurley's Sports, who had been forced to shut down their sports shop, as they couldn't insure it because of ram raiders. Nice place, Eccles. At least this time I knew what breed of nutter I might have to deal with, and I also had door staff to back me up.

Fat Pigs had had its heyday as a restaurant and party venue, and had since gone rapidly downhill. The staff were thieving and lazy bastards, and I was asked to sort it out. Yates's Wine Lodge was at its height in nearby Swinton – where I was later to have my last pub – and I wanted to rename Fat Pigs 'The Swine Lodge', but Mark, the owner, thought better of it.

I got the place a full licence and turned slow Sundays into a busy disco night. We had a good winter. I got the place back on its feet and was taking up to £10,000 a week by Christmas. However, there were quite a few incidents at Fat Pigs, including kidnappings and ransom notes! Mark's pig statues, which were dotted all over the restaurant,

235

ended up all over Salford, and we once got a postcard with a ransom demand from Australia. I would get calls every Monday morning to collect one of our pigs from a venue up and down the precinct.

It was a busy venue, and we ended up with a good strong door team. There were a number of venues within yards of each other, and we all helped each other out when it kicked off. I loved it and would have stayed a lot longer, but I wasn't paid what I was promised and moved on.

The Brook in Swinton was another fine example of a wolf in sheep's clothing, and I had many happy times there, as well as numerous rucks, whilst trying to tame the locals and gain their respect. My first weekend started with an encounter with what can only be described as two of the biggest, ugliest, thickest fuckers I have ever had the misfortune to come across. They approached me in the pub and told me that they were going to do the door for me. 'That's nice,' I said, 'but we are a local pub, and I don't have any vacancies for door staff.'

'No, you don't understand, missus. We are doing yer fucking door, and yer gonna pay us 50 quid a night each.' Again, I politely refused. 'Do you know who I am? Do you know who my fucking uncle is?'

It's amazing how many nephews the top dogs in Salford have. Anyhow, he went on to explain who his uncle was and what he would do to me. Thinking on my feet, I replied, 'Well, do you know who I am? Do you know who my fucking uncle is?' (Of course, they didn't, as Glasgow is a long way from Salford.) 'Go tell your scumbag fucking uncle who my uncle is, and if you still want to do my door, come back and we'll talk.' It was the silliest thing I have ever said. I could hear people laughing in the background, but these two idiots were so confused that they just walked away scratching their heads, and I never saw them again – I guess they didn't want to meet my uncle. I had learned another important lesson: confusion is a great tool when negotiating your way out of a jam.

I formed the Leadership Development Centre back in 2003 after 20 or so years in the licensed and event-and-exhibition-management trades, having decided to eventually sell up and leave my pub and restaurant businesses. I attended college and university to gain the necessary qualifications to teach in adult education. The catalyst had been a British Institute of Innkeeping Awarding Body (BIIAB) course in financial management I attended with an excellent trainer called Sara Bryan. There were ten to twelve people on the course, which lasted three days. I paid £350 to attend, I think, and the most important financial lesson I learned was that Sara and her company had earned approximately £3,500 for three days' work, whereas I was still working ninety or so hours a week in a friggin' pub for a fraction of that. There and then I decided training was the business to be in.

It took a couple of years, but I graduated from university and achieved centre approval from BIIAB to run licensing qualifications. The government was discussing their plans to implement the 2003 Liquor Licensing Act at that time, but the Private Security Act was in full swing, and the SIA had just made their first fuck-up. Everyone had to be conflict-management trained prior to licensing, and guess what? There weren't enough conflict-management trainers. In fact, there were hardly any.

I was invited to do trainer training by a company called Maybo in Birmingham, where I met one of my first door bosses, a bloke by the name of Will Davies, who I later found out ran doors from Manchester and the North East down to Swansea in Wales. Will is a gentleman of the highest order, and I learned more from him that week and on a subsequent physical-intervention course than the so-called instructors had taught me.

On my return to Manchester with my new-found status of conflict-management trainer, I discovered that there was only one other person with the same qualification in all of the north-west of England. Mike worked at Wigan College at that time, and we later became good friends.

One day, I got a call from somebody called Damian, who was running the offices of North Cheshire Security, owned by Mickey Francis. I visited them, met Mickey and a deal was done: I was booked to run my first door course. Once there, I met Lesley Aimes – I was so glad there was a lady on that first course. I don't think she will ever know how much she lifted my confidence, but I was terrified. It was one of those arse-twitching moments; similar, I suppose, to the way you feel on your first night working the doors. Lesley was in charge of that group, some of whom you could only describe as 'big hard bastards', and I learned my first lesson: complete respect is paramount in the security world.

And so it had started. It was now March 2004, and the SIA had stipulated that the lads working the doors in Manchester had to be licensed by 14 November that year, by which time I had trained 2,200 bouncers – now known by the more politically correct title of door supervisors. My life has been a bit of a roller coaster ever since.

Just before the licensing deadline, I had a funny experience when I was asked by the owner of Jilly's Music Box on Oxford Road in Manchester to attend a 'pub watch' meeting that had been called by Greater Manchester Police to discuss how they were going to deal with licensing – or the lack of it at that point – over Christmas. Everyone introduced themselves, as I did when my turn came round. But before the meeting started, I was asked to leave, because 'I represented too many door companies, and my presence was a conflict of interests'. 'Whose?' I thought. There was a bit of an uproar (in my defence), but I left. I didn't want to piss the police off. Later that afternoon, I got a report of what had been too sensitive for me to hear. (Did they really think I wouldn't find out?) Provided that door supervisors had completed their training and could evidence it, they would be allowed to work over Christmas – and this was the bit I wasn't supposed to hear – as long as the police didn't have a problem with the individual, and anyone in the city they wanted off the doors would be gone by the New Year.

As my business had grown really quickly and I had gone to university and achieved a level-four teaching qualification, I could train trainers to level three, the required standard to deliver SIA courses. I got approval to do so from Edexcel – an awarding body – and started to train trainers.

Licences for wheel clampers (most of the industry couldn't spell 'vehicle immobiliser') was the SIA's next fuck-up and my next big triumph. It was virtually impossible to find a wheel clamper anywhere in the UK who had the appropriate teaching qualification in order to be approved and accredited by the SIA to teach the required syllabus for that sector of the industry. You tell me: where are you going to find a wheel clamper who has a teaching qualification? Who the fuck thought that one up? So, I did my research and soon attended my first wheel-clamping lesson, which caused a storm at Salford University, where we were based. Everyone started panicking and coming out of their offices, thinking that they were being clamped by me in the main university car park. They were reassured when reception told them, 'It's just Mol with some of her bouncer geezers.'

And how good for business it was when *The Sun* newspaper (I think) ran the headline 'Pay £500, Go to College for Four Days and Become a Complete Bastard'. Because none of the colleges wanted to run the course, we were the first to get accredited in the north, and we were off and running in our second niche market. God bless the clampers – they always turn up with cash.

I remember when I delivered my first course as a newly qualified clamping expert, I said to the guys, 'Right, lads, this is where I have to show you how to put a clamp on.' They all fell off their chairs laughing at me. (That was the intention, as I was much more confident by then.) I then suggested we go outside and practise the dirty deed, and I could video them to build up my training material. Those boys had the clamps out of the van and on the cars quicker than I could get the camera out of my pocket. 'You don't want to fuck about on your back putting a clamp on someone's car,' one of them explained, 'You don't know who's coming back.'

I then formed a close protection company in late 2005, early 2006, employing two operations managers. Danny, who still works with me to this day, was really old school and commanded lots of respect and loyalty. The other sadly reinvented himself as 007, proved himself to have neither respect nor loyalty, stole from the business and lied so much about his background that I don't think even he knew who he was. He is a fuck-up who will get his just rewards and has already disrespected others with far less patience than me.

The motivation for starting a close protection company was twofold: first, outside of the SIA itself, I probably had one of the biggest databases of door supervisors in the country, and a large number of these door supervisors also wanted to enter the world of close protection. For many in the industry, moving from door work into close protection seemed like a natural career progression. Second, as we started to run level three close protection courses, our client base for this type of training changed from big security companies with hundreds of staff to individuals and door supervisors looking for both accredited training *and* work after completing the course. I therefore felt I could not only bid for our own contracts but network with other established companies on the circuit to help our guys into employment. This was the ultimate goal of starting a close protection company: the ability not only to offer close protection training approved and accredited by the SIA but also to offer our best students close protection work after qualifying and becoming licensed.

BIOGRAPHY OF MOLLY PRINCE

After over 20 years managing pubs and clubs, Molly Prince is now the managing director of Close Protection UK Ltd and the Leadership Development Centre, providing a complete range of security training throughout the UK. She divides her time between England and the Costa Blanca.

Molly can be contacted via www.close-protectionuk.com

19

KEY POINTS TO BEING A GOOD BODYGUARD

BY MARC SAND

Originally receiving the majority of my training in the military, I have been in the security and close protection industry for well over 15 years and have taught literally hundreds of trained professionals – law enforcement officers, military personnel, security professionals, intelligence agents – as well as a great many untrained individuals entering the industry for the first time.

Having met a vast range of people and been in many situations, I believe that there are many things still substandard, missing or lacking in the profession, including effective communication, professionalism, leadership skills and professional courtesy. I have met many bodyguards working on the international circuit in locations such as Africa or South America, where there is still no formal government-recognised and accredited training. Bodyguards in these places have surprisingly little knowledge of the close protection industry. There is also a distinct lack of specific industry skills and basic education, and a definite need for psychological training and evaluations, as well as instruction in conflict resolution and management, thorough risk assessment and general man-management skills. Although this is changing slowly, close protection training in Canada is still significantly behind the training offered in many other countries, including the UK. I also believe that good training should feature a detailed understanding of the dangers faced by close protection agents, a comprehensive analysis of body language, in-depth profiling of possible aggressors, and instruction in dealing with stress and operating in demanding and hostile environments. There is support for soldiers working in Iraq or Afghanistan but very little support for the private contractor.

There are various reasons for close protection assignments in the private industry, and most security companies run background checks on their clients as a matter of course. But if you are tasked as an individual to provide personal protection to someone, you should *always* request a criminal background check on the client and, if necessary, also check with the credit reporting agencies – the last thing you want as a professional close protection officer is to find yourself hired by someone involved in the criminal world.

A decade or so after the Second World War, the close protection profession underwent a revolution of a kind, and celebrities, pop stars, artists and actors all started to employ an entourage of beefy, mean-looking security guards. Bodyguards in the celebrity sector were (and still are) built like brick walls, which certainly made them great to hide behind, although they weren't always the most intelligent. Most people in the protection industry will end up protecting a celebrity at some point, even for just a short period of time, and it will quickly become apparent that for many celebrities it is cool to have bodyguards. Employing a security detail is a trend they feel they have to follow, rather than because of any specific threat against them.

One very important factor in an executive protection assignment is the legal contract between the protection company and the executive or his corporation. This aspect is often missed. It doesn't matter if the contract is for a one-day assignment or for a job lasting six months or more, it is a very important aspect of an operation, as subjects, issues and protocol have to be clearly stated in writing between you and your client, as this could ultimately keep you safe if anything goes wrong. Remember, no one will remember the thousand things that you have done right over the years; the thing people will remember is your one and only screw-up.

Another very important and often neglected aspect of a protection assignment is that you need to assign a liaison officer between the contractor, client and yourself if you intend to use aircraft, limousines or any other method of transportation. If possible, the protection company should organise this, but try not to let the client arrange it, as you personally want to make sure that there are no last-minute delays or fuck-ups, and you have very little control over things if they are managed by the client.

In 2006, I accompanied a client to Mexico on an 18-day assignment. Contracts were all signed and sealed six weeks before the assignment commenced, all the necessary details were arranged, the retainer was cleared and we completed our reconnaissance efficiently and effectively. Everything went to plan until the chartered plane was delayed and the airline overlooked notifying the chief of security, who handled those matters. If a specific liaison officer had been assigned, this would not have happened.

As all of us in the industry know, fuck-ups never come alone, and on this assignment we had started with one. What else would go wrong? We arrived in Mexico at a private airport, and initially everything went well. The transport was smoothly organised, and the local traffic into town was not too much of a killer; however, the client suddenly decided to make changes to his travel arrangements without notifying his chief of security. Clients can sometimes be very difficult people to work with! So, last-minute arrangements had to be made without compromising the executive's safety and comfort. Since the assignment was in Mexico City, where I had an office, we could facilitate this change.

All of our local drivers were trained to the same high standards as our other Canadian, US and European counterparts. However, the armoured vehicle we were using came with its own driver, which happens from time to time, as transportation companies occasionally provide their own for insurance purposes. The driver was checked out and seemed fine, and upon arrival at the hotel and the VIP being settled in his secured suite, I returned to the driver who was stationed at his vehicle and made sure that it could not be compromised in any way. I briefly spoke to the driver, and as I checked over the vehicle I immediately noticed that the fuel gauge was well below halfway, which could be a major security risk, especially with the additional weight of an armoured vehicle plus the possibility of driving in a potentially hostile environment. The thought of running out of petrol with a client sent shivers down my spine. When I asked him why this was the case, he answered that his boss had not given him the money to fuel up before departure! They were now in breach of security procedures, which had been signed off six weeks before the assignment.

In this situation, every good protection officer asks himself, 'What else has happened? Has the driver's integrity been compromised? Will the VIP and protection team be compromised?' Since the local security company was already in breach of contract, we solved the matter by demanding that we immediately relieve the driver of his duties and put our own man in place. Our driver was a native Mexican and knew the streets and routes. However, because we didn't know whether we had been compromised, we changed all the pre-arranged routes, the times for departure and arrival, and everything else the previous driver had been aware of. We were then able to securely complete the assignment without any further problems.

Assignments are never the same, no matter how many times similar procedures are implemented, and lessons will always be learned each time we undertake an operation. It is a never-ending process.

Two of the main attributes that a protection agent should possess are good communication and conflict-resolution skills. Communication is one of the most important aspects of any security or protection detail. No matter which country they originate from, NATO soldiers across the world use English for all their radio communications, because language must be consistent and standard for effective multicultural, multinational security operations. If you are tasked to provide international security to a company that does not use English as a standard form of communication, think twice about joining them. Misunderstanding can lead to injury and death.

Other than to your client, you will not always be recognised as a close protection specialist. You might be introduced as a business associate or colleague, or a personal or public relations assistant, which then enables you to conduct covert protection, as you will be able to stay close to the VIP without generating too much attention. An undercover approach to personal protection can be a very effective form of security.

Some protection assignments are a lot less interesting than others, especially low-profile or long-term assignments that require a certain daily routine in functions and duties. However, never try to create patterns in your assignment: modify your patrol times, change directions of departure and switch vehicles, and advise the client to do the same if his schedule and arrangements allow him to do so.

For long-term assignments, it is very important to build up a rapport with your client and anyone else associated with the operation. Effective communications will not only assist you in having an easier and less stressful assignment, but also keep you up to date on the client's day-to-day activities, especially private and social engagements. Etiquette in social situations with your client is a very important tool in the industry – no one will ever be retained if they embarrass the client in any way or at any time. A good protection agent should feel just as comfortable on the streets of Iraq as at an exclusive event at a foreign embassy.

The most important aspect of any protection assignment is to keep your client safe and secure at all times. Remember, your VIP has a certain position and status, and as well as his life you are also hired to protect his reputation. Don't ever forget, dead clients will never pay their bills. Each day you and your client return home without incident or injury is a great day, and it means you have conducted yourself in a professional manner.

Keep a professional image at all times, and try to be extremely diplomatic and tactful in situations involving the VIP, not to mention those involving your teammates, no matter if they work for the same company or are contracted out. There are too many cowboys out there already, and you don't ever want to be known as one. Keep in mind that a good reputation is hard to build, whereas a bad reputation is hard to shake off.

Close protection is a great industry – enjoy it!

BIOGRAPHY OF MARC SAND

Marc is currently the managing director of VIP Protection, which is based in Canada and has offices in Mexico, China and France. He studied personal protection, weapons, explosives, law and security, and the handling and defusing of highly sensitive explosives at the military academy. He is a certified executive protection specialist, a certified anti-terrorism specialist and an instructor at a military academy, teaching close combat, anti-terrorism, close protection and weapons. He also instructs in hostage negotiations.

Marc can be contacted at marc@vip-protection.ca

20

SPEAKING OF VIRGINS . . .
BY JAMES SHORTT

As with every half-decent story, it starts in a bar, but luckily not the kind that Antonio Banderas's character frequents in *Once Upon a Time in Mexico*. No, this bar was directly opposite the then headquarters of the International Bodyguard Association (IBA) in the aptly named Rue de Bitche in the Parisian suburb of Courbevoie. For those who do not know Paris, Courbevoie is a small suburb nestling alongside its better-known Parisian sister La Defense, with its direct line of sight to L'Étoile and the world-renowned L'Arc de Triomphe. It was August 1989 and I was drinking my typical beverage: 100 centilitres of Jameson's (the Irish whiskey), beloved of my father and grandfather and countless generations of Irishmen before me. Beside me was my mentor, teacher and friend, Major Lucien Ott, the founder of the IBA. Lucien had progressed from *bière* (Kronenbourg, the foreign legion's Vitamin K) to cognac (Rémy Martin – he would never drink Hennessy) and was smoking his customary Villiger cigarillo.

As fate would have it, in strode a brave soldier – or rather a French

Army conscript in his drab-olive *tenue de combat*. Immediately, he was slapped on the back, and the host of the bar and its patrons showered him with *bière* and offers of stronger alcohol. Lucien and I watched this with interest – it is not a bad thing to see those who provide service to their nation feted and appreciated by the citizenry. Within the hour, the conscript, who was by then a lot less steady on his feet, had gained some confidence and started to tell tales of gruesome combat and war in the darkest parts of the 'Dark Continent'. Although it entertained the audience of lounge lizards and bar flies who eagerly sought the conscript's approval and company, it had the opposite effect on Lucien Ott, who detected a strong smell of bovine back splatter (bullshit).

'Ce n'est pas une pucelle qui va t'apprendre à baiser,' Lucien said, his voice carrying across the bar and interrupting the scene of theatre. (Lucien's comment could be loosely translated into English as 'Virgins can't teach you to fuck'.) The conscript probably knew the insult was aimed at him and was about to unleash a torrent of foul-mouthed abuse when, with one hand raised, he was stopped short by our host, *le patron*, who, in a subdued tone, informed the conscript that he was addressing Major Lucien Ott. Beside being the personal bodyguard of President Charles de Gaulle during the OAS crisis, Major Lucien Ott was also a veteran of the 8th BCCP, the famed second demi-brigade of the French SAS, a survivor of Dien Bien Phu and a 'warrior' born into the home of a Foreign Legion senior non-commissioned officer of the 1st Legion Cavalry. The conscript's gaze focused on the miniature ribbons that were pinned to the left lapel of Lucien's suit jacket. Any Frenchman worth his salt would recognise the ribbons of the Médaille Militaire, the Croix de Guerre and others received for combat operations in Indochina and Algeria. What the ribbons did not reveal was that Lucien had been awarded the Croix de Guerre four times and the Médaille Militaire five times.

In 2007, the IBA, which I have led since Lucien Ott's death a year later in 1990, celebrated half a century of activity. As an international non-governmental organisation, the IBA is registered in Brussels with the Union of International Associations (UIA). The IBA is the only bodyguard organisation that has consistently met the UIA's criteria as an international association.

Besides training people of nearly 100 different nationalities, the IBA operate some 80 registered offices around the world, and over the years I have personally trained individuals from most special-force units and government organisations worldwide, as well as individuals from some of the elite warrior nations and races, including Tartars, Mongols, Zulus and Gurkhas. What has made us different is that we have not blindly imitated government protocols, such as those employed by the US Secret Service or UK Royal Military Police, but rather sought to construct our own standard operating procedures and immediate-action drills that are both effective and easily used. These are based on inductive training, as opposed to deductive training. For us, the difference is that inductive training looks at what works, establishes why it works and then creates a theory to support the observations. Deductive training starts with a theory then tries to make the observations fit it, which we believe to be a fundamentally flawed method in close protection, creating the need to make attacks fit the defence. Inductive training is more natural, because the theory has to fit the facts.

The bottom line in our training is your physical presence, followed by the protocols of walking with a principal (escorting), getting them in and out of a vehicle, and transporting them safely in that vehicle. All else is extra.

However, it must also be said that in the world of bodyguarding there are still plenty of people who are not fit for purpose – from practitioners to trainers. They are not bad human beings, but in our world of protection they seek to take short cuts where none exist and operate beyond their capabilities. They only survive on protection details because they fill a space in environments without any real risk or major threat. When they teach, they are the equivalent of swimming instructors in the Sahara: with no water and no possibility of drowning, they can teach any and all forms of swimming without the fear of failure or contradiction. The problems only become apparent when their students 'take to water' and step foot into the real world of close protection. It is a fact that in most countries there is sadly still no legal requirement for close protection training. Unfortunately, in our profession, bluff and bullshit and occasionally outright deception are

249

still heard more loudly than the wise words of the real professionals – men and women who are the genuine mainstream of our profession.

Even supposedly well-trained and experienced operatives should sometimes know better, like a former squadron sergeant major from 22 SAS who thought it a valuable and helpful training aid to shoot at his driver with an AK-47. He might have got away with this piece of 'Hollywood' had the location not been Iraq and the driver an Arab with no knowledge of the ways of the 'Hereford Jedi'. Result: one convoy vehicle in a drainage ditch in an extremely hostile environment. Or take the former British Army soldier who set up his own bodyguard security service company in Germany, even though he had no formal bodyguard training other than reading a couple of books on the subject from Paladin Press. Everything went well until he was asked to protect Whitney Houston and her husband Bobby Brown, plus members of their family and entourage. After an evening out, Whitney, Bobby and the family were transported back to their hotel for the night when the former squaddie decided to 'borrow' Whitney's stretch limo to show his girlfriend the sights and sounds of the city. Enter St Murphy, the patron saint of bodyguards, whose motto is 'To fail to plan is to plan to fail'. On this occasion, St Murphy came in the guise of Whitney's dad, who got up and went to find security to take him clubbing because he was unable to sleep due to jet lag. But neither the driver nor the squaddie were contactable. Furious, Whitney's father woke his daughter's manager, who immediately sacked the entire security crew and 'yellow paged' a replacement team.

The vast majority of celebrity principals are not interested in the details of their security. They simply wish to get from A to B with minimum difficulty and for someone to keep the fans at bay.

In his biography *Let the Good Times Roll*, veteran Australian bodyguard Bob Jones tells a number of stories about incidents that arose because of a lack of proper training or experience. Bob is a friend of mine, and whenever I am in Melbourne we get together over a few whiskeys and 'shoot the breeze'. Bob was once the bodyguard for most of the 'big celebrity names' that visited the country, from the Rolling Stones to the Beatles, and from ABBA to Bob's long-time drinking buddy Joe Cocker. Bob explained to me that when it all started for him he was just a martial artist who worked some of the harder doors in the Melbourne suburbs. 'There was no training, just thinking on your feet and learning from mistakes,' Bob said. In his book, Bob describes how the Rolling Stones considered cancelling their first-ever tour of Australia when Joe Cocker was arrested in the country for possession of drugs. The Rolling Stones' manager struck a deal with the promoter that would allow the tour to go ahead but only if they hired security, and the promoter turned to Bob Jones.

Bob breathed his first short-lived sigh of relief as the Stones were ferried safely from airport to hotel. Security had been put into place and limousines organised. However, he was rudely woken very early the next morning to deal with his first real crisis. An angry woman with an English accent phoned the hotel and subjected Bob to a torrent of abuse: 'Where is my fucking limo? I was promised a limo would be waiting for me. I am Keith Richards' wife, and I have just endured a shit flight from London.' Bob quickly organised the limo, sped to the airport and found a very pissed off Mrs Keith Richards waiting. Once placated, she was taken to the hotel and deposited in the lounge bar while Bob sought out Keith. Luckily, he met the Rolling Stones' guitarist in the lobby and explained that his wife was waiting for him in the lounge. 'Impressive, Bob,' Keith said. 'I have just come off the phone with her. She hates flying and is still in London.'

Discreetly, they both peered around the corner at the mystery woman. 'Fuck. It's my stalker from South Africa. I had a one-night stand with her there, and now she follows me about everywhere.' Bob quickly moved into action, explaining to 'Mrs Richards' that the band had moved to another hotel before breakfast, to which she would now be transported by limo. Six hours of fast driving later, and she was deposited with her luggage at a cattleman's kip hotel in the Australian outback. 'We learned from that one,' reminisced Bob, 'and not just about liars and stalkers.' Bob told me to always have a plan *and* a back-up plan for every situation and to always remember that nothing is as it presents itself.

The life of a bodyguard can be a bit of a circus. Whilst I was looking after Patrick Swayze in Sofia, Bulgaria, during the filming of *Icon*, the actor confided in me that he didn't usually employ professional bodyguards at home in the US. Instead, he brought a pair of Rhodesian Ridgebacks, also known as lion dogs because of their ability to bring down adult lions in a hunt, with him wherever he went. The two dogs would sit by Patrick and his guests during his meal, and fans would keep a respectful distance. 'In some instances, a couple of good dogs are infinitely better than a couple of bodyguards,' he would say with a sly smile on his face.

During the circuit (May–October), there is a flood of bodyguarding jobs across Continental Europe protecting Arab royalty, who demand very different operational procedures and exacting protocols, which can be a nightmare for the untrained or inexperienced bodyguard. For example, Arab royalty will not have bodyguards in their vehicle, and there are no formal embus or debus procedures; instead, the escort team ride in vehicles behind the principals', and it is not so much of a controlled convoy than a dangerous mad-dash pursuit through traffic. Search is always the best weapon of deterrence in the protection officer's armoury, yet there is rarely a search for improvised explosive devices or electronic surveillance devices of Arab royalty's accommodation, venues or vehicles.

Since the creation of the Iraq and Afghanistan conflicts by the US administration, it is common for bodyguards to become involved in high-risk protection roles in which competence with firearms is a must. That competence starts with safety and not with the purchase of the latest designer sunglasses and beige 5.11 Tactical gear. Although procedure and policy say otherwise, common sense says that if you are right-handed you should move to the principal's left – but countless principals in Iraq have been shot not by insurgents but by their own bodyguards, who have nervously stroked a round from an AK-47 or M4 carbine whilst standing to the right behind their charge. Apparently, the favoured site for shooting a principal is in the right leg.

Perhaps the most dangerous feature of our industry is the 'illusion of competence'. A few years ago in a European capital, a high-ranking Arab diplomat approached a very well-known blue-chip security company, which openly boasted of employing the cream of the British ex-Special Forces. The diplomat was worried about his daughter, who apparently led an expensive life of abandon in the company of a rogue of North African origin. The diplomat not only feared for his wayward daughter, but for the scandal in his kingdom should her lifestyle become public. A plan was hatched to place a professional surveillance team on her, and a contract was signed for many hundreds of thousands of pounds. 'Professional' implies people knew what they were doing. The company in question secured the contract by telling the Arab diplomat that they were able to utilise the skills of MI5's A4 department – the surveillance department of the UK security service that taught the Royal Ulster Constabulary's E4 surveillance department. However, an elite ex-member of A4 was not assigned to the case; in fact, it was a female Territorial Army soldier with an acid tongue and ongoing desire to get into the *Guinness Book of Records* for bedding the most UK Special Forces soldiers, both serving and veterans. When she was not playing in the barrack room, her surveillance vehicle was instantly recognisable by the vast amount of 'surveillance debris' she left behind, especially the pile of discarded cigarette butts on the pavement by her window and a dashboard littered with empty polystyrene coffee cups and McDonald's burger bags.

On any surveillance detail, it is always helpful to have a team member on a small motorbike who can get through the congestion in city traffic, but not when that bike is bright yellow and stands out like a sore thumb, as was the case on this operation. Despite all of this, and the glaring incompetence of many of the team's personnel, I hear that the operation is still running.

Close protection is not a game. Instead of celebrating because nothing has happened, you should use your outsiders' eye to ensure that nothing *can* happen in the future. When constructing your protocols and procedures, look at the situation from the point of view of the terrorist or attacker, and actively seek out your weak points instead of covering them over. At the end of the day, it is not what you know that will get you killed – it is what you do not know or forget.

BIOGRAPHY OF JAMES SHORTT

James Shortt has been decorated by the governments of Estonia, Poland, Latvia, Mongolia, Slovenia, Croatia and the Ukraine. He has been the director general of the IBA since February 1990. In conjunction with New College Swindon, the IBA provides close protection training under the UK's SIA licensing scheme through the Edexcel examination board.

James Shortt is also a lecturer in basic bodyguard skills at the University of South Africa (Pretoria) and has trained the Iraqi Police, United Nations bodyguards and US Army Special Forces for deployment in South-east Asia, Iraq and Afghanistan. He has trained Mongolian government bodyguards and has worked with the Australian Institute of Public Safety to create state and federal courses for close protection officers. He has also trained Russian Federation GRAD and SOBR forces, Ukrainian Alpha, Titan, Manguse, Berkyt and Sokul units, the Zulu Regiment of the South African National Defence Forces, the 1st United States Homeland Security Unit, and more recently the Royal Thai Police and Royal Thai Navy SEALs in bodyguard skills, close protection and counter-terrorism.

21

A NEW GIRL ON THE DOOR
ANONYMOUS

I suppose, if I am really honest, I was actually interested in getting into event security rather than working on the doors. I always thought working the door was an occupation for 20-something-stone tattooed giants with big fists and little brains, and it wasn't until I actually started on my first door that this belief was blown straight out of the water.

My interest in security was initially sparked by me being rescued at a Take That concert by a burly steward, who frantically pulled me over the pit barrier when I was being crushed by what seemed like thousands of other girlie teenagers all trying to catch a closer look at Robbie's crotch. I was only 14 at the time, and I looked up at my new hero with awe and respect as his big hands grabbed my tiny waist and pulled me to safety. His shaven head reflected the blues and reds from the stage, and his rough goatee brushed up against my cheek as I held on tight. He was probably old enough to be my dad's dad, but to me he was my conqueror, my hero, someone who I was sure I would spend the rest of my life with – until he dumped me unceremoniously on the ground and swiftly turned away to rescue another pre-pubescent damsel in distress.

Shocked and upset, I ran off to the side of the stage, where someone from the ambulance service rushed me to a seat, asked me if I was all right and briefly checked me over. I was dazed and a little winded, but otherwise I was fine. As I stared back at my hero rescuing damsel upon damsel, and up at the band strutting their gorgeous stuff on stage, deep down I somehow knew that one day I would be doing the same job – saving people at concerts and protecting gorgeous pop stars.

'And what a job it will be,' I thought to myself as I struggled to hear the paramedic confirm that I wasn't concussed or injured. I would work all over the country, maybe even the world. I might work at a pop concert one day and at a football match or horse race the next – I loved horses. Perhaps I might work at private parties, maybe even a Robbie Williams party, where I would protect him from his fans. Of course, Robbie and I would eventually become friends, and I would be invited to his dressing-room so that he could thank me in person for keeping him safe and secure. Yes, the security industry was definitely going to be the one for me.

Years passed, and I was suddenly 19 and about to leave school. Surprisingly, for a dizzy and fairly shy blonde, I found that I did quite well at school and had three A Levels and eight O Levels to my name. Although I considered myself fairly well educated, I didn't really have a direction. However, I did know that I had had enough of sitting in boring classrooms, listening to boring lectures, and I definitely did not want to go to university. I wanted to get out into the world of work and make some money – my parents had bought me a series of five driving lessons to start me off, and I needed to earn some cash to pay for the rest.

I think my teenage lustful dream of following in the footsteps of my heroic saviour faded a few days after the concert, and at school I was preoccupied with more mundane teenage things. I hadn't really thought about security and the security industry, and being a security guard didn't really feature in the lectures from the boring and extremely narrow-minded careers officers. They focused mainly on professional careers, although I never understood why security guards were always deemed to be so lowly and unintelligent. Did they not look after property and people? Were they not first on the scene in an emergency? Were they not the fount of all knowledge in their place of work?

Just after my 19th birthday, I left school and went into retail. I was a shop assistant in Top Shop, which was actually surprisingly good fun for a while. I enjoyed serving people and chatting about clothes and fashion – what teenage girl didn't? While working as a shop assistant, I got to know the security guards and the undercover store detectives, which I think was the spark that ignited new thoughts and feelings about the security industry. I would quickly notice whenever the store detective or security guard had spotted a shoplifter and always ask what the outcome was. Were they arrested? Did they go to the police station? Did they go to jail? After a while, I became more interested in the security guards than doing my job serving the customers and putting out and tidying stock.

On one occasion, I actually managed to follow a shoplifter who had stolen a scarf out of the store. Once outside, I gave chase and grabbed the culprit by the collar, before a security guard arrived, who'd seen me chase someone out of the store. I was so pleased with myself – I'd got the shoplifter and the goods – but upon my triumphant return the manager flipped his lid and was furious with me. He sternly reminded me that it wasn't my role to chase shoplifters. I expected a medal, but instead I got a reprimand and a verbal warning. I knew then that it was time to leave the shop.

After another few months, I handed in my notice and left Top Shop. If I couldn't chase criminals and shoplifters, I didn't want to work at the store at all. I applied and got an office job at a stationery supply company shortly after quitting the retail trade. My role was mainly filing and sorting correspondence, dealing with orders, ordering stock, and doing other mundane things, which I actually hated and which almost drove me insane. It was so incredibly boring and stagnant that sometimes I didn't even leave the building for lunch, taking the half hour allocated to eat my sandwich whilst sitting on a wooden box out in the back corridor daydreaming. After just a few short months, I handed in my notice. It had sent me stir crazy. The only good thing about the job had been that once or twice a week I'd delivered stationery orders to all sorts of people around the city centre, and I'd really enjoyed meeting the customers. It was the only contact I had with the outside world. On one occasion, I got chatting to a security guard at an office I delivered copy paper to. I thought the guard fancied me until I saw the wedding band on his ring finger. Well, maybe he did still fancy me, but married men were not really my cup of tea.

Anyway, I asked him a few questions about his job, as I really wanted to do something for a living that I enjoyed and that would motivate and inspire me, and not just live from weekend to weekend, dreading every Monday morning and yearning for every Friday evening. Surely there was more to life? He suggested I apply for a position with his security company, and I scribbled down the name and address of the company and promised to contact them over the following few days.

However, as is so often the case, it actually took me well over a year to contact the company, as I decided to take some time off work to sort myself out once I'd left the boring office job. What was initially meant to be just a few weeks off work ended up being 18 long months on the dole. I went through a few unpleasant personal events at that time, which had knocked me for six, and I spent quite a while getting myself together and sorting my life out. Because I was fairly young, I think that my personal life affected me more severely than I had originally realised. I had very little self-confidence or motivation and thought myself pretty worthless, but I was still keen on getting into the security industry.

It was 2005 and SIA licences had just been made compulsory. I could barely afford to exist on benefits, let alone afford the cost of a training course and the three-year licence fee. Lots of security companies offered security-guard courses with the promise of employment, but I knew I didn't want to go down that route. I wanted to do some proper training and eventually work in event security looking after celebrities. I was told by a friend of a friend that it would be much better for me if I got my door-supervisors' licence, which would enable me to work in a normal guarding environment as well as in a more specific security role. However, because event security work was not full time, most security companies did not provide training and only tended to take on those who were already licensed.

For the next few weeks, I spent hours searching the Internet and eventually found on a forum for doormen a training course for unemployed women wanting to get into the security industry. The course was funded by the government and would be provided free of charge – but I still needed to find the money for the licence.

Apart from making a beeline for the security guards almost everywhere I went – I think maybe I had a 'thing' for men in uniform – I didn't have any real experience of the security industry, but I somehow knew it was going to be the one for me. I called the company providing the training and was sent an application pack, which I immediately completed and returned. It was a four-day course, held about an hour's underground journey from my house.

On the morning of the first day of the course, I was filled with trepidation and unease. I hadn't studied since my A levels, and I hadn't worked for almost 18 months. Maybe it would be too difficult for me, or maybe I wouldn't get on with any of the other women on the course, or maybe I would find that my desire to work in security was unfounded and that it wasn't the industry for me after all. So many thoughts swirled around my head as I sat on the underground making my way towards Wimbledon.

I had preconceived ideas about who would make a good security guard, what sort of people they were, what they were like and how they behaved, and after just a few hours' training I could honestly say that most of the women on the course were definitely not the sort of people I would want to work with. Maybe it was because it was a course specifically for women on the dole, but I guess it would be fair to say that most were social undesirables – misfits who couldn't do much else with their lives. There were a lot of butch bisexual women who felt bizarrely compelled to boast about their physical prowess, fighting skills and ability to knock people out. Maybe that was what being a butch bisexual was. Or maybe they were trying to impress me a little, because I was blonde and petite. Whatever the reason,

I felt it was a strange, immature and horrible attitude and certainly an approach that the security industry, with its new licences and standardised training, was striving to get rid of.

After four days of security training and first aid, I took the multiple-choice exam and passed the course with flying colours. I was a qualified security guard.

My first day on the doors wasn't actually spent on the doors at all; instead, I worked as a hospitality steward at the Reading Festival. I was very excited but very nervous at the same time, as I had obviously never actually done the job before. In fact, I had never even been to Reading before, and I had never met any of my colleagues, either. Yes, the thought of working at the famous Reading Festival caused me a few sleepless nights.

I wasn't big enough or confident enough to stand in front of the stage, so I was used at the entrance to the site, searching women and dealing with any female issues that my male colleagues couldn't handle or didn't want to handle. I could still hear the music loud and clear, even though I was nowhere near the stage or the pop stars. There was no trouble, everyone seemed happy and sane, and although the days were really long I had a wonderful time.

My next job was at the cricket at Trent Bridge in Nottingham. I applied for the position because my boyfriend happened to be living in the city, and I thought it would be a great idea to stay with him for a few days while I worked. Lots of sunshine and lots of alcohol combined to make lots of rowdy punters. From my position on the front gates, I watched with envy as the four-man response team ran here, there and everywhere, dealing with various incidents. During those few days, I witnessed numerous fights and a few ejections, but nothing major. It was generally just a case of over-the-top but light-hearted fun that occasionally got out of hand.

Although I did thoroughly enjoy my job, I was getting fed up with standing around all day doing very little, and I really wanted to be part of the response team. I wanted some action, but my manager laughed at my wishes, saying that an eight-stone blonde could never do that kind of work. However, I was determined to prove them wrong one day.

During my time in event security, I have witnessed and been

involved in a lot of incidents, especially as a steward at Millwall Football Club, and especially working on the segregation line in the Upper East stand. Whenever a goal was scored, the entire stand would erupt, cheering and jeering and dancing and singing, and we had to try to control the elated crowd and stop them running behind our line. I certainly wasn't prepared for it when I experienced it for the first time, and I nearly fell down the stairs as I tried to hold back two different people and get them into the seating area where they should have been. I was struggling to keep hold of them and at the time stop myself from going arse over tit. It was scary but exhilarating, and after that first day I was much better prepared.

As I slowly proved my worth to my boss, I was given tougher and rougher roles and responsibilities, and one day I was asked if I could handle being placed behind the turnstiles at a football ground to grab anyone who jumped over and then kick them out. 'Of course I am capable,' I almost screamed at my boss, who was very hesitant about giving me my new role. I was put with another guy who boasted about his fighting abilities and expertise in martial arts. I wonder why security guards feel a need to boast all the time, especially when most of them cannot match their words. As my new partner ranted on and on about the various escapades he had found himself sorting out over his few months as a steward, I quickly understood that he was a complete dickhead. I politely listened and nodded, but I was bored out of my brain and hoped he would go and stand somewhere far away.

Suddenly, a big bloke jumped over the turnstiles, and, assuming my colleague would be right behind me, I ran hell for leather and apprehended him. It was only when I was really struggling with this guy who was double my size that I realised I had no back-up. In the end, two stewards from another company came to my assistance. The dickhead 'jacket filler' just stood there watching. 'You couldn't manage him on your own,' he said, smirking. I felt like smashing him square in the teeth.

I love my job as a steward and am currently looking for a nightclub door to work. I also aim to start close protection training as soon as I have saved enough money for a course. I eventually want to work in every aspect of the security industry.

22

A TRUE STORY OF CORPORATE CRIME IN THE RUSSIAN FEDERATION

BY ROBIN BARRATT

In the late 1990s, a US-based global vehicle-battery manufacturer, and one of the biggest auto-component companies in the world, set up an office and a manufacturing plant just outside Moscow, serving their extensive chain of established retailers throughout the Russian Federation. They had, in fact, been trading in Russia since the early '90s but had not actually manufactured their batteries in the country. Everything had been assembled in Ukraine and then imported as a completed unit.

The company had a large turnover, but actually made very little profit in Russia, which baffled the US directors and accountants, as the rest of their global offices had more or less the same margins, yet made much greater profits, no matter where in the world they operated. After a very detailed internal audit, a thorough investigation and a large number of unscheduled visits to retailers around Russia, a huge discrepancy was discovered between the number of units that were imported and those that were actually on the shelves. It was found that there was an estimated four or five times the number of batteries being sold than were registered on the export sheets from Ukraine. This meant that somewhere along the supply chain counterfeit batteries were being manufactured and sold as originals.

Counterfeiting was (and still is) extremely common in Russia; in fact, it has been estimated that probably 75 per cent of all products are fake, and you never really know whether you are buying the genuine product or a cheap counterfeit, repackaged and sold as the original. You need to know exactly what you are buying and be familiar with the supplier, and you always need to make sure that you only shop in the most well-known shops and supermarkets, although even they can occasionally get caught out by unscrupulous suppliers and clever conmen.

One famous case involved an Italian boutique selling very expensive designer coats in Smolenska Passage, an upmarket shopping mall in the centre of Moscow not far from the British Embassy. The coats were supposed to have come directly from Italy and had a huge price tag to match; however, the only thing that came from Italy was the labels – everything else was manufactured in sweatshops on the outskirts of the city. Admittedly, the templates were from actual one-off items bought in Italy, so in theory the coats were made from Italian designs, but they were sold as genuine imports and not cheap imitations made locally with substandard materials and shoddy workmanship. The owner of the boutique went over to Italy on a cheap package holiday once or twice a year, bought a few coats, brought them back to Moscow illegally and then counterfeited them. The owner eventually got caught, not because of a complaint, but because one of the designers instigated a global investigation and the Moscow shop was targeted.

Hundreds if not thousands of Russian retailers do exactly the same – buy templates from abroad while on holiday and have them copied and sold as originals. A major high-street pharmacy and one of the biggest chains in the Russian Federation was recently charged with selling a huge range of counterfeit perfume. Apparently, the main buyer was targeted by the Mafia and bribed to buy products from a company that specialised in counterfeiting fragrances. In the same year, a large supermarket chain was also caught selling hundreds of imitation goods.

Sadly, those who get caught are in the minority, as almost everything is counterfeited, from coffee, tea, olive oil, butter, cigarettes and tobacco to computer chips, car parts, clothing and sports equipment. In some cases, the quality can be awful, especially DVDs and tobacco from market traders, but in many cases the counterfeiting is excellent and only the specialised eye can tell the difference.

The batteries that were being sold as genuine imports were Russian made and of very poor quality. However, they had been cleverly inserted into the supply chain and made to look as though they had been imported from the real company. This did the company no good; first, its reputation was falling to pieces; and second, someone else was making a vast amount of money.

It could not be pinpointed exactly how this crime had been put in place. It also proved to be extremely difficult to ascertain where the counterfeit supply came from – probably because too many people had been paid off and too many people were scared of the consequences of spilling the beans. So, the company decided to import the components directly into Moscow, where they would then be assembled and distributed, which would hopefully make things easier to control.

The Russian financial crisis of 1998 provided a perfect excuse to get rid of the old directors. As banks collapsed and the rouble devalued, most foreign companies pulled out of the country. Many people lost everything in just a few short months – Russia was no longer the get-rich-quick place it had been at the fall of Communism. The very few foreign companies that decided to remain cut their staff and their operating costs and rode the storm. The auto-component company was one of the few that stayed, and new Russian directors were appointed, new systems put in place and a new manufacturing plant opened in Zelenograd, about 30 kilometres north-west of Moscow's outer ring road.

For a few years, everything went smoothly. As the country

recovered, so profits slowly rose, and the company began to grow again. And then suddenly, even though turnover was growing, profits dipped significantly, and the company found itself on the verge of bankruptcy.

I was living in Moscow at the time, providing security, protection and investigation services. I mainly worked for myself, subcontracting to various English security companies. The battery manufacturer contacted a well-known company in the UK, who then contacted me. The contract consisted of two elements: first, the Russian directors needed to be thoroughly yet discreetly investigated; and second, if new directors needed to be found, I'd have to thoroughly investigate their backgrounds before they could be employed.

Money rules in Russia, and the implications of losing it can be extreme. Many businessmen have been assassinated since the demise of Communism, for a whole host of reasons: to get rid of competition, to quickly end business partnerships and even to avenge disputes and debts. Most Russian businessmen and entrepreneurs have teams of bodyguards protecting them from such risks. Ironically, however, most foreign businessmen after the crisis did not require protection and could run a foreign company in relative safety. It seemed that targeting foreigners was more trouble than it was worth for the Mafia, thugs and criminals. At that time, Russia needed foreign investment. If foreigners were targeted, they would quickly pull out again, foreign banks would call in loans, aid would stop and the country would plunge into an even deeper crisis than it had in 1998.

However, even though foreigners living and working in Russia were rarely targeted, if the business was going to be closed and/or the directors sacked, they would become justifiable and legitimate targets. I contacted a Russian investigations company who had previously done a number of very discreet investigations for Western giants, including Philip Morris and Microsoft. Their methods were thorough and systematic, although occasionally a little unorthodox, and their references and results from previous work proved that they could complete the task in hand.

It still is impossible for a foreign company to be wholly owned and managed by foreigners – every foreign company must have at least a

51 per cent Russian ownership. My new clients, the auto-component company, had one director who had worked for them for many years and in various countries. He was asked to move to Moscow from his previous post in Germany. He had an excellent work record and viewed his move to Moscow as a promotion. All the top management knew and trusted him, and he was not a suspect. However, the three Russian directors were.

An initial basic investigation into the three Russian directors was undertaken. After just a few days, it was quickly found that they were also the managing directors of a total of ten other battery companies, all with very similar names. It was also revealed that just a few short months after joining the company all three directors had made large purchases, which had exceeded their salaries. One director had bought a new Audi, another had taken a two-week vacation on a tropical island, while the third had invested in a major refurbishment of his apartment. Of course, they had all done their best to mask their purchases by using either their spouses' names or the names of other family members; however, investigations such as these almost always include every member of the family, as well as close friends.

And so it had gone on, from the period of their appointment to the time of the investigation. Houses and land were bought, and cars were frequently changed and upgraded. The initial report also highlighted a connection between all three directors, even though they were apparently taken on independently of each other. None were reported to have any previous connection with the Mafia or organised crime prior to their appointment. But once they had been appointed and were working for a foreign company, they had put systems in place to rip it off – big-time. It was also found that the bank balances of the ten other battery companies that the Russians were directors of exceeded £100,000, and one of the companies had a bank balance of almost $250,000. That is one very good thing about Russia: if you pay the right people, the right information can be obtained – unlike in England!

It was fraud on a massive scale, but prosecution would be almost impossible. From a Western point of view, a managing director risking his job and his livelihood to steal from his employers when he could have a secure position for the rest of his life might not seem worth it. But because wages in Russia are low compared to Western standards and there is little accountability, stealing and fraud are extremely common. A Russian executive would view £150,000 as a lot of money, and it would last them a very long time. And should a defrauded company push for prosecution, a small percentage of stolen funds could be used to bribe the judge to either delay proceedings or dismiss them. Russian judges are extremely wealthy people but get paid a very small salary, so almost all of them supplement their wages with bribes. Employers and employees know full well that any prosecution would take years to process, and in most cases it simply would not be worth it. Therefore, employees know that they can do more or less what they want – if they are that way inclined and not strictly supervised – and employers know that there is little that can be done about it.

The auto-component company decided to close the Russian branch of the company. After two attempts, they realised that trying to run a legitimate and profitable business in the country was not really worth all the hassle. The company as a whole was bordering on bankruptcy, and the Russian losses were adding to the overall global financial difficulties. They decided that they would find a wholesaler who would buy the units, which would again be assembled in Ukraine and exported to Russia. The wholesaler would buy each unit for a set price and that would, in effect, be that. What happened thereafter would be out of the control of the company, but at least they would have no costs associated with manufacturing and distribution, just a battery being sold for a set price.

Having worked in Moscow for quite some time, I totally agreed with this policy. And this is a route a large number of the major companies take. The quality of manufacturing in Russia is at best questionable, controlling counterfeiting is almost impossible and the logistics of supplying effectively to such a massive country extremely complicated, so exporting products to a Russian company who would then distribute and sell them made infinitely more sense.

We were tasked with providing security and protection to the legitimate director and two company auditors, one of whom was familiar with Russian accounting, who would spend five days in

Moscow closing the business down. The legitimate director knew what was happening; however, at that stage the Russian directors did not know that the company was being closed. They were just told that a high-level visit was going to take place and the manufacturing plant, the offices and all the accounting systems would be thoroughly inspected.

Because of the possible risks and the fact that we had three principals to look after, I asked a colleague whom I had worked with before on another high-level operation in Israel to come over and help me. He was ex-Special Forces, and although he had never worked in Moscow he was very experienced. We also employed a third Russian bodyguard, a guy called Alex, whom I had also worked with before, as well as a team of three armed Russian drivers and their executive vehicles. The budget didn't stretch to much else, and it meant very long days, but we coped with the resources we had.

Security during this fragile and volatile period was extremely tight, and no stone was left unturned in protecting our principals. Two weeks after the operation started, the company submitted its final accounts to the Russian government and ceased trading in the country until a new wholesaler could be found. The operation went smoothly: the company closed down, around 200 people were laid off, property was made vacant and trading more or less stopped overnight. This made a few people very pissed off, from the workers in the factory who lost their jobs to the directors who lost a large amount of income.

Like many foreign businesses starting up in Russia, the auto-component company skimped on detailed initial investigations on both the market and their Russian employees, which cost them dearly in the long run. They also failed to do regular checks and background investigations, and they failed to control their operations, leaving too much responsibility to the Russian directors.

Corruption and crime is endemic in Russia, and it will never change. Because of this, Russia is one of the few places in the world not at war where the word of the bodyguard still rules supreme.